Lecture Notes of the Institute for Computer Sciences, Social Informatics and Telecommunications Engineering 318

More information about this series at http://www.springer.com/series/8197

Paulo Pereira · Rita Ribeiro ·
Ivo Oliveira · Paulo Novais (Eds.)

Society with Future: Smart and Liveable Cities

First EAI International Conference, SC4Life 2019
Braga, Portugal, December 4–6, 2019
Proceedings

 Springer

Editors
Paulo Pereira
Centre for Territory, Environment
and Construction, CTAC
University of Minho
Guimarães, Portugal

Rita Ribeiro
Communication and Society
Research Centre, CECS
University of Minho
Braga, Portugal

Ivo Oliveira
Landscape, Heritage and Territory
Laboratory, Lab2PT
University of Minho
Guimarães, Portugal

Paulo Novais ⓘ
Centro ALGORITMI
University of Minho
Braga, Portugal

ISSN 1867-8211   ISSN 1867-822X (electronic)
Lecture Notes of the Institute for Computer Sciences, Social Informatics
and Telecommunications Engineering
ISBN 978-3-030-45292-6   ISBN 978-3-030-45293-3 (eBook)
https://doi.org/10.1007/978-3-030-45293-3

This Springer imprint is published by the registered company Springer Nature Switzerland AG
The registered company address is: Gewerbestrasse 11, 6330 Cham, Switzerland

Preface

We are delighted to introduce the proceedings of the first edition of the European Alliance for Innovation (EAI) International Conference on Society with Future: Smart and Livable Cities (SC4Life 2019). This conference brought together researchers, developers, and practitioners from around the world who are leveraging and developing new knowledge on the topic of "smart cities", offering more efficiency to main infrastructures, utilities, and services, while creating a sustainable urban environment that improves the quality of life for its citizens and enhances economic development.

However, despite the accepted concept of smart cities, as a result of the utilization of the latest information and communication technologies (ICT), the concepts of smart, sustainable, resilient, safe, inclusive, and liveable cities, must be jointly considered, linking ICT advancements with the most innovative technology and systems of the built and natural environment, as well as with the most relevant component being its citizens, to offer efficient cities and territories. With this context in mind, the theme of SC4Life 2019 was "Society with a Future – Smart and Liveable Cities".

In this first edition, the following main topics were considered: Cities and Territories, Information and Technologies, and Citizen-centred Needs. In addition to papers in the referred topics, contributions with an interdisciplinary nature were particularly encouraged. The technical program of SC4Life 2019 consisted of 13 full papers, presented in oral sessions at the main conference tracks.

Apart from the high-quality technical paper presentations, the technical program also featured a keynote speech by Professor Filippo Practicó from the Università Mediterranea di Reggio Calabria, Italy.

Coordination with the general chair, Paulo Pereira, and the publication chair, Rita Ribeiro, was essential for the success of the conference. We sincerely appreciate their constant support and guidance. It was also a great pleasure to work with such an excellent Organizing Committee and we thank them for their hard work in organizing and supporting the conference. In addition to this, we would like to highlight the great work led by the Technical Program Committee, including Paulo Novais and Ivo Oliveira. We are also grateful to conference manager, Karolina Marcinova, for her support and to all the authors who submitted their papers to SC4Life 2019.

The SC4Life conference series provides a liveable forum for the exchange of scientific ideas and practical results, technological innovations and social challenges, and new visions, from academics, companies, and municipalities, also taking into account the irreplaceable role of the intervention of citizens, fostering the innovations to support a better quality of life with social cohesion.

December 2019   Paulo Pereira

Organization

Steering Committee

Imrich Chlamtac   University of Trento, Italy

Organizing Committee

General Chair

Paulo Pereira   University of Minho, Portugal

General Co-chair

Miguel de Castro Neto   NOVA University Lisbon, Portugal

TPC Chair and Co-chair

Paulo Novais   University of Minho, Portugal
Ivo Oliveira   University of Minho, Portugal

Publications Chair

Rita Ribeiro   University of Minho, Portugal

Web Chair

Karolina Marcinova   EAI

Panel Chairs

Paulo Pereira   University of Minho, Portugal
Paulo Novais   University of Minho, Portugal
Rita Ribeiro   University of Minho, Portugal

Technical Program Committee

Adriano Moreira   University of Minho, Portugal
Ana Melo   University of Minho, Portugal
António Pereira   Polytechnic of Leiria, Portugal
Catarina Sales   University of Beira Interior, Portugal
Cesar Analide   University of Minho, Portugal
Cristina Cavaco   University of Lisbon, Portugal
Daniel Casas Valle   Urban Dynamics, The Netherlands
Davide Rua Carneiro   Polytechnic of Porto, Portugal
Emília Araújo   University of Minho, Portugal

Fernando De La Prieta	University of Salamanca, Spain
Fraya Frehse	University of São Paulo, Brazil
Francesco Pilla	University College Dublin, Ireland
Filippo Practicò	Mediterranean University of Reggio Calabria, Italy
Gianni Vercelli	Università degli studi di Genova, Italy
Ichiro Satoh	National Institute of Informatics, Japan
Ivo Oliveira	University of Minho, Portugal
Jason Jung	Chung-Ang University, South Korea
Javier Bajo Pérez	Technical University of Madrid, Spain
Manuela Almeida	University of Minho, Portugal
Marco Perino	Politecnico di Torino, Italy
Marta Smagacz-Poziemska	Jagiellonian University, Poland
Mimi Sheller	Drexel University, USA
Noel Salazar	University of Leuven, Belgium
Paulo Novais	University of Minho, Portugal
Paulo Ramísio	University of Minho, Portugal
Paulo Ribeiro	University of Minho, Portugal
Pedro Cabral	NOVA University of Lisbon, Portugal
Renato Carmo	Lisbon University Institute, Portugal
Rita Ribeiro	University of Minho, Portugal
Rui José	University of Minho, Portugal
Sara Sucena	Universidade Fernando Pessoa, Portugal
Tatsuo Nakajima	Waseda University, Japan
Xerardo Pereiro	University of Trás-os-Montes and Alto Douro, Portugal

Contents

Cities and Territory

Sustainable Road Infrastructures Using Smart Materials, NDT,
and FEM-Based Crack Prediction 3
    Rosario Fedele, Filippo Giammaria Praticò, and Gianfranco Pellicano

Quantifying the Carbon Dioxide Emissions Resulting
from Awareness-Raising Actions of Sustainable Mobility. 15
    Pétilin Souza, Filipa Paiva, Lígia Silva, and Paulo Pereira

Leak Detection in Water Distribution Networks via Pressure Analysis
Using a Machine Learning Ensemble. 31
    Vivencio C. Fuentes Jr. and Jhoanna Rhodette I. Pedrasa

Solutions for Improving the Energy Efficiency of Buildings Refurbishment. . . . 45
    Maria de Fátima Castro, Joana Andrade, Catarina Araújo,
    and Luís Bragança

Information and Technologies

Image Recognition to Improve Positioning in Smart Urban Environments . . . 59
    Sara Paiva, Pedro Rodrigues, and Benjamim Oliveira

An Hybrid Novel Layered Architecture and Case Study:
IoT for Smart Agriculture and Smart LiveStock 71
    Pelagie Houngue, Romaric Sagbo, and Colombiano Kedowide

Agrilogistics - A Genetic Programming Based Approach 83
    Divya D. Kulkarni and Shivashankar B. Nair

Real World Third-Person with Multiple Point-of-Views for Immersive
Mixed Reality. 97
    Zebo Yang, Mingshu Zhang, Taili Zhang, Linhao Fu,
    and Tatuso Nakajima

Internet of Things for Enhanced Smart Cities: A Review, Roadmap
and Case Study on Air Quality Sensing. 109
    Gonçalo Marques and Rui Pitarma

Citizen-Centre Needs

Smart Pedestrian Network: An Integrated Conceptual Model
for Improving Walkability 125
    Fernando Fonseca, Paulo Ribeiro, Mona Jabbari, Elena Petrova,
    George Papageorgiou, Elisa Conticelli, Simona Tondelli,
    and Rui Ramos

Building Future Societies? A Brief Analysis of Braga's School Bus Project 143
    Emília Araújo, Márcia Silva, Rita Ribeiro, and Filipa Corais

City Rankings and the Citizens: Exposing Representational
and Participatory Gaps..................................... 154
    Ana Duarte Melo

Mobility Time Style: For an Integrated View of Time and Mobility
in Societies with a Future.................................. 170
    Catarina Sales Oliveira and Emília Araújo

Author Index 185

Cities and Territory

Sustainable Road Infrastructures Using Smart Materials, NDT, and FEM-Based Crack Prediction

Rosario Fedele[1]([✉]) [iD], Filippo Giammaria Praticò[2] [iD], and Gianfranco Pellicano[2] [iD]

[1] CNR - Institute of Marine Engineering (INM), Via di Vallerano 139, Rome, RM, Italy
rosario.fedele@unirc.it
[2] DIIES, University "Mediterranea" of Reggio Calabria, Via Graziella, Reggio Calabria, Italy

Abstract. Smart cities need roads with high levels of sustainability. This goal can be reached using different approaches, such as smart materials, Non-Destructive Test (NDT)-based monitoring systems, and Finite Element Method (FEM)-based damage prediction models. The pieces of information provided using the above-mentioned approaches play a crucial role in the work of many stakeholders (citizens, users, road agencies, authorities, driverless vehicles, etc.). Consequently, the main objectives of this study presented in this paper are (i) providing an overview of the current approaches, and (ii) presenting a NDT-, and FEM-based monitoring system that was designed to improve the sustainability of the present and future road pavements by means of the road pavement damage detection and prediction. In more detail, the paper is focused on the set up and the calibration of a FEM model that aims at simulating the vibro-acoustic signatures of un-cracked and cracked road pavements. An NDT apparatus was used to gather the vibro-acoustic signatures of road pavement (data set) that was progressively damaged. Subsequently, the data set mentioned above was used to set up the FEM model. Results show that, even though the FEM model is able to replicate only in part the measured signals, this model can be successful used for predicting the variation of the structural health status of the road pavement. Hence, the proposed approach can be used to improve the sustainability of the current road pavements.

Keywords: Finite element modeling · Vibro-acoustic signature · Road crack prediction

1 Introduction

Smart cities require roads with high levels of sustainability, which can be reached using different approaches. Among all the possible solutions, the study presented in this paper is focused on three promising approaches (see Fig. 1), i.e., the use of smart materials, the implementation of Non-Destructive Test (NDT)- and sensor-based monitoring systems, and the application Finite Element Method (FEM)-based damage prediction models. In more detail: (i) smart materials can be used to obtain self-healing road pavements, to carry out energy harvesting, and to save resources (e.g., raw material, and

P. Pereira et al. (Eds.): SC4Life 2019, LNICST 318, pp. 3–14, 2020.
https://doi.org/10.1007/978-3-030-45293-3_1

energy); (ii) using NDT- and sensor-based monitoring system, instead of the traditional destructive ones (e.g., coring), can improve the sustainability of the roads because of the fact that it positively affects the management process (e.g., maintenance based on real time information about the road conditions); (iii) FEM models can be used to predict the temporal and spatial behavior of the road pavements, i.e., to forecast the occurrence of possible failures (e.g., internal cracks) or the reduction of the performances (e.g., clogging). For these reasons, the following subsections contain an overview of noteworthy applications of the three approaches listed above.

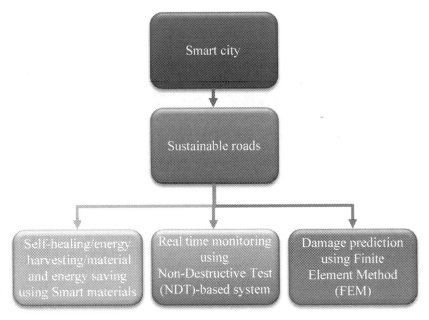

Fig. 1. Three possible solutions to obtain sustainable roads for smart cities.

1.1 Smart Material for Road Pavements

A material can be defined "smart" if it has the ability of changing its properties to react to an external condition [1]. In order to obtaining smarter, and more sustainable and efficient materials for road pavements, several types of wastes can be used in the asphalt concrete mixture, such as Reclaimed Asphalt Pavement (RAP) [15], by-products (e.g., crumb rubber, plastics, blast furnace slag, fly ash, leachate, glass, concrete, wood ash) [12, 14], graphene [7], and fibers [3, 8, 21]. These latter are used in applications that principally aim at conferring to the asphalt concrete healing properties (i.e., make the material able to easily repair the damages due to different causes, such as vehicular traffic, or thermal excursions) [4, 11, 16–19]. Furthermore, smart materials be used to produce or harvest energy from the road pavements. The energy derived from the roads can be used for typical applications, such as street lighting [22], and sensors based monitoring systems [5, 13], or for innovative applications, such as feeding electric vehicles [2, 9].

1.2   NDT Solutions for Monitoring the Road Pavements

Infrastructure monitoring can be carried out using [6] traditional destructive testing (DT), or innovative semi-destructive testing (SDT) and non-destructive testing (NDT). Usually, DT-based monitoring is the most used although it provides sample-based information (i.e., discrete points of the pavement), and requires energy and money for extracting (e.g., coring), analyzing, and landfilling pavement samples. On the other hand, SDT- and NDT-based methods, which are driven by the increasingly insistent demand for smart cities, are growing because they offer high performance (e.g., extended measurements), sustainability (e.g., energy and time savings), and efficiency (e.g., high measurement frequency, and/or technologically advanced devices). The main NDT-based monitoring drawbacks are related to the costs (i.e., instrumented infrastructures are more expensive than traditional ones), and to the worker's skill (i.e., skilled worker are required to set up, use, and tune sophisticated devices/systems, and/or to handle and analyze huge amounts of data). From an energy point of view, it should be underlined that the NDT methods tend to be more sustainable than the DT methods, because they use efficient and advanced systems (e.g., [10]).

Noteworthy NDT methods applied or designed for the Structural Health Monitoring (SHM) of the road pavements refer to: (i) audio-visual inspections and image analysis [20, 23]; (ii) heavy and light instrumented vehicles, unmanned aerial vehicles, satellite, smartphones on vehicles using several devices (e.g., the smartphone's gyroscope) [24, 25]; (iii) ultrasonic guided waves, ultrasonic wave propagation, and ultrasonic tomography [26–28]; (iv) electromagnetic, e.g. the Ground Penetrating Radar (GPR), or using nuclear and non-nuclear electromagnetic gauges, or microwave imaging to scan the surface layers [29, 30]; (v) seismic methods (e.g., MASW), or devices such as the Light Weight Deflectometer (LWD), the Falling Weight Deflectometer (FWD), and the Rolling Wheel Deflectometer (RWD [31, 32]; (vi) Ground Penetrating Radar (GPR) and thermo-cameras [33–35]; (vii) self-powered, or low- and ultralow-powered, wireless sensor networks [36–38].

1.3   FEM Models Applied on Road Pavements

This section contains relevant examples of the application of FEM on road pavements, which were used to simulate and study the behavior of these pavements under different load conditions, and to forecast their performances and sustainability over time. The examples mentioned below were grouped based on the software used to build the model, as follows: (a) ABAQUS was used to derive natural frequencies, dynamic moduli, fatigue cracking performance, and response to a given load. The above mentioned software was used also to simulate crack propagation, and interactions between deformable tires and pavements [39–41]; (b) ANSYS was used to study the bridge-vehicle interactions, and the resultant vibrations perceived by pedestrians [42]; (c) COMSOL Multiphysics was used to simulate structural responses to dynamic loads [43, 44]; (d) CAPA-3D was used to model tire-road contacts, and distress mechanisms [45]; (e) Matlab was used for the prediction of ground-borne vibrations due to road unevenness-tire interactions [46]; (f) the combination of SAFEM and ABAQUS was used to analyze mechanical performances of asphalt pavements (e.g., deflection, and strain/stress), and their dynamic responses to moving loads [47]; (g) SAFEM was used to simulate deterioration of asphalt pavements under heavy vehicle loads [48]; (h) SURFER was used to derivate ground borne vibrations, induced by vehicles, for different soils [49].

Despite the fact that, in the last decades, several solutions were proposed to improve the overall quality of the road pavements, it is still difficult to apply them in real contexts. Possible motivations can be the complexity, the cost, and the poor attention to the them by the authorities. For this reason, this paper aims at presenting a simple, and cheaper solutions that can be easily used to effectively improve the sustainability of the road pavements, in terms of smart monitoring and efficient maintenance. In more detail, the objectives of the study presented in this paper are: (1) to present a NDT-based monitoring system able to gather the vibro-acoustic responses of the road pavement to different loads; (2) to set up a FEM model able to simulate road pavement cracks and forecast any possible variations of the responses cited above due to a change of the structural status of the pavement.

Note that, this study is part of the research projects SICURVIA (project funded by Region Calabria, Italy).

2   Method

This paper describes a method that was developed to increase the sustainability of road pavements acting on two of the three approaches discussed in the previous section (see Fig. 1). In particular, the method is based on (1) the real time assessment of the structural conditions of the road (using an innovative monitoring system described in Sect. 2.1), and (2) on the prediction of the occurrence of road cracks due to repeated or extraordinary loads (using the FEM model described in Sect. 3). The method could be applied by authorities and companies that are responsible for the management of the road infrastructures, or could be used as a key component of the smart cities because of its ability to provide crucial information about the availability and reliability of the road infrastructures, which can be shared (Internet of Thing, IoT, approach) with users, or vehicles or other infrastructures (i.e., allow vehicle-to-infrastructure communication, and infrastructure-to-infrastructure communication).

2.1   NDT-Based Monitoring System and Data Gathering

An innovative NDT-based monitoring system was designed, based on the concept of vibro-acoustic signature. In more detail, the ground-borne response of the road pavement to vibration and noise generated by a mechanical source (e.g., vehicle, hammer, Light Weight Deflectometer, LWD) are considered as the vibro-acoustic signature of the road pavement. It is expected that the signature will be affected by any significant change of the structural conditions of the pavement. Hence, a system that is able to gather the above-mentioned signature can be used for monitoring purposes. The system used in this study consists of a broad-band and omnidirectional microphone located (NDT) on the surface of the road, which is able to gather the sound produced by the waves generated by a mechanical source that travels on the road. Importantly, this microphone must not be affected by the air-borne noise, and for this reason a sound-insulating dome was used to avoid undesirable effects due noise and wind. The structural condition of the road pavement was changed by means of drilled holes. Figure 2a shows the road pavement used in this study. Two different conditions were taken into account in this study, i.e., the structural condition 0, without holes, and the structural condition 1, with one line of 15 holes (diameter $= 0.01$ m, same depth as the one of the asphalt concrete layers $=$ 15 cm, spaced 5 cm each other). A well-known mechanical source was used to load the road pavement, i.e., a LWD (see Fig. 2 left). This device is commonly used to measure the elastic modulus of pavements and is able to produce an impulse load that is suitable for the purposes of the study. The data set consists of 100 acoustic signals (50 for each condition), which were gathered with a sample frequency of 192 kHz.

Fig. 2. (Left) experimental set up used to gather the data set used in the study, i.e. LWD, microphone + dome (Mic), and holes (structural condition 1); (Right) main elements of the FEM model: (a) isolating dome of the microphone; (b) LWD's steel plate; (c) dome-cracks-steel plate; (d) road pavement.

3   Set up of a FEM Model for Crack Prediction

The software COMSOL Multiphysics® was used to build the FEM model. In particular, the "Acoustic-Solid Interaction" interface, and the study "Pressure Acoustics Transient" were selected. Figure 1 right shows the main elements of the model, i.e. the road pavement, the drilled holes, the LWD base plate, and the dome of the probe. While, Table 1 summarizes the input parameters used to feed the FEM model.

Table 1. Input parameters of the FEM model.

Parameter	Details
Sampling	Sampling frequency of 2000 points per 200 ms, i.e., 10000 Hz, was selected
Geometry	LWD plate (height = 0.01 m, radius = 0.15 m). Pavement layers (thicknesses of the wearing course $d_0 = 0.1$ m, of the subbase course $d_1 = 0.3$ m, and of the subgrade course $d_2 = 10$ m; length of the layers = 10 m; width of the layer = 10 m). Boundary condition = "low reflection"
Sensors	One microphone (acoustic pressure detection) placed $h_0 = 0.005$ m far from pavement surface
LWD-road interaction	LWD steel base plate (Young's modulus = 200 GPa, density = 7850 kg/m³; plate dimensions (diameter = 0.3 m, and height = 0.01 m)
Air-born noise insulating dome	Dome is a semi-sphere of radius = 0.05 m, thickness $d_d = 0.005$ m, filled with a material with Young's modulus = 50 MPa (with clay), density = 1800 kg/m³, and Poisson's ratio = 0.3. Boundary conditions = "low-reflecting"
Impulse load	LWD's load function over time produced a maximum force on the steel plate cited above of 9 kN (that is due to a mass of 10 kg falling from 0.83 m, on five rubber buffers with an elastic constant of about 362 kN/m). The pulse time is 15 ÷ 30 ms
Layers	On average, lower moduli correspond to slower and bigger signals over time. Densities (2200 kg/m³ for friction course, 2000 kg/m³ for subbase course, and 1800 kg/m³ for subgrade), and moduli ($E_0 = 1000$ MPa for friction course, $E_1 = 500$ kg/m³ for subbase course, and $E_2 = 90$ kg/m³ for subgrade course)
Temperatures	Bituminous layers elastic modulus is affected by the temperature, and it, in turn, affects the speed of the propagating waves. During the experiments, the road surface temperature was in the range 25–35 °C, and the reference temperature for air was assumed equal to 20.0 °C
Induced cracks	Drilled holes were modelled according to Sect. 3. Importantly, the air trapped into cracks was modelled itself
Speed of propagation	Vibrations propagate into the road pavement with a speed $v_1 = 670$ m/s, while the sound speed in air v_2 was derived from the air temperature

4   Results

The results of this study refer to the calibration of the FEM model presented in the previous section. In more detail, the calibration was carried out using meaningful features of the measured signals related to the peaks amplitude and time-lags. The peaks that were taken into account are shown in Fig. 3.

Fig. 3. Peaks used to represent the signals (features).

The time lags refer to the x-axis and the following feature were derived (the numbers point out the peak showed in Fig. 3): x2-x1, x3-x2, x4-x3, x5-x4, x6-x5, and x7-x6. The peak amplitude refers to the y-axis, and the features that were derived are: y1/y3, y2/y3, y3/y3, y4/y3, y5/y3, y6/y3, and y7/y3. After two rounds of calibration, the FEM model was able to provide the signals of Fig. 4 using the input parameter reported in Table 2.

Table 2. Main inputs of the calibrated FEM model.

ID	Main inputs											
	E_0	E_1	E_2	Ta	$Tpav$	d_d	$\emptyset_d$	v_1	v_2	μ	σ	F
	MPa	MPa	MPa	K	K	M	M	m/s	m/s	ms	ms	kN
1st	1000	500	90	293.15	293.15	0.01	0.05	670	n.a.	15	2	9
2nd	2000	600	200	299.75	304.25	0.008	0.075	1208	347.4	15	1.5	9

Symbols. ID = Round of calibration; Ei = moduli of the layers, with i = 0, 1, and 2; Ta = air temperature; $Tpav$ = pavement temperature; d_d = dome thickness; $\emptyset_d$ = dome diameter; $v_{1,2}$ = speeds of propagation in the transmission media 1 and 2; μ, σ = impulse peak position and width, respectively; F = impulse force.

Figure 4 shows the comparison between the measured vibro-acoustic signatures and those simulated using the FEM model. Based on the results shown in Fig. 3, it is possible to state that the procedure used to build and set up the FEM model can be effectively used to try to replicate real damage of a road pavement. Hence, this method can be also used to forecast the occurrence of any type of damages (e.g., surface or hidden cracks, or cracks due to thermal excursion, or fatigue failures).

Finally, the validation of the study was carried out comparing a set of the measured signals (42 signals) with a set of simulated data (42 signals). In particular, experiments showed an instrumental uncertainty (LWD) of about ± 5% (8.55–9.45 KN), which can

Fig. 4. Superposition of the measured and simulated vibro-acoustic signature of the road pavement in the structural conditions 0 (without holes) and 1 (with one line of holes).

be considered, together with the holes, the main cause of signal changes. Hence, further simulations were carried out, using the same parameters reported in Table 2, and changing the LWD load to obtain a simulated data set that takes into account the experimental uncertainties. Subsequently, a third round of calibration was carried out in order to find two calibration factors, i.e. one for the structural condition 0, and one for the structural condition 1. In more detail, each simulated signal (referred to the given condition) was divided for a reference signal (properly selected, measured signal) obtaining one corresponding matrix of factors. Then, from the elements of the given column an average was derived. The resulting two vectors (one *per* conditions) were used as calibration factors. These latter were multiplied by the simulated signals obtaining the final simulated data set. Finally, the two abovementioned data sets (measured and simulated after three rounds of calibrations) were used as input of a hierarchical clustering algorithm (implemented in Matlab®) that aimed at classifying the signals into two classes, i.e., structural condition 0 and 1. The result of the classification was expressed in terms of model accuracy (i.e., the ratio between the number of signals correctly classified and the total number of signals belonging to the testing data set to be classified), derived from confusion matrixes (i.e., a matrix that shows how many observations were associated to each cluster). The average model accuracy resulted of about 85% (i.e., 83% and 86% for the structural condition 0 and 1, respectively), which can be considered sufficient to validate the FEM model.

5   Conclusions

Smart cities need roads with high levels of sustainability, and this goal can be reached using, e.g., smart materials, Non-Destructive Test (NDT)-based monitoring systems, and Finite Element Method (FEM)-based damage prediction models. Consequently, the main objectives of this study are (i) providing an overview of the current approaches, and (ii) presenting a NDT-, and FEM-based monitoring method (road damage detection and prediction). The proposed method has the potentialities to contribute to a more sustainable environment because it is based on (1) the real time assessment of the structural conditions of the road (using an innovative monitoring system), and (2) on the prediction of the occurrence of road cracks due to repeated or extraordinary loads (using the FEM model). The FEM model was calibrated using a data set gathered during an experimental investigation on road pavements that was progressively damaged with drilled holes. A simple NDT apparatus was used to gather the vibro-acoustic signatures of road pavement (data set). Results show that, the procedure used to build and set up the FEM model can be effectively used to replicate real damage of a road pavement, and that this method can be used to forecast the occurrence of any type of damages. Hence, the proposed solution can positively affect both the maintenance efficiency of authorities and companies that are responsible for the management of the road infrastructures, and the road sustainability by means of the ability to share crucial information (road availability and reliability) with users, or vehicles or other infrastructures (IoT approach).

Finally, based on the promising results, possible further research steps are: (1) reproducing typical cracks of the road pavements and, then, using the monitoring system to detect the vibro-acoustic responses and the FEM model to predict the variation of the above mentioned responses due to the propagation of the induced cracks; (2) using the FEM model to design new smart materials and forecast their behavior; (3) improving the system using low-power electronics (e.g., MEMS sensors, low-power and ultra-low power wireless transmitters) for large-scale production and application. The future researches listed above will require interactions with other research fields such as the machine learning one to face the increase of the data set size due to the use of the monitoring system (big data), and the micro-electronics to improve the performances of the monitoring system.

References

1. Neelakanta, P.: Smart Materials (2013). https://doi.org/10.1201/9781420049763.ch58
2. Praticò, F.G., Vaiana, R., Giunta, M.: Pavement sustainability: permeable wearing courses by recycling porous European mixes. J. Archi. Eng. (2013). https://doi.org/10.1061/(ASCE)AE.1943-5568.0000127
3. Wang, T., Xiao, F., Zhu, X., Huang, B., Wang, J., Amirkhanian, S.: Energy consumption and environmental impact of rubberized asphalt pavement. J. Cleaner Prod. (2018). https://doi.org/10.1016/j.jclepro.2018.01.086
4. Praticò, F.G., Moro, A., Noto, S., Colicchio, G.: Three-year investigation on hot and cold mixes with rubber. In: 8th International Conference on Maintenance and Rehabilitation of Pavements, MAIREPAV (2016). https://doi.org/10.3850/978-981-11-0449-7-085-cd
5. Le, J.L., Marasteanu, M.O., Turos, M.: Mechanical and compaction properties of graphite nanoplatelet-modified asphalt binders and mixtures. Road Mater. Pavement Des. (2019). https://doi.org/10.1080/14680629.2019.1567376
6. Du, Y., Chen, J., Han, Z., Liu, W.: A review on solutions for improving rutting resistance of asphalt pavement and test methods. Constr. Build. Mater. (2018). https://doi.org/10.1016/j.conbuildmat.2018.02.151
7. Wang, H., Yang, J., Liao, H., Chen, X.: Electrical and mechanical properties of asphalt concrete containing conductive fibers and fillers. Constr. Build. Mater. (2016). https://doi.org/10.1016/j.conbuildmat.2016.06.063
8. Li, H., et al.: Investigation of the effect of induction heating on asphalt binder aging in steel fibers modified asphalt concrete. Materials (2019). https://doi.org/10.3390/ma12071067
9. Sun, D., Li, B., Ye, F., Zhu, X., Lu, T., Tian, Y.: Fatigue behavior of microcapsule-induced self-healing asphalt concrete. J. Cleaner Prod. (2018). https://doi.org/10.1016/j.jclepro.2018.03.281

10. Sun, Y., Wu, S., Liu, Q., Li, B., Fang, H., Ye, Q.: The healing properties of asphalt mixtures suffered moisture damage. Constr. Build. Mater. (2016). https://doi.org/10.1016/j.conbuildmat.2016.10.048

11. García, A., Norambuena-Contreras, J., Bueno, M., Partl, M.N.: Single and multiple healing of porous and dense asphalt concrete. J. Intell. Mater. Syst. Struct. (2015). https://doi.org/10.1177/1045389X14529029

12. Hasheminejad, N., et al.: Digital image correlation to investigate crack propagation and healing of asphalt concrete. In: Proceedings of the Eighteenth International Conference of Experimental Mechanics, p. 5381. MDPI, Basel (2018). https://doi.org/10.3390/icem18-05381

13. Patti, F., Mansour, K., Pannirselvam, M., Giustozzi, F.: Mining materials to generate magnetically-triggered induction healing of bitumen on smart road pavements. Constr. Build. Mater. (2018). https://doi.org/10.1016/j.conbuildmat.2018.03.160

14. Zhang, H., Bai, Y., Cheng, F.: Rheological and self-healing properties of asphalt binder containing microcapsules. Constr. Build. Mater. (2018). https://doi.org/10.1016/j.conbuildmat.2018.07.172

15. Fedele, R., Merenda, M., Praticò, F.G., Carotenuto, R., Della Corte, F.G.: Energy harvesting for IoT road monitoring systems. Instrum. Mesure Metrologie 17(4), 605–623 (2018). https://doi.org/10.3166/I2M.17.605-623

16. Yoomak, S., Ngaopitakkul, A.: Optimisation of lighting quality and energy efficiency of LED luminaires in roadway lighting systems on different road surfaces. Sustain. Cities Soc. (2018). https://doi.org/10.1016/j.scs.2018.01.005

17. Praticò, F., Della, F., Merenda, M.: Self-powered sensors for road pavements. In: 4th Chinese–European Workshop on Functional Pavement Design, CEW (2016). https://doi.org/10.1201/9781315643274-151

18. Hasni, H., Alavi, A.H., Chatti, K., Lajnef, N.: A self-powered surface sensing approach for detection of bottom-up cracking in asphalt concrete pavements: theoretical/numerical modeling. Constr. Build. Mater. (2017). https://doi.org/10.1016/j.conbuildmat.2017.03.197

19. Bansal, R.C.: Electric vehicles. In: Emadi, A. (ed.) Handbook of Automotive Power Electronics and Motor Drives, 1st edn. Taylor & Francis, Boca Raton (2017)

20. Miller, J.M.: Hybrid electric vehicles. In: Emadi, A. (ed.) Handbook of Automotive Power Electronics and Motor Drives, 1st edn. Taylor & Francis, Boca Raton (2017). https://doi.org/10.1201/9781420028157

21. Hola, J., Schabowicz, K.: State-of-the-art non-destructive methods for diagnostic testing of building structures – anticipated development trends. Arch. Civ. Mech. Eng. (2010). https://doi.org/10.1016/S1644-9665(12)60133-2

22. Praticò, F.G., Vaiana, R.: A study on the relationship between mean texture depth and mean profile depth of asphalt pavements. Constr. Build. Mater. (2015). https://doi.org/10.1016/j.conbuildmat.2015.10.021

23. Zhang, Y., et al.: Kinect-based approach for 3D pavement surface reconstruction and cracking recognition. IEEE Trans. Intell. Transp. Syst. 19, 3935–3946 (2018)

24. Carlos, M.R., Aragon, M.E., Gonzalez, L.C., Escalante, H.J., Martinez, F.: Evaluation of detection approaches for road anomalies based on accelerometer readings-addressing who's who. IEEE Trans. Intell. Transp. Syst. (2018). https://doi.org/10.1109/TITS.2017.2773084

25. Cafiso, S., D'Agostino, C., Delfino, E., Montella, A.: From manual to automatic pavement distress detection and classification. In: 5th IEEE International Conference on Models and Technologies for Intelligent Transportation Systems (MT-ITS) (2017). https://doi.org/10.1109/mtits.2017.8005711

26. Pahlavan, L., Mota, M.M., Blacquière, G.: Influence of asphalt on fatigue crack monitoring in steel bridge decks using guided waves. Constr. Build. Mater. (2016). https://doi.org/10.1016/j.conbuildmat.2016.05.138

27. Mounier, D., Di Benedetto, H., Sauzéat, C.: Determination of bituminous mixtures linear properties using ultrasonic wave propagation. Constr. Build. Mater. (2012). https://doi.org/10.1016/j.conbuildmat.2012.04.136
28. Hoegh, K., Khazanovich, L., Yu, H.: Ultrasonic tomography for evaluation of concrete pavements. Transp. Res. Rec. J. Transp. Res. Board (2011). https://doi.org/10.3141/2232-09
29. Praticò, F.G., Moro, A., Ammendola, R.: Factors affecting variance and bias of non-nuclear density gauges for PEM and DGFC. Baltic J. Road Bridge Eng. **4**, 99–107 (2009)
30. Bevacqua, M.T., Isernia, T.: Boundary indicator for aspect limited sensing of hidden dielectric objects. IEEE Geosci. Remote Sens. Lett. (2018). https://doi.org/10.1109/LGRS.2018.2813087
31. Iodice, M., Muggleton, J., Rustighi, E.: The detection of vertical cracks in asphalt using seismic surface wave methods. J. Phys. Conf. Ser. (2016). https://doi.org/10.1088/1742-6596/744/1/012059
32. Pitoňák, M., Filipovsky, J.: GPR application - non-destructive technology for verification of thicknesses of newly paved roads in Slovakia. Procedia Eng. **153**, 537–549 (2016). https://doi.org/10.1016/j.proeng.2016.08.184
33. Solla, M., Lagüela, S., González-Jorge, H., Arias, P.: Approach to identify cracking in asphalt pavement using GPR and infrared thermographic methods: preliminary findings. NDT Int. (2014). https://doi.org/10.1016/j.ndteint.2013.11.006
34. Ouma, Y.O., Hahn, M.: Wavelet-morphology based detection of incipient linear cracks in asphalt pavements from RGB camera imagery and classification using circular Radon transform. Adv. Eng. Inform. (2016). https://doi.org/10.1016/j.aei.2016.06.003
35. Grace, R.: Sensors to support the IoT for infrastructure monitoring: technology and applications for smart transport/smart buildings. In: MEPTEC IoT Conference, San Jose, CA (2015)
36. Fedele, R., Della Corte, F.G., Carotenuto, R., Praticò, F.G.: Sensing road pavement health status through acoustic signals analysis. In: 13th Conference on Ph.D. Research in Microelectronics and Electronics (PRIME) (2017). https://doi.org/10.1109/prime.2017.7974133
37. Lenglet, C., Blanc, J., Dubroca, S.: Smart road that warns its network manager when it begins cracking. IET Intell. Transp. Syst. **11**, 152–157 (2017). https://doi.org/10.1049/iet-its.2016.0044
38. Xu, X., Cao, D., Yang, H., He, M.: Application of piezoelectric transducer in energy harvesting in pavement. Int. J. Pavement Res. Technol. (2018). https://doi.org/10.1016/j.ijprt.2017.09.011
39. Alavi, A.H., Hasni, H., Lajnef, N., Chatti, K.: Continuous health monitoring of pavement systems using smart sensing technology. Constr. Build. Mater. (2016). https://doi.org/10.1016/j.conbuildmat.2016.03.128
40. Hernandez, J.A., Al-Qadi, I.L.: Tire–pavement interaction modelling: hyperelastic tire and elastic pavement. Road Mater. Pavement Des. (2017). https://doi.org/10.1080/14680629.2016.1206485
41. Moghimi, H., Ronagh, H.R.: Development of a numerical model for bridge-vehicle interaction and human response to traffic-induced vibration. Eng. Struct. (2008). https://doi.org/10.1016/j.engstruct.2008.06.015
42. Pedersen, L.: Viscoelastic Modelling of Road Deflections for use with the Traffic Speed Deflectometer. Kgs. Lyngby: Technical University of Denmark (DTU). IMM-PHD-2013, No. 310 (2013)
43. Stamp, D.H., Mooney, M.A.: Influence of lightweight deflectometer characteristics on deflection measurement. Geotech. Test. J. (2013). https://doi.org/10.1520/GTJ20120034

44. Casey, D.B., Airey, G.D., Grenfell, J.R.: Relative pavement performance for dual and wide-based tire assemblies using a finite element method. J. Test. Eval. **45**, 1896–1903 (2017). https://doi.org/10.1520/JTE20160589
45. Lak, M.A., Degrande, G., Lombaert, G.: The effect of road unevenness on the dynamic vehicle response and ground-borne vibrations due to road traffic. Soil Dyn. Earthq. Eng. (2011). https://doi.org/10.1016/j.soildyn.2011.04.009
46. Liu, P., Wang, D., Oeser, M.: Application of semi-analytical finite element method coupled with infinite element for analysis of asphalt pavement structural response. J. Traffic Transp. Eng. (2015). https://doi.org/10.1016/j.jtte.2015.01.005
47. Liu, P., Wang, D., Hu, J., Oeser, M.: SAFEM – software with graphical user interface for fast and accurate finite element analysis of asphalt pavements. J. Test. Eval. **45**, 1301–1315 (2017). https://doi.org/10.1520/JTE20150456. ISSN:0090-3973
48. Liu, P., Otto, F., Wang, D., Oeser, M., Balck, H.: Measurement and evaluation on deterioration of asphalt pavements by geophones. J. Int. Measure. Confederation (2017). https://doi.org/10.1016/j.measurement.2017.05.066
49. Astrauskas, T., Grubliauskas, R.: Modelling of Ground Borne Vibration Induced by Road Transport. Vilnius Gediminas Technical University, Vilnius (2017). https://doi.org/10.3846/mla.2017.1060

Quantifying the Carbon Dioxide Emissions Resulting from Awareness-Raising Actions of Sustainable Mobility

Pétilin Souza$^{(\boxtimes)}$ (ID), Filipa Paiva (ID), Lígia Silva (ID), and Paulo Pereira (ID)

University of Minho, Rua da Universidade, 4710-057 Braga, Portugal
petilindesouza@gmail.com, filipa_paiva@sapo.pt,
{lsilva,ppereira}@civil.uminho.pt

Abstract. Currently, the transport sector is a major contributor to global greenhouse gases emissions. The evaluation of projects that promote the decarbonization in cities is mainly focused on calculating the reduction of CO_2 emissions. The calculation methodology takes into account the characteristics of the city car fleet where these projects are implemented. In the case of the "SchoolBus" project, promoted by the Braga Municipal Council during the 2018–2019 school year, the average value of reduction was of 34.9 $tonCO_2eq$/year. The number of vehicles circulating in the study area, the emission factor related to the type of vehicle and its fuel and the distance traveled by them were the main parameters used to calculate CO_2 emissions. The impacts of the "SchoolBus" project on stakeholders and awareness-raising actions of sustainable mobility can be quantified in terms of CO_2, by analyzing the population's interest in joining more sustainable modes of transport. Thus, it is possible to evaluate the potential of the awareness-raising actions, applied in the study area, in the decarbonization in a larger area (i.e. the whole municipality). At the same time, it is possible to compare and analyze the calculated values in relation to the quantified potential range of effects of policy measures on CO_2 emissions using transport demand for the year 2030, indicated by the European Commission and adapted to the area of study, by introducing measures of sustainable mobility in the territory.

Keywords: Cities decarbonization · Sustainable urban mobility · Public participation

1 Introduction

Nowadays, people are moving from rural areas to cities in order to search better opportunities of labor. According to the study carried out by the United Nations, an urban population growth was observed in Portugal in 1995 [1]. Worldwide, it was determined that 55.7% of the population lives in urban areas, with an expected increase to 68.4% by 2050 [1]. However, in Portugal it is expected a future increase of 79.3% of the urban population [1].

P. Pereira et al. (Eds.): SC4Life 2019, LNICST 318, pp. 15–30, 2020.
https://doi.org/10.1007/978-3-030-45293-3_2

The growth of the urban population has created impacts on the environment, whether directly or indirectly. According to IPCC [2], the direct and indirect impacts are as follows: (i) the increase in temperatures in cities; (ii) the higher concentration of air pollutants, including carbon dioxide emissions; (iii) the increase in noise, mainly from road traffic; and (iv) floods or droughts, creating water crises in urban areas [2].

Road traffic is one of the main sources of pollution, both air and noise, causing adverse effects on human health [3]. Increasingly, the combustion of fuels from road vehicles (60% of air pollutants emitted in urban and surrounding areas) is one of the largest air pollutants [4].

Greenhouse gases (GHG), when present in the atmosphere, absorb and emit part of the infrared radiation, making it impossible the Earth to lose heat to space. Carbon dioxide (CO_2) is a greenhouse gas, although it is not a toxic gas, and its emissions are the main cause of global warming. The increase in CO_2 emissions is therefore one of the most important issues in an urban area [2, 4].

The case study of this article is based on the project developed by Braga City Council (CMB), Braga Urban Innovation Laboratory Demonstrator (BUILD), with the aim of reducing greenhouse gas emissions. The BUILD project aims to solve car traffic issues, improving the urban environment, based on the implementation of technological and innovative solutions in the city. The project also aims to raise awareness in the community, in order to make them aware of the importance of decarbonization and the consequent impact on raising quality of life. The area chosen for the implementation of the BUILD project is located in the parish of São Vicente, and there are seven educational institutions in this area.

Based on the analysis of the results of the actions carried out under the BUILD project, this study aims to quantify the CO_2 emissions resulting from sustainable mobility awareness actions, analyzing and comparing the quantified values in relation to the potential CO_2 emission reduction values established by the European Commission, which have been adapted to the area under study.

Currently, there are a great range of technological equipment capable of providing effective tools, such as electronic sensors to collect information on traffic and air pollution concentrations, thus enabling support for public policy decisions. However, a change in community habits is highly important in order to decarbonize the city and contribute to the reduction of environmental impacts. This change is only possible with the application of sustainable policies and through the participation of the community in this objective.

The present study evaluates different approaches of urban planning in the context of the BUILD project, in order to improve urban quality of life and mitigate the climate changes. More specifically, BUILD aims to promote sustainable and inclusive urban mobility, prioritizing pedestrian mode, cycling and public transport over individual transport, with the decarbonization of the study area as its main purpose. Moreover, the BUILD stimulates the potential of awareness actions, as well as the application of measures developed within the framework of Sustainable Mobility to reduce emissions in the study area. The influence of different approaches from BUILD project on CO_2 emissions in the study area were compared and evaluated according to the method indicated by the European Commission, which was adapted to the study area, defined as PER Framework.

In the following sections the theoretical approach, the adopted methods, the case study exposition and the conclusions obtained from it are presented.

1.1 Urban Mobility and Traffic Pollution

Across the EU cars remain the dominant mode of passenger transport and account, approximately, 12% of total carbon dioxide (CO_2) emissions, the main greenhouse gas (GHG) [5]. Economic and population growth have been the most important factors in increasing CO_2 emissions from fossil fuel combustion [6]. In 2010, the transport sector accounted for 14% of total direct anthropogenic greenhouse gas emissions (gigatons of CO_2-equivalent per year, $GtCO_2$-eq/year) [2].

The GHG emissions from transport have not reduced in line with other economic sectors, although CO_2 emissions of new passenger cars have been steadily decreasing since 2007, reaching an value of 118.5 g/km in 2017 [5]. Thus, CO_2 emissions per km decreased by 10.4% between 2012 and 2017 [5]. To decarbonize cities, increasing their resilience to climate change, it is necessary to change lifestyles and current mobility patterns, which focus on individual transport [2]. Thus, the impact on environment by choosing between more or less sustainable transportation modes represents a challenge for decarbonization.

The planning process of transportation has changed throughout time, but to improve the cities is required a careful planning [7]. Traditional urban planning was carried out by traffic engineers, focusing on traffic modes, infrastructure and transportation modals [8]. Currently, urban mobility planning is focused on people, presenting integrated actions to achieve cost-effective solutions in a balanced development of all relevant transport modes, regarding the transition towards cleaner and more sustainable transport modes. On the other hand, city planning began to be carried out by interdisciplinary teams with stakeholder involvement.

The decarbonization of cities has been materialized by several policy objectives focused on urban mobility, such as the sharp reduction in CO_2 emissions from the transport sector to zero between 2040 and 2050; a marked reduction in emissions of air pollutants; almost zero fatalities in road transport in 20 to 40 years, depending on the current situation; drastic reduction of traffic congestion; improving the quality of urban life in general [7]. This shows the need to continually act on mobility in order to achieve a more sustainable scenario.

1.2 Sustainable and Inclusive Urban Mobility as a Goal

The year of 2015 marked a turning point towards sustainable development around the world. World leaders adopted a new global framework for sustainable development at the 70th UN General Assembly on 25 September 2015: the 2030 Agenda for Sustainable Development, based on the Sustainable Development Goals (SDGs). The 2030 Agenda represents a commitment to eradicate poverty and achieve sustainable development by 2030. The 17 SDGs and their 169 associated objectives are global in nature, universally applicable and interlinked [6].

The Paris Climate Agreement (COP21), the Addis Ababa Action Agenda, as an integral part of the 2030 Agenda, and the Sendai Framework for Disaster Risk Reduction also began to be implemented in 2015 [6]. The 2015 Paris Agreement represents a remarkable landmark in the global fight against climate change. In turn, the SDG 13 represents the EU's path to a low-carbon and climate resilient economy, through setting an ambitious economy-wide domestic target of reducing GHG emissions in at least 40% by 2030. The target is based on global projections that are in line with the medium term ambition of the Paris Agreement [6].

The SDG 11 marks, in the following, the importance of the sustainable mobility, providing access to safe, affordable, accessible and sustainable transport systems for all. It also enhances inclusive and sustainable urbanization and capacity for participatory, integrated and sustainable human settlement planning and management in all countries.

Urban mobility planning is a challenging and complex task. Planners need to manage many demands at the local and international levels, such as the European climate change and energy efficiency targets. The complexity increases in the event of political change and severe financial constraints, as is the situation in many European countries today. A Sustainable Urban Mobility Plan (SUMP) contributes to achieving the European energy and climate objectives set by EU leaders [8].

A SUMP is a strategic plan aimed at improving the quality of life of cities and surrounding areas, taking into account the mobility needs of people and businesses, which is based on existing planning practices and considers the principles of integration, participation and evaluation. The basic principles of a Sustainable Urban Mobility Plan are: Long-term vision and clear implementation plan; Participatory approach; Balanced and integrated development of all modes of transport; Horizontal and vertical integration; Evaluation of current and future performance; Regular monitoring, review and reporting; and consideration of external costs for all modes of transport [8].

1.3 Mobility Projects to Promote Decarbonization

Echeverri [9] and Grandim [10] refer that more than 70% of carbon dioxide emissions are produced by cities, making the discussion of urban challenges relevant to achieve a reduction in them. These urban challenges come from different dimensions, including urban infrastructure, transport, buildings and waste, presenting at the same time difficulties and opportunities at the technical and economic level [10]. Therefore, these mitigation challenges address the following levels: (i) institutions; (ii) behaviors; (iii) values; and (iv) technologies.

A relational perspective of these levels of urban dynamics allows us to understand that the various types of relationships that make up cities are what really create and change cities. Looking at how urban development is structured by its political economy and investigating how material forces and non-human agency are molding urban life, an adaptable relationship between both everyday practices and urban infra-structure becomes evident and results in unequal patterns of urban energy request and well-being [10].

With the implementation of new energy and mobility infrastructures in urban areas, there is potential for reducing carbon emissions [10]. Grandim et al. [10] address the complexity behind the implementation of new technologies or the investment of a public transport project but, more than that, a cultural and political social challenge.

The European Commission's report determined the expected impact of urban sustainable mobility measures on reducing CO_2 emissions for urban areas and examined the NUT-3 areas for Europe in order to establish the interval of the potential impact [11]. The report sets out the following 21 sustainable mobility measures, each with 7 categories: (i) public transport services; (ii) urban logistics and distribution; (iii) mobility management; (iv) incorporation of transport modes; (v) road transport; (vi) marketing and educational campaigns; (vii) access restriction schemes. In order to quantify the defined measures, a range corresponding to the total at European level was established and, thus, the total value of the contribution of each dimension was defined for each country [11]. These dimensions address the need to replace unsustainable transport with sustainable transport. Taking this into account, the study conducted by Souza [12] defined the values adopted for the country where the area under analysis is located, and stipulated the reduction coming from the expected impact values for the dimensions of the study area [12].

In recent decades, the number of parents travelling by individual transport to take their children to school has increased substantially, thus reducing the number of journeys by students on public transport. The aim of school mobility plans is to improve accessibility to schools by enabling pupils to travel independently to schools in a sustainable and safe manner [11]. There are several alternative modes of sustainable mobility, including collective bus travel, walking, cycling or car sharing between parents, which promote more sustainable behaviour in children with regard to environmental and safety issues [11].

In 2014, in Cordoba, Spain, a 14-week free Walking School Bus pilot project was developed. This project, carried out in a public school with the participation of 450 students, and consisted in students going to school, accompanied by monitors. The monitors had access to an application that allowed them to add the children's participation data and provide the group's location.

School Mobility is an important aspect for the control of road traffic and, as well as for the mobility improvement in the city of Braga [13]. Thus, as part of the European Mobility Week, in 2017, the CMB developed activities in the city in order to experiment solutions to reduce road traffic in the BUILD area. The activities developed were the "PeddyBus" and the "SchoolBus". The "PeddyBus" activity consisted in the movement of students, in groups and under the supervision of adult volunteers, to schools. In a first trial, about 10 children participated in the activity [13]. At the same time, the pilot project "SchoolBus" was under development, and its function was the free transportation of students by bus to previously established schools, with the participation of 700 children in the project [13].

2   Methods

Several measures that change urban infrastructure or mobility patterns are good options to reduce CO_2 emissions, for instance central urban areas closure for vehicles with pedestrian networks (SMM 5); integrated systems of public transportation (SMM 3); implementation of complete streets (SMM 14); scholar mobility plans (SMM 8) and implementation of low emission zones (SMM 21).

As previously mentioned, although traditional planning has a great focus on traffic, the discussion of sustainable urban mobility planning considers people as more important [8]. Therefore, it is extremely necessary to have an approach with participatory actions through a transparent relation. And so, the population and general stakeholders participate since the beginning of the plan development until the implementation phase. This participatory approach guarantee that the population own a Sustainable Urban Mobility Plan and the policies related to it [8].

The acceptance of a sustainable mobility plans, through long-term actions, and their permanence on the territory have greater chances to last with the involvement of the population [11, 15]. Therefore, willing to achieve the objectives previous presented, the actions will be developed along with stakeholders to promote sustainable and inclusive urban mobility.

2.1 Awareness-Raising Actions

In order to promote the "SchoolBus" project among the scholar community, several activities aimed at the target public, were applied. The awareness-activities developed were: (i) mobility as a game; and (ii) sustainable mobility workshops. The barriers of the involvement of the population in planning are the idea of a high need of effort and time [15]. Regarding it, it is important to use approaches, such as playful participatory processes (PPP), that insure a more attractive activities and beaten these mentioned issues. A few examples of PPP are story-telling, walking activities, sketching or drawing and games [15]. Thus, regarding the awareness-raising actions, more specifically for the engagement of the students, the activity will consist in two games that address the theme of sustainable mobility, in order to disseminate this concept and, therefore, increase the perception of different modes of transport's impact on the environment.

The Sustainable Mobility Workshop (SMW) developed to reach the goals of raising awareness engaged general stakeholders, focusing on students, willing to help to transition from the ongoing mobility paradigm towards more sustainable options,, and was based on the activity developed in Sao Paulo, Brazil, by ITDP Brasil [14]. Therefore, the students were first invited to fill a board with their daily transportation mode on the commuting to school, between the options of by foot, by bicycle by motorcycle, by car, by taxi or by public transport.

To motivate the participation it is possible to apply free-style drawing, beyond the options of playing a game or drawing, since it is possible to comprehend either objects and situations in the geographic environment [15].

Regarding it, the students later should draw their route in a mental map form, considering the path from home to school. It was important to highlight a few reference points, as well as some obvious figures for them, like people, things or landscapes, always emphasizing their transportation mode.

In an attempt to gather more individual information, the students could share theirs drawings, by explaining to their friends their creations. At the same time, the technical team would support the description by asking some previous agreed questions, about their feeling during the journey, their routine activities meanwhile travelling, if it was pleasant for them or would they consider some aspect to change. If the students mentioned an aspect to change, they could mark in red these modifications.

To assess the impact of the actions it will be calculated the number of people who confirmed to be willing to transition towards a more sustainable transportation mode, and this quantity of people will be considered as vehicles that will no longer drive in that area, allowing the calculation of the CO_2 emission reduction.

2.2 PER Framework

The Joint Research Centre (JRC) from the European Commission [11] calculated in their report 21 sustainable mobility measures' potential impact on reducing CO_2 emissions in an urban environment, thorough defining the effects of those measures for each NUTS-3 zone in Europe. To better understand the NUTS (Nomenclature of Territorial Units for Statistics) zoning, it is a classification through a hierarchical system which separates the European Union (EU) economic territory regarding its dimensions considering different intentions (European Commission, n.d.). The division of the territory comes in basically three different levels, the first is for major socio-economic regions, the second basic regions in which the regional policies are applied, finally in a third level for small regions that need specific analysis to more accurate diagnosis. In the case of Portugal, the division of NUTS-1 is Continent, Azores, and Madeira; NUTS-2 is five regions and two autonomous regions; finally, NUTS-3, concern groups of municipalities.

In the study of JRC [11] it was considered the demand of transportation by the year of 2030 through MODEL-T JRC, and the estimated CO_2 emissions resultant for each NUTS-3 zone, in order to quantify the potential interval of policies' effects on reducing CO_2 emissions. The potential effects of the policies of sustainable mobility were asset by an analysis which considered the differences between European territories and weighted scores from a group of experts regarding tendencies of transport behavior in each NUTS-3 zones. Once each European city distinguished itself for its size, density, population, and other aspects, the weighing method of scoring considered it, since it could certainly differ between cities [11]. Consequently it were analyzed different aspects of the cities, such as density, accessibility, employment, population and commuting characteristics of each particular zone.

The values presented by JRC [11] were adapted in the PER Framework (Table 1) to the dimensions of the study area.

To develop this scale-down approach, Souza [12] calculated each sustainable measure contribution regarding the values range of A-S-I dimensions for Portugal potential values. As a result, Portugal represented 1.27% of the European total emission of CO_2.

Afterwards, Souza [12] considered the more refined spatial dimension of sub-NUTS-3, that are more precise dimensions, and through the correlation of these sub zones with the Functional Urban Area (FUA) of each NUTS-3 zone it was possible to scale the values from Portugal to the dimensions of the city of Braga. The FUA analyzed in combination with NUTS-3 zones allowed a greater precision in the estimation of each transport activity specification by area. Through the method of Random Forest model, it was set a matrix of 642 (FUAs) × 21 (measures) × 3 (coefficients: A-S-I), that represented the net impact on emissions reduction across all modes in relative terms (as a share of estimated total urban transport emissions of each FUA) [16].

Some simplifications on the calculation were considered by Souza [12] since in the matter of the present study is analyzed a specific area of a city instead a comparison between different cities. Conclusively it was create a framework (PER Framework)

Table 1. PER Framework [12]

PER Framework			[tonCO$_2$eq/year]	
Sustainable mobility measures			Min	Max
Public transport services				
1	Investment and maintenance, including safety, security and accessibility		34	43
2	Public transport coverage & frequencies		44	55
3	Interoperable ticketing and payment systems		23	28
4	Taxi services (individual and collective)		28	35
5	Dedicated walking and cycling infrastructure investment and maintenance & Bike sharing schemes		38	47
City logistics and distribution				
6	Improvement of the efficiency of city logistics by the use of ICT		46	57
7	Measures to improve the energy efficiency and environmental performance of vehicles and/or use of alternative modes		30	37
Mobility management				
8	Corporate, school and personalized mobility plans (or workplace travel plans)		33	41
9	Car sharing & carpooling schemes		21	27
10	Telecommunications		49	61
Integration of transport modes				
11	Multimodal connection platforms		15	18
12	Multimodal travel information provision		41	51
13	Park and Ride areas		25	31
Road transport				
14	Reallocation of road space to other modes of transport, e.g. dedicated bus lanes		48	59
15	Parking management		38	47
16	Dynamic traffic management measures		20	25
17	Low speed zones		23	29
Marketing campaigns and education				
18	Information and marketing campaigns		30	38
19	Promotion of eco-driving		7	9
Access restriction schemes				
20	Congestion charging zones		72	90
21	Low emission zones		41	51

which allows the assessment and analysis of the potential reduction of CO$_2$ emission by each measure considered in the calculation.

The impact of the sustainable mobility measures can be asset through the PER once it calculates the quantity of CO$_2$ that will no longer be emitted, considering the dimension of the study area in comparison with the interval set by the framework. The calculation evaluation is presented in the following section.

3   Case Study: Awareness Activities Under Sustainable Mobility Theme - The BUILD Project

Braga City Council developed a project in the form of Living Lab, called Braga Urban Innovation Laboratory Demonstrator (BUILD), which focused on the decarbonization of the city, allowing an urban environment accessible to innovation, through the actions of local authorities, companies, the University of Minho (UM), the International Iberian Nanotechnology Laboratory (INL), the Center for Computer Graphics (CCG), citizens and local communities. As part of this study and after the success of the "SchoolBus" pilot project carried out during the mobility week, the CMB permanently implemented the "SchoolBus" project during the 2018/2019 school year. This project consists in transporting students by bus to the respective schools, located in the city centre and belonging to the BUILD intervention area, from points located on the border of the city centre, previously defined in the project. BUILD's intervention area is located in the city of Braga, more specifically in a parish in the northeast area, São Vicente, which integrates the historical centre area and the Braga East area. The area represents one of the most recent growth areas of the city's urban area, with around 14 hectares, being highly influenced by its proximity to the city centre [14]. The north and northwest border of the area is delimited by the Regiment Street of Infantry 8 and along the east border is the cemetery of Braga and the street Dom António Bento Martins Júnior. The south border of the area is delimited by the Monte de Arcos square, the Conselheiro Bento Miguel street, the Conselheiro São Januário street and Dr. Domingos Soares street. According to the Geographic Information Reference Database (BGRI) and analyzing the Census 2011, there are 75 buildings in the BUILD area, 62 of which are exclusively residential and the rest with residential and commercial use. The study area presents a high difference between the areas close to the historical center, where the residential buildings are new and large, and the northern areas, where the buildings are smaller, usually single-family, and older [14]. The area under analysis has a high road traffic, due to the high concentration of educational institutions. The area contains two leisure areas, among them there is the Monte d'Arcos Square, which acts as living area, and the public park called the Pachancho Children's Park (Fig. 1).

Fig. 1. BUILD area and reference points in which (1) Dom Diogo de Sousa School (2) Leonardo Da Vinci School (3) Sá de Miranda School (4) British Institute (5) Enguardas School (6) Teresiano School (7) Francisco Sanches School [12]

The study area presents considerable road traffic congestion, mainly during the period of entry and exit of students from the various educational institutions. It also presents a problem of lack of inclusive mobility and soft modes, under the existing conditions of urban public life and access, especially in relation to abandoned and damaged public spaces. Thus, the main objective of the "SchoolBus" project is to improve accessibility, safety and, above all, the mobility in the vicinity of schools, with a perspective of decarbonizing the BUILD area. The "SchoolBus" project started in September 2018 and, in January 2019, 410 students participated in the project. The CO_2 emissions calculation took into account the characteristics of the vehicle fleet of Braga, depending on the percentage of the different fuels used during the year 2017 in Portugal. Whereas in light vehicles there is a clear predominance of gas oil (64.1%), the percentage of gasoline in heavy vehicles is practically insignificant, since diesel is used in 99.49% of these vehicles. In this way, all heavy vehicles were considered to use diesel (100%). On the other hand, DEFRA [17] indicates that the amount of fuel per kilometer (kg/km) consumed by type of vehicle (light and heavy vehicles) and fuel used is 0.07 and 0.06 kg/km for diesel and petrol vehicles, respectively, and 0.24 kg/km for heavy (diesel) vehicles. Based on the number of vehicles circulating in the intervention area, CO_2 emissions from the study area were calculated using Eq. 1.

$$CO_2 \text{emissions} \left(\text{kgCO}_2\text{e} \right) = \Sigma \left(N_{i,j} \times D_{i,j} \times EF_{i,j} \right) \qquad (1)$$

In which:

$N_{i,j}$ – Number of vehicles of category "i" with fuel "j"
$D_{i,j}$ – Distance traveled by vehicles of category "i" with fuel "j" (km)
$EF_{i,j}$ – Emission factor of category "i" vehicles with "j" fuel (kgCO$_2$-eq/km)

The conversion factors for calculating the greenhouse gas emissions considered the parameters set by the British Government [17, 18]. Considering the vehicles fleet composition for light vehicles the emissions factors were 0.17887 kgCO$_2$eq/km and 0.18568 kgCO$_2$eq/km for diesel fuel and gasoline respectively. Regarding heavy vehicles the emissions factors were 0.9339 kgCO$_2$eq/km for heavy-duty diesel vehicles and 1.2194 kgCO$_2$eq/km for buses.

The reduction of CO_2 emissions resulting from "SchoolBus" project was determined considering the daily number of students who used the buses assigned to the project, from the interfaces to the respective educational institutions, in each month since the beginning of the project. In order to facilitate the calculation of the distance traveled by the buses, two centroids were considered: (i) Centroid of the BUILD (CEB) Schools; (ii) Centroid of Schools not BUILD (CENB). The center of the BUILD Schools is the middle center of the bus route that passes through the Dom Diogo de Sousa School, the Leonardo Da Vinci School and the Teresiano School. The centroid of the Schools BUILD is the middle center of the bus route that passes through the School EB2,3 Francisco Sanches, Calouste Gulbenkian School and School EB2,3 André Soares. Knowing the route made by the buses, from the interfaces to the centroids, it was determined the distances traveled by them (Fig. 2).

The reduction of motor vehicle traffic after the implementation of the "SchoolBus" project was obtained by considering that the number of students using the bus as equal to

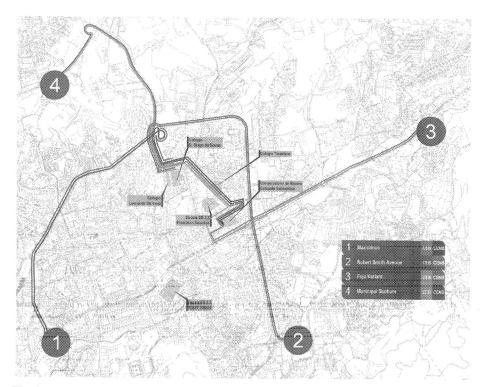

Fig. 2. Routes between interfaces and centroids considered for the calculation of CO_2 emissions (Source: Authors)

the number of private light vehicles that stop circulating in the BUILD area, applying the 1:1 rule. The Table 2 shows the routes traveled by buses and their distances traveled, as well as the number of private vehicles associated with the number of students using the

Table 2. Number of vehicles associated with the number of students using School Bus and the routes and their distances traveled by buses (Source: Authors)

Routes		Travelled distance [Km]	Average number	
Departure	Arrival		Diesel cars	Light cars petrol
Municipal stadium	CENB	10.6	7	4
Municipal stadium	CEB	8.0	15	8
Fojo variant	CENB	6.4	2	1
Fojo variant	CEB	9.4	9	5
Robert Smith avenue	CENB	10.8	2	1
Robert Smith avenue	CEB	8.2	35	19
Maximinos	CENB	11.2	5	3
Maximinos	CEB	8.6	5	3

bus. Finally, through Eq. 1, the contribution of the "SchoolBus" project was calculated for the decarbonization of the BUILD area, which translated into the average annual reduction of 33.8 tonCO$_2$eq.

From the 546 students involved in the awareness actions carried out, 141 students were as well in the sustainable mobility workshops from the Dom Diogo de Sousa School and the Leonardo Da Vinci School (Table 3).

Table 3. Number of stakeholders engaged in each activity (Source: Authors)

Awareness-raising actions		Students engaged
Mobility as a game	Leonardo Da Vinci School	140
	School EB2,3 André Soares	20
	School EB2,3 Francisco Sanches	225
	Calouste Gulbenkian School	20
Sustainable mobility workshops	Dom Diogo de Sousa School - Art students	11
	Dom Diogo de Sousa School - 4th class	108
	Leonardo Da Vinci School	22

One of the awareness-raising actions was a game in which Leonardo Da Vinci school pupils, in groups of 10, had to rank which modes of transport they considered to be more and less sustainable, and which would have the greatest impact on the environment, among several pre-defined modes of transport (walking, cycling, metro, bus, motorcycle and car). This game triggered discussions among the various groups of pupils about the results they had initially considered.

Another carried out action was the game called "Big Mobility" which consisted in answering questions about mobility, in order to address concepts and clarify issues related to the environmental impact created by each mode of transport, involving students and residents in it. This game had already been developed in 2017, by the CMB, during the European Mobility Week. The BUILD project's technical team adapted the idea to the awareness-raising activities carried out, having achieved a participation of 100 students in the "Big Mobility" games.

Students who participated in the Sustainable Mobility workshops indicated that they traveled to school in private cars, as illustrated in Fig. 3. Still, 30% of the total showed a willingness to change to a more sustainable mode of transport, of which 64% mentioned the "SchoolBus" as a choice. On the other hand, 68% of the students indicated that they enjoyed the transportation they currently use to get to school, while 64% traveled by car.

In the awareness actions carried out, it was observed that 50% of the students would like the city to have less road traffic or, in some cases, that it entirely did not exist. The children mentioned the desire to have a city with less air and noise pollution, with fewer road accidents and, in this way, make the city a more attractive place with more green areas (Fig. 4).

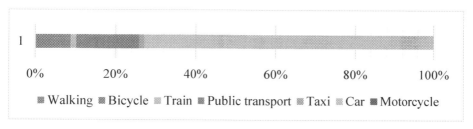

1

0%   20%   40%   60%   80%   100%

▩ Walking ▩ Bicycle ▩ Train ▩ Public transport ▩ Taxi ▩ Car ▩ Motorcycle

Fig. 3. Modal distribution of students on the commuting to the educational institution [12]

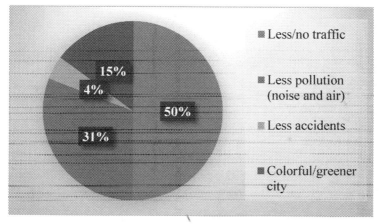

▩ Less/no traffic

▩ Less pollution (noise and air)

▩ Less accidents

▩ Colorful/greener city

Fig. 4. How the children would like the city to be different from Mental Maps [12]

In the awareness-raising actions there was a potential increase of the CO_2 emissions reduction of the "SchoolBus" project, since 27 new students showed interest in joining the project in the future. Evaluating the impact of these future inscriptions, it was verified that these 27 students would cause a decrease of CO_2 emissions of 7.19 tonCO$_2$eq, which is equivalent to 21% of the current value reached by the "SchoolBus" during this school year (reduction of CO_2 emissions from 33.8 tonCO$_2$eq to 40.9 tonCO$_2$eq).

The "SchoolBus" project, as started in September 2018, may have contributed to its success in achieving large numbers in reducing CO_2 emissions. However, the potential impacts of awareness-raising actions in increasing the reduction of CO_2 emissions allowed to achieve results closer to the maximum values of the range established by the PER Framework method, instead of approaching the minimum values, as shown in Table 4.

The awareness-raising actions carried out made it possible to verify that progressive investments in Sustainable Mobility Measures, through public participation, represent a possibility of greater contribution, even more so when the objective is to achieve the decarbonization goals of a city.

Table 4. Values from PER Framework compared with calculated values of BUILD interventions [12] (Adapted)

Sustainable mobility measure	Intervention	Interventions calculated values [tonCO$_2$eq/year]	PER framework [tonCO$_2$eq/year]	
			Min.	Max.
Corporate, school and personalized mobility plans (Or workplace travel plans)	"SchoolBus" – Current value	**33.8**	33	41
Corporate, school and personalized mobility plans (Or workplace travel plans)	"SchoolBus" – Considering the utilization increase	**40.9**	33	41

4   Conclusions

The correlation of the city as a meeting place, that enabled the social contact of the population get lost with the raise of private transportation modes. That because it kept the population away from the urban environment as an extension of their daily life. It could only lead to an alienation of the public space, and so the scales of the city turn into impersonal relations with the built urban environment.

Considering that, there is a need of increase more active modes of transportation, that are, at the same time, more sustainable modes. This shift can approximate again the population with the city, and consequently it is important to promote a shift from expert technicians into interdisciplinary teams. It will create the possibility of the population to be heard by technical people, at the same time building up a positive relation between society and built environment. That is because it is already clear that the effectiveness of the city planning process is strictly connected with the comprehension by population that the planning is a method able to improve their quality of life.

Furthermore, the Mobility Games as a tool for public participation truly engage the stakeholders and acted as an efficient tool during the phase of motivational increase of the actions. It was a great challenge for the stakeholders to avoid mistakes while answering the questions about sustainable mobility and local traffic laws. At the same time, it was a really ludic activity for young students and helped, in a more functional perspective, in spreading the sustainable mobility concept.

Furthermore, there is much of work in progress, since the impacts of the promoted actions in contribute to a behavioral change regarding sustainable mobility can definitely rise. Once, only 30% of the students could demonstrate the comprehension of co-responsibility on transition to a more sustainable modes of transportation, which means that they also have to change their transportation mode for a more sustainable one, although a great number of the students identified the need of a city with less traffic.

To achieve the goals of the global sustainability agenda not only governmental policies are needed, but indeed the local actions of awareness raising had great impact on behavior, since they were mainly addressed to the young population of the study area. At the same time it was an opportunity to contribute with a transformation of the technicians' perspectives, once approaching the needs of the city-users more closely. Moreover, by creating alternative solutions, such as addressing the Scholar Mobility, that was a great concern on the study area, through the project "SchoolBus", it was possible to actually impact directly issues of urban mobility. Therefore, bringing effective solutions regarding the mobility planning of the city.

Lastly, the confirmation of the continuation of the "SchoolBus" project for the scholar year of 2019/2020 creates an opportunity for future works. It will make possible the further analysis along the months of the raise tendency of students using the service, and thereupon the effective impact calculation of the project. Although the need of continuation of these actions, it is certain that this is already a piece of contribution for the sustainable mobility promotion in the city of Braga.

References

1. United Nations: World Urbanization Prospects: The 2018 Revision (2018)
2. IPCC, Climate Change 2014: Synthesis Report. Contribution of Working Groups I, II and III to the Fifth Assessment Report of the Intergovernmental Panel on Climate Change. Geneva, Switzerland: IPCC (2014)
3. Silva, L.T., Mendes, J.F.G.: City noise-air: an environmental quality index for cities. Sustain. Cities Soc. **4**, 1–11 (2012)
4. Petrovic, N., Bojovic, N., Petrovic, J.: Appraisal of urbanization and traffic on environmental quality (2016)
5. European Union: Sustainable Development in the European Union 2018. Publications Office of the European Union, Luxembourg (2018)
6. European Commission: Next steps for a sustainable European future: European action for sustainability. COM(2016), p. 739 (2016)
7. Korver, W., Stemerding, M., Van Egmond, P., Wefering, F.: CIVITAS Guide for the Urban Transport Professional - Results and Lessons of Long Term Evaluation of the CIVITAS Initiative, Graz, Austria (2012)
8. Wefering, F., Rupprecht, S., Bührmann, S., Böhler-Baedeker, S.: Guidelines. Developing and Implementing a Sustainable Urban Mobility Plan (2014)
9. Gomez Echeverri, L.: Investing for rapid decarbonization in cities. Curr. Opin. Environ. Sustain. **30**, 42–51 (2018)
10. Grandin, J., Haarstad, H., Kjærås, K., Bouzarovski, S.: The politics of rapid urban transformation. Curr. Opin. Environ. Sustain. **31**, 16–22 (2018)
11. Lopez-Ruiz, H.G., Christidis, P., Demirel, H., Kompil, M.: Quantifying the effects of sustainable urban mobility plans, JRC Technical report, vol. EUR 26123 (2013)
12. Souza, P.: People-centered Urban Measures towards Sustainable Mobility, University of Minho (2019)
13. Braga Municipal Council: Plano de Implementação do Braga Urban Innovation Laboratory Demonstrator (BUILD) (2017)
14. ITDP Brasil: Intervenção urbana temporária (Re)pensando a rua em Santana, pp. 1–55 (2018)
15. Poplin, A.: Playful public participation in urban planning: a case study for online serious games. Comput. Environ. Urban Syst. **36**, 195–206 (2012)

16. Pisoni, E., Christidis, P., Thunis, P., Trombetti, M.: Evaluating the impact of 'Sustainable Urban Mobility Plans' on urban background air quality. J. Environ. Manage. **231**, 249–255 (2019)
17. DEFRA: UK Government GHG Convertion Factors for Company Reporting (2017)
18. CTAC: Assessoria técnica no âmbito da avaliação dos impactos decorrentes das ações implementadas, Braga (2018)

Leak Detection in Water Distribution Networks via Pressure Analysis Using a Machine Learning Ensemble

Vivencio C. Fuentes Jr.$^{(\boxtimes)}$ ⬤ and Jhoanna Rhodette I. Pedrasa ⬤

University of the Philippines, Diliman, 1101 Quezon City, Philippines
vivencio.fuentes@eee.upd.edu.ph, jipedrasa@up.edu.ph

Abstract. Water distribution networks (WDNs) are vital infrastructure which serve as a means for public utilities to deliver potable water to consumers. Naturally, pipelines degrade over time, causing leakages and pipe bursts. Damaged pipelines allow water to leak through, incurring significant economic losses. Mitigating these losses are important, especially in areas with water scarcity, to allow consumers to have adequate water supply. Globally, as the population increases, there is a need to make water distribution efficient, due to the rising demand. Thus, leak detection is vital for reducing the system loss of the network and improving efficiency.

Monitoring WDNs effectively for leakage is often a challenging task due to the size of the area it covers, and due to the need to detect leaks as early as possible. Traditionally, this is done via pipeline inspection or physical modeling. However, such techniques are either time-consuming, resource intensive, or both. An alternative is machine learning (ML), which maps the relationship between pipeline data to detect leakages. This allows for a faster, yet reasonably accurate model for detection and localization. Machine learning techniques could be utilized together as an ensemble, which allows these techniques to work in conjunction with each other. Wavelet decomposition will be performed on the data to allow for a smaller dataset, as well as utilizing possible hidden features for the machine learning model.

Keywords: Water distribution networks · Leak detection · Machine learning

1 Introduction

1.1 Water Distribution Networks

Water distribution networks (WDNs) are systems designed and implemented to deliver potable water from a source to a consumer. However, pipeline

This work is supported by a Commission on Higher Education (CHED) Philippine California Advanced Research Institues (PCARI) grant under Project IIID54 - Resilient Cyber Physical Societal Scale Systems.

P. Pereira et al. (Eds.): SC4Life 2019, LNICST 318, pp. 31–44, 2020.
https://doi.org/10.1007/978-3-030-45293-3_3

infrastructure gradually experience deterioration, which could be due to natural aging, environmental damage, or unauthorized human interference [1]. Damaged pipelines allow water to leak through, which would cause significant economic losses. As the world population grows, there is a need for distributing water efficiently due to scarcity in water supply. Mitigating losses is key, especially in areas with water scarcity, making leak detection an important part for improving the efficiency of a network.

1.2   Leak Detection

Without using automated sensing or analytical methods, leakages are traditionally reported via water utility personnel examining above-ground meters along the WDN [2]. Due to the nature of human involvement, this is a time-consuming method that could possibly incur significant losses before it is addressed.

As leakage events follow hydraulic principles, sensors could be used to monitor characteristic changes within the pipeline. Pressure drops and flow imbalance in certain areas could imply disruption in normal pipeline operations [1].

Data acquired from sensors in pipelines could be studied to develop analytical models. By combining known hydraulic equations and state analysis of the pipeline, physical modeling could be performed for a network [3]. Further analyses of data could be done by applying machine learning techniques to establish correlation between different factors, and distinguish false positives from actual leaks [4]. More often than not, a combination of certain aspects of these techniques are used to improve accuracy of leak detection [5].

1.3   Data Analysis

Datasets containing real-world data could be used to model existing water distribution networks and possible leakage occurrences in conjunction with actual demand patterns [6]. However, in the absence of real-world data, EPANET software would be used to simulate leakage in water distribution networks [7]. Components such as pipes and valves could be implemented in simulations to reflect physical models. Datasets are constructed from such simulations, and could be used for analysis. For this study, the datasets are generated with emphasis on varying sensor density and topology. Datasets from these networks would then be evaluated to test the machine learning model. Using machine learning, leakage detection in these networks could be performed [8].

1.4   Overview

The main objective of this research is to perform simulations on different water distribution networks, and develop a machine learning approach for leak detection. Factors affecting WDN operations such as water demand and physical characteristics of the WDN will be taken into consideration. Performance of the machine learning model will be evaluated on different network topologies and sensor density.

2   Related Work

2.1   Leak Detection Methods

Without the usage of other leak detection techniques, on-site inspections by water utility personnel are relied upon [2]. Above-ground sensor reading equipment must be deployed along the WDN for a technician or engineer to be able to note sensor data. As the response highly involves human intervention, the system could possibly undergo significant losses before the appropriate action is implemented [1].

Acoustic sensors could be installed along the WDN to detect sound signals, which could be used with signal processing techniques to detect and localize leakages [2]. Signals would be higher in amplitude near the leaks, allowing for localization. This method has the advantage of not needing a complex mathematical model. However, acoustic sensing techniques are easily affected by the physical environment around it; external noise might interfere with sensor readings [9]. The cost of implementing the hardware for the system would be high as well, especially for larger networks [1].

Another technique used for leak detection are balancing methods. Under normal operation, input and output mass flow rate of each pipeline are equal [2], which is supported by the law of conservation of mass. Thus, imbalances of these metrics would imply leakage within the pipeline. The balance between input and output flows could be represented by the equation

$$M_I - M_O = \Delta M_{pipe} \qquad (1)$$

where M_I and M_O represent mass in the inlet and outlet of the pipe, respectively, while ΔM_{pipe} represents the imbalance between the two. As mass is proportional to the flow rates, input and output flows could also be represented by the equation

$$Q_I - Q_O = \Delta Q_{pipe} \qquad (2)$$

where Q_I and Q_O similarly represent flow rates in the inlet and outlet of the pipe, respectively, while ΔQ_{pipe} represents the imbalance between the two [1]. To be within range of possible errors in sensor readings, an alarm threshold is implemented based on pressure or flow values. While rather simplistic in theory, utilizing pressure and flow data is a fundamental basis for techniques that rely on data processing of hydraulic models.

Transient analysis could also be utilized as a leak detection method [10]. Transient information generated by leakage scenarios could be extracted and then evaluated accordingly. The main idea of transient analysis is to compare signals received by a sensor in a leakage event to signals under normal operation. Focusing on the transient signals can offer more information rather than simply monitoring the WDN at its steady state [10,11].

Model-based methods could be assessed, to determine the state of subsections of a WDN based on water hammer equations [3]. The underlying fundamental principle relating flow and pressure could be summarized in equations

$$\frac{\partial H}{\partial t} = -\frac{c^2}{gA}\frac{\partial Q}{\partial z} \tag{3}$$

$$\frac{\partial Q}{\partial t} = -Ag\frac{\partial H}{\partial z} - \frac{fQ|Q|}{2DA} \tag{4}$$

where t and z represent coordinates in time and space, respectively, H representing pressure, c representing wave speed, g representing Earth's gravity, Q representing flow rate, D representing the diameter of the pipeline, A representing the cross-sectional area of the pipe, and f representing the friction coefficient [3].

While model-based methods based on physical properties of a WDN yield high accuracies in fault detection, it is not feasible to use in large-scale networks due to the amount of parameters and data involved [12,13]. An alternative is to use machine learning techniques, which generate similarly high accuracies, but require less computational load [8,14]. Machine learning maps the dependent and independent parameters of a given system, with little prior process knowledge. Performance of machine learning techniques are based on the design of the technique, which could be improved over time with data [13].

Machine learning techniques and their properties could be incorporated into a single learning algorithm called an ensemble method [15]. Ensemble methods are multiple machine learning techniques that are trained cooperatively to produce better predictive performance. In the field of hydrology, there have been proposals to utilize ensemble methods to improve the performances of WDNs [14,16]. Pairing up single methods with each other could help decrease unwanted levels in bias and variance, which could ultimately increase predictive performance.

2.2 EPANET

EPANET is a simulation software for modeling water distribution networks and examine hydraulic behavior in pipe networks. It is able to simulate different WDN entities, such as pipes, tanks, valves, and reservoirs. Factors such as water pressure, water flow, and chemical concentrations could be monitored within the system. EPANET also provides a visual simulator to help the user build pipe networks and edit properties such as pipe diameter or valve function [7].

By simulating emissions within a water distribution network, EPANET is able to model leakage events, and the properties of the network during such an event could be studied. EPANET has been used in modeling and detecting leakages in WDNs of real-life communities and small-scale testbeds [17,18] (Fig. 1).

EPANET takes advantage of combining demand patterns and leakage properties to model leaks within a specified time frame. This would help in detecting the possibility of leakage within the WDN [18]. A relation used in EPANET to model leakage is as follows [17]:

$$Q = E_c * P^{P_{exp}}, \tag{5}$$

where Q represents flow, E_c represents the emitter coefficient, P represents pressure, and P_{exp} represents the pressure exponent, which is usually set to 0.5 for water networks.

Fig. 1. EPANET window simulation

3   Methodology

The methodology is composed of three major tasks: simulations, feature extraction, and classification. Simulation modeling includes the construction of a functional and realistic water distribution network in simulation software. Simulations involving leakage events are carried out afterwards, done on WDNs with varying topology and sensor density.

The proposed solution is to apply wavelet series decomposition on pressure data, and to use the energy of each wavelet as a feature for the machine learning model. Specifically, a CNN ensemble is implemented as part of the machine learning model to analyze the data. The CNN ensemble would effectively classify the pressure profiles from the sensors as to whether or not they have a leak. Instead of using each recording from each sensor node as a feature, the energy of each wavelet is used, effectively reducing the size of the dataset. This allows the machine learning model to learn from another feature, which could result in better detection.

3.1   Hydraulic Simulations

In the absence of datasets for real-life water distribution networks, simulations are performed in EPANET to produce data from networks with similar characteristics. Water distribution networks are constructed in EPANET by implementing elements such as pipes, junctions, and reservoirs. These networks in the EPANET program reflect certain parts, if not the whole, of actual WDNs.

For the analysis, three distinct EPANET networks are used: the Cherry Hills/Brushy Plains network, the New York City Tunnel network, and the

Fossolo network. These networks are derived from actual implementations of existing water distribution networks [19,20], and are distributed with EPANET releases [7].

The simulations would incorporate hourly water demand profiles used by households [18]. A profile could be constructed via analysis of previous consumption data [21], or sociological analysis [22]. For example, usage in residential areas is typically at lowest after midnight, and would peak during early mornings or early evenings [23]. Accuracy of leak detection would depend on how much volume of water is taken into consideration within pipelines.

Pipes, junctions, and other elements close to the emitter nodes are monitored for changes. The model for the water distribution networks is able to capture key characteristics, and these will be the basis for leak detection. Such characteristics include pressure, water flow, water head, and water quality. Out of these, pressure changes are most reflective of leakage scenarios [4], making it the ideal data input for the proposed solution. Pressure data are recorded accordingly based on EPANET's time reporting step, which was set to every 30 s. Changes in the pressure profile is then analyzed to determine and localize leaks.

Changes on leak sizes and leak locations are then performed. These combinations of changes are used to create datasets for machine learning. To introduce leakage events, the emitter coefficients of the nodes within the network are be increased. Shown in Fig. 2 are the differences between the pressure profile of a node in the Cherry Hills/Brushy Plains network within a 24-h period upon increasing the emitter coefficient. The drop in pressure is found to be consistent with hydraulic principles.

To facilitate leak detection, sensor nodes are implemented into every EPANET simulation of a water distribution network. These are assigned out of existing junction nodes, and the placement of these would have an impact in detecting leaks. This allows for a mechanism to monitor and record pressure profiles within the network, which would then be analyzed accordingly [18].

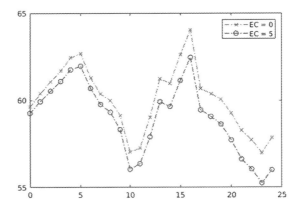

Fig. 2. Pressure profile of the same node at $E_c = 0$ and at $E_c = 5$

To test the effect of sensor density, sensor placement is done differently on each simulation. Specifically, different simulations have sensors that are placed on locations that are 1-, 2-, and 3-hop distances from non-sensor junction nodes, without overlap.

3.2   Feature Extraction and Wavelet Decomposition

The data streams that will be observed are pressure streams coming from sensor nodes. Intuitively, pressure data observed from components away from the leakage event would be inversely proportional to the distance from the leak. Generally, leakage within the vicinity would result in more drastic pressure drops.

Furthermore, wavelet transforms could be applied to these signals, where they would be decomposed into their respective approximation coefficients and detail coefficients [4,24]. The approximation coefficient corresponds to the lower frequency of the original signal, while the detail coefficients correspond to the higher frequency of the original signal. Different levels of the detail coefficient could possibly detect transients in the signal, which could be correlated with detecting leakages in the pipeline, as leakage events come with changes of pressure. The detail coefficients also capture the noise element of the signal, while the approximation coefficient resemble the original signal (Fig. 3).

The energy of the coefficients would be computed, and used as the feature vectors for each sensor, effectively reduceing the input size of the dataset. Utilizing the energy of the pressure signals instead of raw pressure data allow for minimizing energy consumption of the sensors in sending data over a network [18], as well as allowing the CNN ensemble to possibly find more hidden features [4].

These data would then be analyzed via machine learning by a CNN ensemble. It is expected that the different networks would provide different pressure profiles for the CNN ensemble to learn.

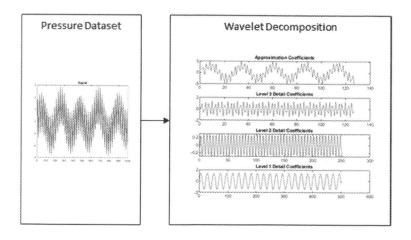

Fig. 3. Wavelet Decomposition

3.3   Classification via Machine Learning Ensemble

The main concern of the study is to identify the occurrence of leakage scenarios given a profile of a water distribution network. The study also aims to compare the effectiveness of the proposed solution on different network topologies and different sensor densities.

A machine learning ensemble is implemented by training multiple machine learning sub-models then stacking them together to form an ensemble. Specifically, an ensemble consisting of a stacked convolutional neural network (CNN) sub-models is used to classify leakage events by learning patterns from the generated wavelets. A CNN is a machine learning implementation used for feature extraction [25] and has been used extensively in the field of hydrology [8,26]. This could be utilized to reveal hidden features relevant for leak detection. The CNN ensemble would act as a binary classifier for leak detection, where its output would be to determine whether or not a leak exists within the network. Adjustments in configurations are made to maximize performance for a specific network model.

Data generated from EPANET simulations are used as input for the machine learning model. The models are implemented in Python using Keras and Tensorflow as framework, with a 70/30 split of the dataset for the training and test set.

3.4   Evaluation Metrics

The techniques above will be evaluated with respect to certain metrics: classification accuracy, true positive rate (TPR), false positive rate (FPR), and the area under the curve (AUC) of the receiver operating characteristic (ROC) [17,27]. A summary of these metrics is as follows:

$$Accuracy = \frac{correct}{total} * 100 \tag{6}$$

$$TPR = \frac{TP}{TP + FN} \tag{7}$$

$$FPR = \frac{FP}{FP + TN} \tag{8}$$

where TP, TN, FP, and FN represent the total amount of true positives, true negatives, false positives, and false negatives respectively. A true positive (TP) is defined as correctly identifying a leakage scenario occurring in the WDN, while a true negative (TN) is defined as correctly identifying that the WDN is operational without leaks. A false positive (FP) is defined as incorrectly noting a leak in the WDN.

The AUC-ROC is an often used evaluation metric for machine learning [27], which is generally characterized by plotting the true positive rate against the false positive rate. The area is a measure of how much the model is able to distinguish between classes. A higher AUC corresponds to a better classifier.

4   Results and Discussion

Shown in Table 1 are the physical attributes of the tested networks. These serve as a baseline on how network topologies physically differ from one another.

Table 1. Physical characteristics of different network topologies

Metric	New York tunnel	Cherry plains	Fossolo
Nodes	19	34	36
Avg. Node Connections	2.105263	2.294118	3.194444

Tables 2, 3, 4 present the performance of the proposed leak detection method. The ensemble CNN method was able to reach accuracies of more than 90% in each topology, even when considering the differences in sensor density. While this is the case, the accuracy of the model is dependent on how complex or large the network; leak detection on networks with more connections between nodes tend to be slightly less accurate than networks with fewer connections. Similarly, the true positive rate for all topologies and sensor densities reach an adequate percentage for leak detection. This metric is relevant as there is a need to correctly determine the presence of leaks in the event of one occurring. In all region sizes, it is seen that the Fossolo network has the lowest true negative rate, while the Cherry Plains network has the highest. The true negative rate of the Fossolo network is at its lowest when using data from the 3-hop node distance region. This may be due to the fact that the dataset is mostly comprised of leakage scenarios, with non-leakage scenarios only taking up roughly 14% of the datasets, and compounded further by having generated less data from a network configuration with less sensors. It is likely that the CNN ensemble fails to find more hidden features in these networks, where the pressure profiles are comprised of more nodal connections; hence the low true negative rate. Generally, this is more acceptable than the opposite, where there is a low true positive rate, and a high negative rate, as inaction for an existing leak would entail more economic losses than routinely checking on pipe operations.

Table 2. Performance of the model for leak detection of different network topologies, with the sensor density based on 1-Hop node distances

Sensor density based on 1-Hop node distances		
Metric	New York tunnel	Cherry plains	Fossolo
Regions	8	14	10
Accuracy	0.987737584	0.98560658	0.96956944
TPR	0.994318182	0.98458498	0.990661188
TNR	0.946188340	0.992268041	0.832524272

Table 3. Performance of the model for leak detection of different network topologies, with the sensor density based on 2-Hop node distances

Sensor density based on 2-Hop node distances			
Metric	New York tunnel	Cherry plains	Fossolo
Regions	4	6	4
Accuracy	0.984671980	0.977039068	0.966655876
TPR	0.994318182	0.973913043	0.988793425
TNR	0.923766816	0.99742268	0.822815534

While there is not much difference in the accuracy and true positive rate metrics between sensor densities, a noticeable trend is seen in the true negative rate. As the sub-regions of the network become larger, a decline in the true negative rate can be noticed. This is corroborated by the decrease in the AUC-ROC for the Fossolo network, as shown from Figs. 4, 5, 6, as it is affected by the increase in false negatives. It is possible that covering a large area within the

Table 4. Performance of the model for leak detection of different network topologies, with the sensor density based on 3-Hop node distances

Sensor density based on 3-Hop node distances			
Metric	New York tunnel	Cherry plains	Fossolo
Regions	3	4	3
Accuracy	0.984671980	0.979095271	0.946260926
TPR	0.995028409	0.980237154	0.987672768
TNR	0.919282511	0.971649485	0.677184466

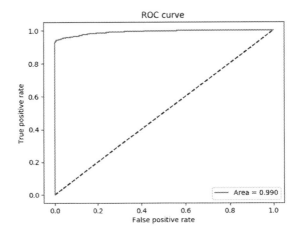

Fig. 4. ROC curve of the Fossolo network, 1-hop region size

WDN makes it more difficult for the machine learning model to learn connections in the pressure profile and correctly classify non-leakage scenarios. Having more connections on average for each junction further exacerbates this problem, as nodal pressures are more affected by neighboring nodes.

In general, the model was able to correctly classify leakage and non-leakage scenarios correctly. From the results gathered, significant increases in accuracy, TPR, and TNR for leak detection can be achieved by allowing the model to be trained further, as each network configuration was trained using the same machine learning model and the same amount of training periods. Networks with higher connections between nodes require more training as well, to find more connections between the different pressure profiles generated by each node.

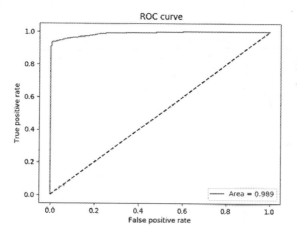

Fig. 5. ROC curve of the Fossolo network, 2-hop region size

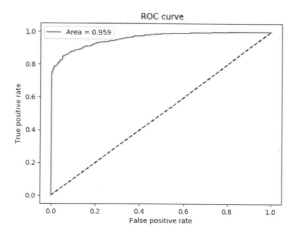

Fig. 6. ROC curve of the Fossolo network, 3-hop region size

5   Conclusions

This study explored the problem of detecting leakages in water distribution systems. The proposed solution of using a CNN ensemble with wavelet decomposition was able to determine occurrences of leaks within the pipeline. Wavelet decomposition allowed the data used for machine learning features to be relatively small, while retaining information regarding changes in the pressure profile. By using a CNN as a classifier, connections in the pressure profiles were analyzed and yielded sufficient performance by the model. Generally, the model is able to perform well on different network topologies, different sensor densities, and certain combinations thereof.

5.1   Limitations of the Study

The research dealt exclusively with simulated data, as real-life datasets were found to be incomplete or hard to come by. Sensor placement within the simulated networks were also not optimized. While the sensors were physically distributed equitably over the network, a study was not done on how specific sensor placements affect the overall performance of the model. Determining where the leak is located is likewise not incorporated into the study. As the study simply aims to detect whether or not a leak exists in the system, the utility of this knowledge depends on the size of the network and how easy it is for the leak to be alleviated. The trained model was not used in actual implementations of water distribution networks. This is primary due to the scale of the simulated networks, and the difficulty in implementing small-scale ones.

5.2   Future Work

Improvements in the implementation of the CNN ensemble could still lead to better performance. From the results, it could be seen that the model performs worse on networks that are relatively large and have a higher number of connections per node; better results could be achieved by optimizing the layers and parameters of the model. A better model would also allow for a better classifier, allowing for the classification of more regions within the network or more dense sensor distributions.

Similar to leak detection, machine learning techniques could also possibly be used for determining the location of the leak within the network. The CNN could be used as a multiple classifier, where outputs are different regions within the network, narrowed down to a smaller area.

References

1. Adedeji, K.B., Hamam, Y., Abe, B.T., Abu-Mahfouz, A.M.: Towards achieving a reliable leakage detection and localization algorithm for application in water piping networks: an overview. IEEE Access **5**, 20272–20285 (2017). https://doi.org/10.1109/access.2017.2752802

2. Wan, J., Yu, Y., Wu, Y., Feng, R., Yu, N.: Hierarchical leak detection and localization method in natural gas pipeline monitoring sensor networks. Sensors **12**(12), 189–214 (2011). https://doi.org/10.3390/s120100189

3. He, Y., Li, S., Zheng, Y.: Distributed state estimation for leak detection in water supply networks. IEEE/CAA J. Autom. Sin. **PP**(99), 1–9 (2017). https://doi.org/10.1109/JAS.2017.7510367

4. Gupta, G.: Monitoring Water Distribution Network using Machine Learning. KTH Royal Institute of Sweden, Stockholm (2017)

5. Xu, Q., Liu, R., Chen, Q., Li, R.: Review on water leakage control in distribution networks and the associated environmental benefits. J. Environ. Sci. (China) **26**(5), 955–961 (2014). https://doi.org/10.1016/S1001-0742(13)60569-0

6. Conejos, M.P., Alzamora, F.M., Alonso, J.C.: A water distribution system model to simulate critical scenarios by considering both leakage and pressure dependent demands. Procedia Eng. **186**, 380–387 (2017). https://doi.org/10.1016/j.proeng.2017.03.234

7. EPANET. https://www.epa.gov/water-research/epanet. Accessed 23 May 2018

8. Kang, D., Lansey, K.: Novel approach to detecting pipe bursts in water distribution networks. J. Water Resour. Plan. Manage. **140**(1), 121–127 (2014). https://doi.org/10.1061/(ASCE)WR.1943-5452.0000264

9. Fang, C.M., Lin, S.C.: 5.4 GHz high-Q bandpass filter for wireless sensor network system. In: IEEE SENSORS 2009 Conference (2009). https://doi.org/10.1109/ICSENS.2009.5398458

10. Colombo, A.F., Lee, P., Karney, B.W.: A selective literature review of transient-based leak detection methods. J. Hydro-Environ. Res. **2**(4), 212–227 (2009). https://doi.org/10.1016/j.jher.2009.02.003

11. Wang, X., Ghidaoui, M.S.: Identification of multiple leaks in pipeline: linearized model, maximum likelihood, and super-resolution localization. Mech. Syst. Signal Process. **107**, 529–548 (2018). https://doi.org/10.1016/j.ymssp.2018.01.042

12. Quiñones-Grueiro, M., Verde, C., Llanes-Santiago, O.: Demand model in water distribution networks for fault detection. IFAC-PapersOnLine **50**(1), 3263–3268 (2017). https://doi.org/10.1016/j.ifacol.2017.08.460

13. Goyal, M.K., Ojha, C.S.P., Burn, D.H.: Machine learning algorithms and their application in water resources management. In: Sustainable Water Resources Management, pp. 165–177. American Society of Civil Engineers (2017). https://doi.org/10.1061/9780784414767.ch06

14. Kang, J., Park, Y., Lee, J., Wang, S., Eom, D.: Novel leakage detection by ensemble CNN-SVM and graph-based localization in water distribution systems. IEEE Trans. Ind. Electron. **65**(5), 4279–4289 (2018). https://doi.org/10.1109/TIE.2017.2764861

15. Dietterich, T.G.: Ensemble methods in machine learning. In: Kittler, J., Roli, F. (eds.) MCS 2000. LNCS, vol. 1857, pp. 1–15. Springer, Heidelberg (2000). https://doi.org/10.1007/3-540-45014-9_1

16. Shi, F., Liu, Z., Li, E.: Prediction of pipe performance with ensemble machine learning based approaches. In: 2017 International Conference on Sensing, Diagnostics, Prognostics, and Control (SDPC), Shanghai, pp. 408–414 (2017). https://doi.org/10.1109/SDPC.2017.84

17. Nasir, M.T., Mysorewala, M., Cheded, L., Siddiqui, B., Sabih, M.: Measurement error sensitivity analysis for detecting and locating leak in pipeline using ANN and SVM. In: 2014 IEEE 11th International Multi-Conference System Signals Devices, SSD 2014, pp. 7–10 (2014). https://doi.org/10.1109/SSD.2014.6808847

18. Gupta, K., Kishore, K., Jain, S.C.: Modeling and simulation of CEERI's water distribution network to detect leakage using HLR approach. In: 2017 6th International Conference on Reliability, Infocom Technologies and Optimization (ICRITO) (Trends and Future Directions) (2017). https://doi.org/10.1109/ICRITO.2017.8342440

19. Rossman, L.A., Clark, R.M., Grayman, W.M.: Modeling chlorine residuals in drinking-water distribution systems. J. Environ. Eng. **120**(4), 803–820 (1994). https://doi.org/10.1061/(ASCE)0733-9372(1994)120:4(803)

20. University of Exeter Centre for Water Systems. http://emps.exeter.ac.uk/engineering/research/cws/resources/benchmarks/. Accessed 23 May 2018

21. Delorme-Costil, A., Bezian, J.J.: Forecasting domestic hot water demand in residential house using artificial neural networks. In: 2017 16th IEEE International Conference on Machine Learning and Applications (ICMLA), Cancun, pp. 467–472 (2017). https://doi.org/10.1109/ICMLA.2017.0-117

22. Domene, E., Sauri, D.: Urbanisation and water consumption: influencing factors in the metropolitan region of Barcelona. Urban Stud. **43**(9), 1605–1623 (2006). https://doi.org/10.1080/00420980600749969

23. Letting, L.K., Hamam, Y., Abu-Mahfouz, A.M.: Estimation of water demand in water distribution systems using particle swarm optimization. Water, 9(8) (2017). https://doi.org/10.3390/w9080593

24. Fagiani, M., Squartini, S., Severini, M., Piazza, F.: A novelty detection approach to identify the occurrence of leakage in smart gas and water grids. In: Proceedings of the International Joint Conference Neural Networks, vol. 2015, September 2015. https://doi.org/10.1109/IJCNN.2015.7280473

25. Wu, Z.Y., El-Maghraby, M., Pathak, S.: Applications of deep learning for smart water networks. Procedia Eng. **119**, 479–485 (2015). https://doi.org/10.1016/j.proeng.2015.08.870

26. Xu, Y., Zhang, J., Long, Z., Chen, Y.: A novel dual-scale deep belief network method for daily urban water demand forecasting. Energies **11**(5), 1068 (2018). https://doi.org/10.3390/en11051068

27. Sokolova, M., Lapalme, G.: A systematic analysis of performance measures for classification tasks. Inf. Process. Manage. **45**(4), 427–437 (2009). https://doi.org/10.1016/j.ipm.2009.03.002

Solutions for Improving the Energy Efficiency of Buildings Refurbishment

Maria de Fátima Castro, Joana Andrade, Catarina Araújo, and Luís Bragança(✉)

CTAC, University of Minho, Guimarães, Portugal
info@mfcastro.com

Abstract. The buildings sector contributes to 30% of annual greenhouse gas emissions and uses about 40% of energy. In this scenario and regarding the sustainable concerns, different strategies and directives have been developed. However, this consumption can be reduced by between 30% and 80% through commercially available technologies.

A critical and evolutionary way of thinking about the energy (and other resources) demand, management, and supply is necessary, because there is a clear concern about irreversible impacts to the world and a scarcity of the resources as well. Energy supplies should be mostly or entirely through renewable resources and highly efficient technologies put in place to achieve solution such as nearly Zero Energy Buildings (nZEB). The strategies and the rehabilitation benefits are more and more recognised, used and increasingly considered by the stockholders. So, the aim of this article is to: critical analyse the state-of-art regarding this matter; discuss the existing solutions, directives, and strategies; and present a case study where the energy performance and the economic viability are discussed. The case study is a Portuguese building model which represents the conventional construction between 1960 and 1990. On it, three scenarios of refurbishment were tested, and their benefits and costs are presented.

Keywords: Energy efficiency · nZEB · Building rehabilitation · Building retrofit

1 Introduction

The connection between climate change and carbon emissions is impossible to decouple, since emissions are strongly linked to energy production and use. Measures are therefore being taken to reduce energy use, promote energy efficiency and increase the use of renewable energy. Improving the energy performance of buildings is one of the most economically viable measures to achieve European climate change objectives and to stimulate sustainable growth [1]. This not only leads to environmental benefits, but also promotes important social and economic benefits by reducing energy poverty, improving thermal comfort and indoor air quality, improving health and productivity, creating jobs, and promoting finance [2].

Buildings are responsible for about 40% of the total energy use in the European Union (EU) and for 36% of total CO_2 emissions. Furthermore, it is inside buildings

© ICST Institute for Computer Sciences, Social Informatics and Telecommunications Engineering 2020
Published by Springer Nature Switzerland AG 2020. All Rights Reserved
P. Pereira et al. (Eds.): SC4Life 2019, LNICST 318, pp. 45–56, 2020.
https://doi.org/10.1007/978-3-030-45293-3_4

that people spend 90% of their life [3]. It is estimated that in the EU, Switzerland and Norway, there are about 25 billion square meters of constructed floor space. So, if the entire constructed area were to be concentrated, the occupied land would be equivalent to the territorial area of Belgium – 30,528 km^2 [4]. On the other hand, it is known that 75% to 90% of the existing building will still be in use by 2050. Much of it was built before 1990 (before EU legislation) and is considered energetically inefficient. So, it is necessary to increase the energy rehabilitation rate by at least 3% to achieve the objectives of the Paris Agreement and the European Energy Efficiency Directive [5].

1.1 Methodology and Objectives

This paper intends to present a critical analysis of the state of the art, discussing existing solutions, directives, and strategies with the aim of improving the energy efficiency of the existing building and presenting a case study about its economic viability. For this, a review of the most relevant literature on the subject, namely the EU directives and concepts defined by them, was carried out. Finally, five rehabilitation scenarios and their economic viability were tested in a case study of a conventional building model of a Portuguese building between the 1960s and 1990s.

2   Strategies and Directives for Improving Energy Efficiency

Considering the need to reduce energy consumption and improve its efficiency, the European Union released the Directive 2002/91/EC, known as EPBD - Energy Performance of Buildings Directive, which has since been reformulate by Directive 2010/31/EU, recognised as EPBD-recast, and amended by Directive (EU) 2018/844.

2.1 Directive of Energy Performance of Buildings

The Directive 2002/91/EC, approved in December of 2002, aimed to promote the improvement of the energy performance of buildings in the EU by means of economic feasibility, considering the climate and the local conditions of each member state (MS). The purpose was to increase the energy efficiency of building and thereby improve their quality (new buildings or renovated), reduce the external energy dependency, decrease the emission of greenhouse gas (GHG) and increase the population awareness and information. The EPBD imposed the energy certification system to demonstrate their performance level, through an integrated calculation method. This method should account for thermal characteristics of the building, heating and cooling systems, domestic hot water (DHW) preparation, ventilation, lighting, or passive solar systems, among others. The EPBD imposed also minimum requirements for the energy performance of new buildings and subject to major renovation works, and the need to regularly inspect boilers and air-conditioning systems and the heating system at each 15 years [6].

This directive implementation had some obstacles such as the MS diversity of the built environment and the low ambitions in some. The low renovation rate was also responsible for aggravating compliance with the objectives, as well as the lack of credibility of some energy certificates and the of the obligation to report the national implementation results.

In 2010, the EPBD was reformulated by the Directive 2010/31/EU (EPBD-recast). This new directive intended to: (i) reduce the CO_2 emissions to mitigate the climate change and, (ii) promote the development of sustainable and energy efficient solutions. Therefore, the following goals were established until 2020: (i) 20% reduction in energy, (ii) 20% reduction in CO_2 emissions and, (iii) 20% increase in use of renewable energy.

This requires the MS to establish minimum energy requirements considering cost-optimal levels and to revise their energy standards in building regulations, at regular intervals, which shall not be longer than five years. The EPBD-recast also established the concept of nZEB – nearly zero energy buildings – for new buildings from 2019 (public sector) and 2021 (all new buildings). The cost-optimal levels of the minimum energy performance requirements mean the energy performance level which leads to the lowest cost during the estimated economic lifecycle, see Fig. 1 [7].

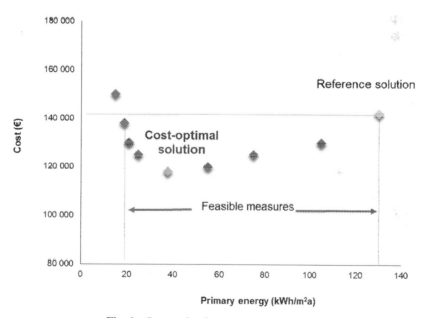

Fig. 1. Cost-optimal concept representation.

As a result of the reduction of the minimum energy requirements, the maximum allowed values, as for instance, the thermal transmission coefficient (U – W/m² °C), were lowered regarding the requirements imposed by Directive 2002/91/EC. In Portugal, the U-value for external walls decreased from 1.4 W/m² °C to 0.4 W/m² °C and from 0.9 W/m² °C to 0.35 W/m² °C for roofs.

All MS were compelled to implement national plans for energy efficiency or policies with alternative measures that enable reducing the final energy. The decrease of energy consumption after the implementation of EPBD and EPBD-recast can be seen in Fig. 2.

The mean annual final energy consumed which decreased 2.1 kWh/(m^2·year) until 2006, is now decreasing at higher rate of 3.8 kWh/(m^2·year).

Recently, Directive 2018/844 of 30 May 2018 amending Directive 2010/31/EU on the energy performance of buildings and Directive 2012/27/EU on energy efficiency was published. The main goal of this new directive is to increase the average renovation rate in a cost-effective manner, i.e., (i) introduce building automation and control as an alternative to physical inspections; (ii) encourage the implementation of efficient mobility infrastructures and, (iii) introduce a smart readiness indicator to measure the technologic capacity of buildings. Thus, the following amends can be highlighted [5]:

- Insertion of new definitions as "building automation and control system";
- Implementation, until 2050, of a long-term renovation strategy to support the renovation of the building stock, into a highly energy efficient and decarbonised one;
- Convene the Commission to the implement of an optional common Union scheme for rating the smart readiness of buildings;
- Establishment of regular inspections of heating systems or of systems for combined space heating and ventilation, with an effective rated output of over 7 kW;
- Determination of the primary energy use in kWh/(m^2·year) as a numeric indicator to express the energy performance of a building for the purpose of both energy performance certification and compliance with minimum energy performance requirements.

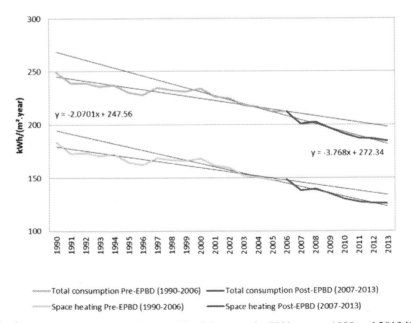

Fig. 2. Energy use evolution in the residential sector, the EU between 1990 and 2013 [8].

2.2   nZEB – nearly Zero Energy Buildings

The nZEB concept arose with the EPBD-recast. This concept refers to buildings that have a very high energy performance (Directive 2010/31/EU, 2010). According to the Directive definition the amount of energy required should be "nearly zero or very low" and "should be covered to a very significant extent by energy from renewable sources, including energy from renewable sources produced on-site or nearby". Nevertheless, none precise definition was established, and each MS should draw up their definition, considering the following:

- Period – time rate used for the energy balance (annual, monthly, and weekly);
- Boundary – on-site and nearby system boundary (building, site, neighbourhood, …);
- Weighting system – which weighting factors to consider in the energy balance, dynamic or static;
- Energy flow – which use to consider (heating, cooling, lighting, DHW supply, …).

Therefore, it is of major importance to establish a holistic nZEB approach, considering not just the reduction of energy use in the building through solar passive design measures, but also satisfying the remaining needs with energy from renewable sources (Fig. 3).

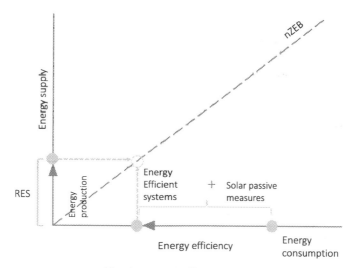

Fig. 3. nZEB holist approach.

3   Existing Buildings and Rehabilitation

It is essential to stimulate and promote the rehabilitation of the existing residential buildings, considering the European objectives already presented. Non-residential buildings, on the other hand, account for about 25% of the European built constructions, which is a more heterogeneous sector and therefore more complex than the residential sector. Additionally, according to an analysis of energy efficiency certificates in Europe, about 97.5% of the building constructions should be improved so that it could be made up of highly efficient buildings, and thus the objective of decarbonisation until 2050 will be reached [4].

3.1 Directive of Energy Performance of Buildings

The concept of rehabilitation is defined as an intervention, more or less extensive, necessary to do in a building or property, aiming to increase its useful and service life, its economic value, the quality of life of the inhabitants and the implementation of good practices of energy efficiency [9]. In this way, the thermal and energy rehabilitation of buildings is imperative as it allows correcting of other existing anomalies in buildings, as well as facilitating the compliance with the existing directives and the reduction of the energy needs, thus reducing the use of energy and emissions of GHG [10]. Therefore, rehabilitation allows implementing measures of energy efficiency and sustainability, providing the increase of thermal and acoustic comfort, and indoor air quality.

The thermal and energy rehabilitation of a building can act on several fronts, such as:

- The opaque building envelope - through the introduction of thermal insulation for correction of thermal bridges and reduction of heat losses;
- The non-opaque building envelope - by improving the type of glass used in the spans, the frame and the material that constitutes it;
- Passive solar systems - through, for example of the orientation and design of the spans, promoting natural ventilation and heat collection systems. These systems can be divided into passive direct, indirect, and isolated gain heating systems and passive cooling systems by natural ventilation, soil cooling, evaporative and radiative;
- Active systems - through, for example, solar systems such as photovoltaic panels or solar thermal collectors. These systems transform energy from renewable sources into energy for use.

4   Energy Rehabilitation of Residential Buildings

Nowadays, around 35% of the European building stock has more than 50 years [5]. An analysis to the energy certificates performed by BPIE (Buildings Performance Institute Europe) has concluded that around 97.5% of the building stock presents a label lower than class A [2]. However, the percentage of buildings being rehabilitated annually in Europe is low, ranging from 0.4 to 1.2% [2]. Thus, the rehabilitation of the building stock has a high energy saving potential. This section presents a discussion on the energy and economic performance of different energy rehabilitation scenarios, through a case study.

4.1 Methodology for Energy and Economic Performance

The energy performance of the case study building was assessed through a dynamic simulation using the *EnergyPlus* software [11], which reliability has been amply demonstrated [12]. To perform such simulations the energy balance method CTF (Conduction Transfer Functions) [11] was used. The CTF method allows to perform dynamic simulations with the necessary precision concerning current building solutions [13]. A life cycle approach of 30 years was considered both in energy and economic performance.

The economic performance was assessed using the methodology proposed by delegated regulation n° 244/2012 of January 16th [14], as presented on Eq. 1.

$$C_g(\tau) = C_I + \sum_j \left[\sum_{i=1}^{\tau} \left(C_{a.i_{(j)}} \times R_d(i) - V_{f.\tau}(j) \right) \right] \tag{1}$$

Where:
T: Calculation period
Cg (T): Global cost across calculation period
CI: Initial investment for measure j
Ca,I (j): Annual cost across year i for measure j
Rd (i): Annual cost across year i for measure i
Vf,T (j): Residual value of measure j in the end of the calculation period

A discount rate of 3% and an evolution of the energy costs were considered [7]. For the period between 2013 and 2030 the energy costs used were based on the EU predictions [15]. For the period between 2030 and 2046 the costs predicted in the Energy Roadmap 2050 [16] were considered. Finally, the investment costs were obtained through the CYPE price generator [17].

4.2 Case Study Building

A typical Portuguese single-family building model was used as case study building (Fig. 4). The building was considered to be located in Lisbon at an altitude of 71 m and have the following: (i) two bedrooms; (ii) a total built area of 110 m^2; (iii) an unventilated attic between the living area and the roof, (iv) an air conditioning through mobile heating and cooling systems (COP = 1; SREE = 3.5); (v) no mechanical ventilation system, thus being only naturally ventilated; (vi) three inhabitants being in there from 7 pm to 8 am in week days and all day during the weekends.

Fig. 4. Outline of the case study.

Table 1 presents the case study building solutions. These solutions were defined considering the most common building solutions used between 1960 and 1990 (period to which most of the existing buildings in the country belong) in Portugal [19].

Table 1. Case study building solutions.

Building element	Construction solutions	U (W/m^2 °C)
Walls	Single masonry wall with 22 cm with 2 cm of plaster both sides	1.8
Superior slab	Lightweight slab	2.8
Roof	Pitched roof with lightweight slab	3.0
Ground floor	Concrete slab covered with ceramic tile	1.7
Glazing	Single glazing (6 mm) and wooden frame	4.1

The thermal comfort temperatures recommended by the Portuguese thermal regulation [18] – 18 °C for the heating season and 25 °C for the cooling season – were considered for the analysis. The ventilation was assessed trough dynamic simulation using the *EnergyPlus AirFlowNetwork* module [11].

4.3   Rehabilitation Scenarios

Five rehabilitation scenarios were analysed (Table 2). In Scenario 1 only passive measures were considered. In Scenario 2, beyond the passive measures, more efficient building systems were defined. In Scenario 3 the measures from Scenario 1 were combined with a heat pump. Scenario 4 and 5 are the combination between Scenario 2 and 3 with a self-consumption photovoltaic kit.

Table 2. Case study building solutions.

Scenario	Description
Scenario 1	Application of 12 cm of thermal insulation (expanded polystyrene) on the externa walls (U = 0.24 W/m^2 °C) and on the superior slab (U = 0.27 W/m^2 °C), and substitution of the glazing systems for double glazing with aluminium frame (U = 2.8 W/m^2 °C)
Scenario 2	Passive measure of Scenario 1 and substitution of building acclimatization equipment for an air conditioning system (COP = 4.12; SREE = 8.53) for heating and cooling and of the DHW system by a gas condensing heater (COP = 0.97)
Scenario 3	Passive measure of Scenario 1 and substitution of building acclimatization equipment for a heat pump for heating, cooling and DHW preparation
Scenario 4	Measures from Scenario 2 with the addition of a self-consumption photovoltaic kit with a production of 1,500 W (Eren = 2,290 kWh·year)
Scenario 5	Measures from Scenario 3 with the addition of a self-consumption photovoltaic kit with a production of 1,500 W (Eren = 2,290 kWh·year)

4.4 Results

Figure 5 presents the energy consumptions obtained in each rehabilitation scenario.

Fig. 5. Energy consumption for each rehabilitation scenario (khW/m^2·year).

It is worth to mention that the simple adoption of passive measures leads to a decrease of around 44% of the building energy consumption. These passive measures combined with more efficient but conventional building systems allow decreasing the energy consumption in 76%, approximately. The adoption of a heat pump, which is a more efficient but usually also a more expensive equipment, allows a better energy performance. However, the benefits of this system may not be sufficiently appealing to convince the user to adopt it [20]. The combination of Scenarios 2 and 3, with renewable energy production systems lead to an 87% decrease in the building energy consumption in Scenario 4 and in 91% in Scenario 5.

Table 3 presents the economic analysis regarding the implementation of the five scenarios.

Table 3. Case study building solutions.

Scenario	Initial cost (€)	Operational cost (€)	Life cycle cost (€)	Annual savings (€/year)	Payback time (years)
Ref. scenario	0	35,571.00	40,062.00	0.00	0.00
Scenario 1	9,823.00	24,692.00	36,325.00	363.00	27.00
Scenario 2	13,424.00	20,318.00	35,660.00	508.00	26.00
Scenario 3	17,171.00	24,689.00	44,415.00	363.00	47.00
Scenario 4	15,898.00	17,101.00	32,444.00	616.00	26.00
Scenario 5	19,645.00	21,472.00	41,198.00	470.00	42.00

According to the results, the payback time is too long in all five rehabilitation scenarios. Nevertheless, the scenarios with the best payback time are Scenario 2 and 4, corresponding to the adoption of passive measures, an air conditioning system, and a gas condensing heater (DHW preparation), without and with renewable energy production systems, respectively. The scenarios using a heat pump have twice the payback time than the other options. It was also noticed that regarding the payback time, the scenario based only in passive measures (Scenario 1) presents a very similar performance to the scenarios that combine such measures with more efficient energy systems (Scenario 2 and Scenario 4).

The results show that the initial cost has a very significant influence on the economic analysis of residential buildings rehabilitation measures [20]. Even in scenarios with relevant annual savings, the initial cost of the solutions makes the payback only possible in the last years of the life cycle.

5   Conclusions

Five energy rehabilitation scenarios were analysed, focusing on their energy and economic performance. This study corroborated the importance of economic analysis of rehabilitation scenarios in residential building. Here, it allowed to understand that the adoption of a heat pump may not be an interesting solution, as cheaper systems lead to a similar energy performance. However, the adoption of energy rehabilitation scenarios in residential buildings should not be seen as a way of obtaining a return of the investment. Instead, it should be a way to increase the building comfort and quality, and to decrease the building's environmental impact by using the smallest investment possible.

The energy performance of buildings in the EU is not in the overwhelming majority of cases, efficient. Its potential for improvement is significant, which can be reflected in high savings and thus, have significant contribution to a more sustainable future. In this sense, the implementation of Directive 2002/91/EC has led to a representative change in the energy dimension of buildings throughout Europe. Buildings became more energetically efficient and the population more sensitive and informed about these issues.

However, energy savings were below expectations (42%), since not all countries were able to implement the requirements entirety.

With the implementation of the EPBD-recast, in 2014, an additional 48.9 Mtoe of final energy reduction was achieved, compared to the base value of 2007, being in line with that forecast for 2020–60 to 80 Mtoe reduction of final energy [8]. Thus, with the new Directive (EU) 2018/844 reinforcements are made to the previous EPBD-recast and new targets imposed. In turn, the cost-optimal approach reveals an incentive to energy efficiency and the promotion of nZEB. However, more energy efficiency measures need to be disseminated as well as more incentive to rehabilitate.

References

1. Araújo, C., Almeida, M., Bragança, L., Barbosa, J.A.: Cost-benefit analysis method for building solutions. Appl. Energy **173**, 124–133 (2016)
2. BPIE Factsheet - 97% of buildings in the EU need to be upgraded. http://bpie.eu/wp-content/uploads/2017/12/State-of-the-building-stock-briefing_Dic6.pdf. Accessed 07 June 2018
3. BPIE Facts & Figures. http://bpie.eu/publications. Accessed 07 June 2018
4. BPIE: Europe's buildings under the microscope. BPIE, Brussels (2011)
5. EC Buildings. https://ec.europa.eu/energy/en/topics/energy-efficiency/buildings. Accessed 10 June 2018
6. EU: Directive 2002/91/EC of the European Parliament and of the Council of 16 December 2002 on the energy performance of buildings. Journal of the European Communities L 1/65 from 4.1.2003. EU, Brussels (2002)
7. EU: Directive 2010/31/EU of the European Parliament and of the Council of 19 May 2010 on the energy performance of buildings (recast). Journal of the European Communities L 153/13 from 18.6.2010. EU, Brussels (2010)
8. EU: Good practice in energy efficiency. EU, Brussels (2017)
9. Santos, J.; Sá, M.; Pereira, C.: Futureng. http://futureng.pt/reabilitacao. Accessed 10 June 2018
10. Pontes, J.: Análise multicritério de soluções construtivas para reabilitação de edifícios. Master Thesis. University of Minho, Faculty of Engineering, Guimarães (2018)
11. USDE: EnergyPlusTM Version 8.7 Documentation - Engineering Reference. US Department of Energy, U.S.A (2010)
12. Anđelković, A.S., Mujan, I., Dakić, S.: Experimental validation of an EnergyPlus model: application of a multi-storey naturally ventilated double skin façade. Energy Build. **118**, 27–36 (2016)
13. Tabares-Velasco, P.C., Christensen, C., Bianchi, M., Booten, C.: Verification and validation of EnergyPlus conduction finite difference and phase change material models for opaque wall assemblies. Technical report NREL/TP-5500-55792. NREL, Colorado, U.S.A. (2012)
14. EU: Commission Delegated Regulation (EU) no 244/2012 of 16 January 2012. Official Journal of the European Communities. https://eur-lex.europa.eu/legal-content/PT/TXT/PDF/?uri=CELEX:32012R0244&from=PT. Accessed 10 June 2019
15. EC: EU Energy Trends to 2030 – Update 2009. https://ec.europa.eu/energy/sites/ener/files/documents/trends_to_2030_update_2009.pdf. Accessed 10 June 2019
16. EC: Communication from the European Parliament, The Council, The European Economic and Social Committee of the Regions - Roadmap to a Resource Efficient Europe, COM (2011) 571 Final. UE, Brussels (2011)
17. CYPE Ingenieros, S.A.: Gerador de Preços. Portugal. http://www.geradordeprecos.info/. Accessed 07 June 2019

18. DR: Lei no58/2013 de 20 de Agosto. Diário da República, 1.a série - N. ° 159 - 20 de agosto de 2013. DR, Lisbon (2013)
19. INE, & LNEC. O Parque habitacional e a sua reabilitação - análise e evolução 2001-2011. Instituto Nacional de Estatística & Laboratório Nacional de Engenharia Civil, Eds.) (2013). ISBN 978-989-25-0246-5
20. Araújo, C.: Análise da viabilidade de implementação dos princípios da construção sustentável em operações de reabilitação de edifícios residenciais portugueses. Doctoral thesis, University of Minho, Faculty of Engineering, Guimarães (2019)

Information and Technologies

Image Recognition to Improve Positioning in Smart Urban Environments

Sara Paiva(✉), Pedro Rodrigues, and Benjamim Oliveira

Instituto Politécnico de Viana do Castelo, Viana do Castelo, Portugal
sara.paiva@estg.ipvc.pt, sara.paiva@ieee.org,
{pmiguelrodrigues,benjamimoliveira}@ipvc.pt

Abstract. This paper describes a solution and algorithm to enhance positioning in outdoor environments with high buildings to be used in a mobile application to aid visually impaired people for navigation purposes. We used an image recognition algorithm and adjusted the android app algorithm to decrease the initial error average of 85 m (without any correction from GPS obtained signal) to a 5 m error, in the final version of our solution.

Keywords: Image recognition · Outdoor positioning · Outdoor navigation · Urban mobility · Visually impaired people

1 Introduction

Obtaining a precise position is necessary in several applications we use in our day-to-day life and its improvement gains increasing importance as we witness new research and studies in these areas. The need for precise positioning can happen indoors (inside buildings) or outdoors (outside buildings). Each situation has its own particular and specific approach. We will focus on this paper in the outdoor location that is associated in the vast majority of cases to the use of GPS. In fact, most of the applications we have on our mobile phones need only this technology to guide the user on the road while driving or while walking on foot to a certain location. But when we speak of location, sometimes a margin of error of 5 m is acceptable, in other cases not. We know that the GPS position obtained has a margin of error that can be considerable, especially if we are in urban environments where there are many buildings, sometimes high, that make it impossible to receive a better GPS signal. In fact, achieving a high precision in urban environments is clearly still an issue to solve [11]. If we consider the traditional applications developed for drivers on the road, it can be considered that the current state of these applications is already advanced, considering that the effectiveness and real usefulness to end users, in this case drivers, is already quite good. However, if we look at other types of applications, such as assisting visually impaired people (VIP) people to make footpaths in the historical centers of cities, the accuracy achieved with the GPS of a commercial smartphone is still clearly insufficient. World Health Organization

---

S. Paiva—IEEE Senior Member.

Published by Springer Nature Switzerland AG 2020. All Rights Reserved
P. Pereira et al. (Eds.): SC4Life 2019, LNICST 318, pp. 59–70, 2020.
https://doi.org/10.1007/978-3-030-45293-3_5

(WHO) [1] stated in 2018 that globally, it is estimated that approximately 1.3 billion people live with some form of vision impairment. The International Classification of Diseases classifies vision impairment into two groups, distance and near presenting vision impairment.

With regards to distance vision, 188.5 million people have mild vision impairment, 217 million have moderate to severe vision impairment, and 36 million people are blind. With regards to near vision, 826 million people live with a near vision impairment. Globally, the leading causes of vision impairment are uncorrected refractive errors and cataracts. According to the study published in 2017 by The Lancet Global Health, compared to 1990, the number of blind people increased by 17.6% and that of individuals with moderate and severe problems about 35.5%. The same study also predicts that by 2020 there will be 237.1 million people with moderate to severe vision impairment and the number of blind people will be 38.5 million. By 2050, these figures are estimated to be about 587.6 million and 114.6 million individuals [14]. In Portugal, according to the 2011 Census, there are 900,000 cases of visual impairment, of which 28,000 are estimated to be entirely blind [2]. Approximately 80% of all vision impairment globally is considered avoidable. The majority of people with vision impairment are over the age of 50 years. A person's experience of vision impairment varies depending upon many different factors. This includes for example, the availability of prevention and treatment interventions, access to vision rehabilitation (including assistive products such as glasses or white canes), and whether the person experiences problems within accessible buildings, transport and information. According to this reality, technological research related to the promotion of accessibility and quality of life of the VIP has been under study for several years. Several solutions have also been developed sustained by the evolution of computational processing and data processing. Technologies have evolved and reached a big level of maturity that allow new technologies, approaches and algorithms to solve problems related to VIP more effectively, always with the goal of making their lives less affected by this deficiency to the greatest extent possible. In this article, we present a practical case study in the city of Viana do Castelo, Portugal, where we worked alongside an association of blind and partially sighted people (with whom previous work has already been done to help them through computer solutions in bus navigation in the center as well as pedestrian navigation [7, 10]). In this paper, we present an algorithm we developed and that is incorporated in a mobile app to make image recognition in order to allow the correction of a received GPS position. Images are captured from the visually impaired people (VIP) smartphone camera which triggers the algorithms to identify that image with a pre-loaded geo-referenced image in a dataset, so the GPS position of the user can be corrected and enhanced compared to the position directly obtained from the GPS.

The rest of the paper is structured as follows: the next section presents a literature review on positioning technologies. Section 3 explains the methodology followed for this project and the next chapter has all details about its implementation. Section 5 presents results and discussion and Sect. 6 presents main conclusions.

2 Positioning Technologies

GPS (Global Positioning system is probably the major outdoor positioning technology we have at the current moment, assisting several location-based services. It is used in industries such as aviation, nautical navigation, and land surveying, to personal and commercial applications such as driving navigation, people tracking, location sharing [21]; also, it can be of great help and fundamental to make a difference in the lives of people with disabilities facilitating day-to-day tasks. We have referred already to the imprecision of GPS position, namely in places with high-building, that can go from 1 to 20 m. Considering this, one study to overcome this situation is to use GPS to implement a high-accuracy global positioning solution and human mobility captured by mobile phones [22]. Authors developed a prototype system, named GloCal, and conduct comprehensive experiments in both crowded urban and spacious suburban areas. The evaluation results show that GloCal can achieve 30% improvement on average error with respect to GPS. Another study combines GPS with smartphone-enabled dead reckoning to produce a high-accuracy global positioning solution based on GPS and human mobility captured by mobile phones [21]. The performance comparison of four self-position fixing methods is made in [8] where authors analyze RSS Statistics, Least squares, Weighted LS (WLS) and Constrained WLS. Other authors provide a solution that makes use of a handheld device [3]. Their ideas to estimate the 3D location and 3D orientation of the phone camera based on the knowledge of the street objects. The use of vision process to generate a3D model with inertial and magnetic measurements is yet another proposal to update a Pedestrian Dead-Reckoning process and to improve the positioning ac-curacy [4]. Other contribution investigates the spatial correlation of multi-path error to estimate the multipath error at a pedestrian by using a regression model and leveraging the multipath errors at nearby points [12]. In [20] authors propose a new positioning algorithm based on signals only with pseudo range error modeling in association with an adapted filtering process. Another approach corrects signals using the European Geostationary Navigation Overlay Service (EGNOS) [19] and also presents an overview of the accuracies that can be achieved with different modes of GPS positioning. In [18] a method to mitigate multiple path in GNSS applications is proposed. Their principle is based on the addition, to the geographic map of a city or a neighborhood, of a supplementary information that consists of the correction of error caused by the multiple paths. Issues and problems associated with GNSS are presented and discussed in [13]. GPS and GLONASS were chosen for a comparison on accuracy and precision. The tightly-coupled single-frequency multi-GNSS RTK/MEMS-IMU integration is proposed in [9] to provide precise and continuous positioning solutions in urban environments. In a similar way, authors in [23] describes and applies a DGNSS-correction projection method to a commercial smartphone. An example of the use of images to enhance positioning is used in [15] where authors use the camera and a GPS-tagged image database to identify with precision the position the user stands. In [6] authors propose to improve the localization of scene items based on state-of-the-art map data, combined with a coarse and cheap position estimation as provided by standard GNSS. In [16] authors propose a method to geo-locate a mobile device by recognizing what is captured by its camera. A visual recognition algorithm in the cloud is used to identify geolocated reference images that match the cameras view. Some case studies are also presented and found in the literature. A study on the performance of BeiDou Navigation Satellite System in urban environments have been made [5] in Wuhan, central China. The compared data (visibility, position dilution of precision and the positioning accuracy) showed that the single point positioning accuracy of the GPS/Beidou dual system is much better and more stable than single BeiDou system. The POI Explorer mobile application aims to help VIP in their spatial orientation and urban navigation, using a smartphone, its sensors and data connectivity. Interaction is made through text-to-speech and notifications [17].

3   Methodology

The methodology followed for this project consisted in the concrete identification of the type of signal collected in the historical center of the city of Viana do Castelo, in one of its busiest streets. The goal was to realize the real mistake and therefore the impossibility of using only GPS to develop an application that allows VIP to move around the city and get relevant information about their location that allows them to gain more autonomy. After that, we designed an algorithm that compares captured camera image from the commercial smartphone to compare it to a preloaded geo-referenced image in a dataset so position can be enhanced compared to GPS received position. We made first round of tests that showed necessary improvements to be incorporated in the algorithm which we did to create a second version of it. Final results will be presented based on this second version of the algorithm and tests made in the field.

4   Implementation

Stage 1 - GPS Precision Analysis
As aforementioned, the first step was to pick a strategic street in the historical center and gather some data on the reliability and precision obtained. The street is shown in

Fig. 1. Street chosen for the tests made

Fig. 1 and it is possible to see it has high buildings which naturally affects received GPS signal.

The tests made included going down from one side and then going up from the other side, covering both sides of the beginning of the street. 167 positions were chosen, the exact position was marked in a map using a mobile app and the received position was compared to it. The average error received, in meters, was of 85.5. The minimum error obtained was 6.3 m and the maximum 205.1 m. Figure 2 shows the exact location of tester going down the road (green markers) and the obtained position through GPS (red markers). It is possible to see that most locations were received has been on the other side of the road, which makes it completely impossible to use only GPS to create a location-based app to aid VIP in their navigation needs.

Fig. 2. Correct position vs. received GPS position without any correction (Color figure online)

Stage 2 – First Algorithm

This stage consisted in developing the algorithm that would allow for an image from the VIP cellphone camera to be compared with a dataset of geo-referenced images, so a better position than the GPS could be returned to a mobile app to be used for navigational purposes to aid VIP. For building the dataset we captured some relevant objects throughout the street that could serve as a reference point and allow for the image recognition to be successful. At this point, we were aware that the success of the entire algorithm was mostly related to the performance of the image recognition algorithm.

Choosing the Image Recognition Algorithm
OpenCV (Open Source Computer Vision Library) is a well-known open source computer vision and machine learning software library, with different comparison methods. The Histogram Comparison Method is the fastest and simplest to adapt regarding image comparison. After we have analyzed this algorithm, we concluded it would not be appropriate to use in this case, because images are compared mostly by color, and as there are several buildings with the same color, it could lead to a huge margin of error, since two images containing buildings of the same color would be considered the same. The Template Matching method basis its comparison mainly depending of its size, which would also not work in this project, since all the images would be considered equal, assuming they would be captured through the smartphone camera. A more thorough search has allowed us to choose the Feature Matching Algorithm. Initially the key points of a given image (in this case the image already stored in the database) are chosen and later compared with the key points of another image (the image captured by the smartphone camera). The algorithm keeps track of the points so that they can be detected and recognized regardless of how the image is, either re-scaled or turned.

The Android App Algorithm
After choosing the algorithm for image recognition, it was time to incorporate it in the global algorithm to be executed in the Android mobile app to make the tests to conclude about enhancement on precision. The behavior of the first version of the algorithm, shown in Fig. 3, is as follows:

- We receive the GPS coordinates from the mobile app. These are the coordinates we will try to enhance since, as we know, they will most likely be wrong by a few tens of meters;
- Check if the quality of the signal is good enough, using the "accuracy" parameter received alongside the GPS coordinates;
- Depending on the GPS quality: (a) If the GPS signal is considered to be good enough, we use the coordinates provided by the GPS. The algorithm ends. (b) If the GPS signal is considered "weak" we computed a search area (based on the "accuracy" parameter) and retrieve all the images geo-referenced inside that same area;
- Two parallel actions are made at this point: (a) Obtain images on the range of the search area. Each image on our dataset is geo-referenced. Using the area previously calculated we retrieve all the images that are inside it. (b) Obtain image from the smartphone camera;
- Compare captured image with images from the dataset. To find out which image matches best the image retrieved by the smartphone we have to loop through all of the images we have filtered;
- Retrieve position of the most similar image. Once the previous loop ends, we will retrieve the image with more similarities to the image being captured by the smartphone camera;

- Place a marker on the map in the new corrected position and use it to inform the user of his location or nearby obstacles.

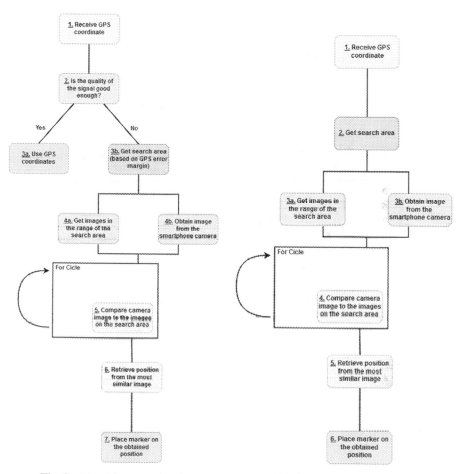

Fig. 3. Algorithm - version 1   **Fig. 4.** Algorithm - version 2

When testing on the field this first version, two main problems were noticed. The first has to do with the "accuracy" parameter returned by the GPS. It cannot be used to decide about precision of the signal as plenty of signals are marked as having a good accuracy with tens of meters of errors. The second change has to do with how the dataset was being created. Figure 5 shows some images in the dataset, with which captured images on the smartphone were to be compared with. The image recognition algorithm did not have a good behavior as its strength is to detect recognizable symbols which are small in these first images and therefore, we had few matches.

Fig. 5. Examples of images from the first dataset

So, we developed a second version of the algorithm shown in Fig. 4. The main changes were the removal of step 2 regarding accuracy, for the reasons already mentioned. In this last version, we also narrowed dataset number of images directly after receiving GPS coordinates. This is an important and necessary step as image recognition takes some milliseconds and, depending on the number of images on the dataset, and considering GPS position can be gathered from the smartphone every 2 or 3 s, the algorithm had to be ran in a fast way. To achieve this, images in the dataset had to have a considerable small size, otherwise several seconds would be needed to run the algorithm which would not suit the mobile application itself.

5   Results and Discussion

As previously explained, this project consisted of three main phases. The first one analyzed the accuracy of the signal obtained without any correction. In a second phase, a dataset of images was defined and developed a first algorithm. Finally, in phase 3, an improved version of the algorithm was developed, according to tests made in phase 2. In each phase, our purpose was to measure the accuracy of the signal received compared to the real location of the user. In the first phase we obtained an average of 85 m of error comparing the real position with the obtained GPS position. In the second phase, we used the first version of the algorithm and the average error was of 54 m. At this point, we expected to have better results and understood the result was very much originated by the incorrect match/recognition of the image the smartphone was capturing, comparing to the ones on the dataset. At this point, we adjusted the algorithm and also changed the dataset of images, so they are mainly composed of brands/logos or very relevant and significant sub-parts of the image being captured by a camera. Figure 6 shows some images used in the second dataset which are significantly different from the ones used in the first dataset shown in Fig. 5. This allowed the image recognition algorithm to have a much better behavior and recognize images more successfully.

Fig. 6. Examples of images from the second dataset

With the changes made in the second algorithm, which corresponds to phase 3 of our process, the obtained average error went down to 5 m, as can be seen in Fig. 7.

Similar to Fig. 2, we have measured correct position versus position obtained with version 2 of the algorithm and results are, as can be seen in Fig. 8, much more accurate.

The improvement was significant (reduction of approximately 80 m in average compared to phase 1 and reduction of approximately 50 m compared to phase 2), but we know it can be even better and we need it to be we this algorithm can be used in mobile solutions for visually impaired people. Images are correctly detected, and position is corrected but 2 or 3 m ahead, the recognition of the image is still done, and corrected position keeps being the same of the coordinates in the image from the dataset which contributes to some errors. To further decrease the obtained error number and solve this problem, we need also to use smartphone sensors, so we detect how much the user has walked since the first correction considering a given image and introduce an additional correction, that not only is based on the coordinate of the image that made a match but also on the user's movement.

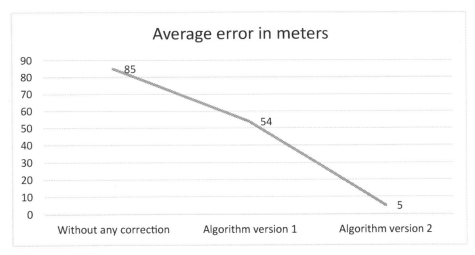

Fig. 7. Comparison of average meters obtained in each of the 3 phases

Fig. 8. Correct position vs. received GPS position using algorithm version 2 (Color figure online)

6   Conclusions

In this paper we have presented an on-going work that has the main goal to develop an algorithm to achieve better precision in positioning that can be used in a mobile application to aid visually impaired people to walk in a more autonomous way within cities. For this, we used image recognition to correct the GPS position received by the satellite that has, as we know and if used alone, still a big error. Our approach started by choosing a street with much usage in the city of Viana do Castelo and understand precision of GPS received signal. We found out average error is approximately 85 m, considering that are high buildings. So, we implemented the first version of an android app algorithm that makes use of an image recognition algorithm so the captured image from the smartphone camera is compared to a preloaded dataset of geo-referenced images. This first approach allowed us approximately to a 54 average error meter. It was still a big number mainly because of the images in the dataset were not the most appropriate as they captured a large part of the buildings. We had to change to significant markers and symbols only so recognition could be more successful. The second version of the algorithm achieved a 5 m error average which was a significant increase. To obtain further results we will, in a next stage, combine work done so far with smartphone sensors to allow to narrow down the error m obtained.

References

1. Blindness and vision impairment (2018). https://www.who.int/news-room/fact-sheets/detail/blindness-and-visual-impairment. Accessed 13 June 2019
2. Associação dos cegos e amblíopes de Portugal (2019). http://www.acapo.pt/deficiencia-visual/perguntas-e-respostas/deficiencia-visual. Accessed 13 June 2019
3. Antigny, N., Servires, M., Renaudin, V.: Hybrid visual and inertial position and orientation estimation based on known urban 3D models. In: 2016 International Conference on Indoor Positioning and Indoor Navigation (IPIN), pp. 1–8 (2016)
4. Antigny, N., Servires, M., Renaudin, V.: Pedestrian track estimation with hand-held monocular camera and inertial-magnetic sensor for urban augmented reality. In: 2017 International Conference on Indoor Positioning and Indoor Navigation (IPIN), pp. 1–8 (2017)
5. Xiang, X., Bian, S.: Research on BeiDou positioning performance in urban environments. In: 2013 IEEE International Conference on Signal Processing, Communication and Computing (ICSPCC 2013), pp. 1–5 (2013)
6. Cao, G., Damerow, F., Flade, B., Helmling, M., Eggert, J.: Camera to map alignment for accurate low-cost lane-level scene interpretation (2016)
7. Faria, P., Curralo, A.F., Paiva, S.: A case study for the promotion of urban mobility for visually impaired people. In: Paiva, S. (ed.) Mobile Solutions and Their Usefulness in Everyday Life. EICC, pp. 65–82. Springer, Cham (2019). https://doi.org/10.1007/978-3-319-93491-4_4
8. Krishna Reddy, D., Achanta, D., Satya, V.: Mobile position estimation with RSS based techniques in an urban city with multiple multi-storied structures, pp. 234–234 (2014)
9. Li, T., Zhang, H., Gao, Z., Chen, Q., Niu, X.: High-accuracy positioning in urban environments using single-frequency multi-GNSS RTK/MEMS-IMU integration. Remote Sensing **2018**, 205 (2018)
10. Lima, A., Mendes, D., Paiva, S.: Mobile solutions for visually impaired people: case study in Viana do Castelo Historical Center. In: 2017 12th Iberian Conference on Information Systems and Technologies (CISTI), pp. 1–6 (2017)
11. Lin, H., Ye, L., Wang, Y.: UWB, multi-sensors and wifi-mesh based precision positioning for urban rail traffic. In: 2010 Ubiquitous Positioning Indoor Navigation and Location Based Service, pp. 1–8 (2010)
12. Patou, Y., Obana, S., Tang, S.: Improvement of pedestrian positioning precision by using spatial correlation of multipath error. In: 2018 IEEE International Conference on Vehicular Electronics and Safety (ICVES), pp. 1–8 (2018)

13. Przestrzelski, P., Bakua, M.: Study of differential code GPS/GLONASS positioning. Ann. Navig. **21**, 117–132 (2014)
14. Bourne, R.A., et al.: Magnitude, temporal trends, and projections of the global prevalence of blindness and distance and near vision impairment: a systematic review and meta-analysis. The Lancet Global Health **5**, e888–e897 (2017)
15. Salarian, M., Manavella, A., Ansari, R.: Accurate localization in dense urban area using google street view image, pp. 485–490 (2015)
16. Sanjuan, D.M., Adamek, T., Bonnin, A., Trzciski, T.: Enhancing global positioning by image recognition (2011)
17. Skulimowski, P., Korbel, P., Wawrzyniak, P.: POI explorer a sonified mobile application aiding the visually impaired in urban navigation, pp. 969–976 (2014)
18. Titouni, S., Rouabah, K., Attia, S., Flissi, M., Khababa, O.: GNSS multipath reduction using GPS and DGPS in the real case. Positioning **08**, 47–56 (2017)
19. Verbree, E., Tiberius, C., Vosselman, G.: Combined GPS-galileo positioning for location-based services in urban environment. LBS TeleCartography **66**, 99–107 (2003)
20. Viandier, N., Nahimana, D.F., Marais, J., Duflos, E.: GNSS performance enhancement in urban environment based on pseudo-range error model. In: 2008IEEE/ION Position, Location and Navigation Symposium, pp. 377–382 (2008)
21. Wu, C., Yang, Z., Xu, Y., Zhao, Y., Liu, Y.: Human mobility enhances global positioning accuracy for mobile phone localization. IEEE Trans. Parallel Distrib. Syst. **26**(1), 131–141 (2015)
22. Wu, C., Yang, Z., Zhao, Y., Liu, Y.: Footprints elicit the truth: improving global positioning accuracy via local mobility. In: 2013 Proceedings IEEE INFOCOM, pp. 490–494 (2013)
23. Yoon, D., Kee, C., Seo, J., Park, B.: Position accuracy improvement by implementing the DGNSS-CP algorithm in smartphones. Sensors **16**, 910 (2016)

An Hybrid Novel Layered Architecture and Case Study: IoT for Smart Agriculture and Smart LiveStock

Pelagie Houngue[1], Romaric Sagbo[1(✉)], and Colombiano Kedowide[2]

[1] Institut de Mathématiques et de Sciences Physiques, Dangbo, Benin
{pelagie.houngue,romaric.sagbo}@imsp-uac.org
[2] Université TELUQ, Québec, Canada
colombiano.kedowide@gmail.com

Abstract. The meteoric rise in the number of connected objects in our daily lives is proof that data transmission and improvement of services related to our activities are a permanent and urgent concern. Communicating objects transform our behaviors, our habits and our society in general. Despite the significant progress in the field of Internet of Things (IoT), much remains to be done especially in developing countries. In the field of e-agriculture, digital production techniques are not enough to guarantee a better yield and safeguard crops. Thus, in this work, we have focused on the resolution of the problems related to transhumance, given the expansion of the phenomenon in developing countries. Indeed, during transhumance, passages intended for animals, called corridors may not be followed by the breeders. This can lead to deadly clashes between herders and farmers. Our vision is to help through the implementation of a smart guidance system based on IoT Technologies, herders to better control their livestock following the predefined corridors from north to south of Benin and vice versa. In order to help farmers to save their crops in case of flood, our system will integrate a prediction module that will enable them to anticipate natural events such as flooding in the heavy rainy season. In this paper, our researches will therefore focus on the proposal of a multi-level architecture that can enable us to achieve the aforementioned objectives.

Keywords: IoT · Smart · Prototype · Sensors · E-agriculture · Smart-village · Livestock · Farmer · Big data

1 Introduction

One of the latest breakthroughs in the Internet world was the Internet of Things (IoT). The term IoT dates back to 1999 [1] and is a science that allows multiple objects to communicate with each other and/or with the cloud. This technology currently promises to positively and dramatically change human's life through

P. Pereira et al. (Eds.): SC4Life 2019, LNICST 318, pp. 71–82, 2020.
https://doi.org/10.1007/978-3-030-45293-3_6

these connected objects. Connected objects rely on embedded chips and sensors that connect them to the Internet and give them new features. Thanks to IoT, it is also possible to facilitate the convergence between several disciplines such as embedded systems, Artificial Intelligence, Big Data, Open Data, Cloud computing, Machine-to-Machine communication (M2M), etc. Once upon a time, isolated [2]. Gartner Institute predicts that nearly 21 billion connected devices could be in circulation by the end of 2020, two-thirds for private uses and the rest for the professional world. The Internet of Things has become today, a required tool for the rapid expansion of several sectors such as health, agriculture, transport, livestock, manufacturing, logistics, building, home automation, etc.

The fields of agriculture and livestock are of particular interest to us in this paper, as agriculture and livestock are the keys to economic development and poverty reduction in developing countries. For a long time and for a variety of reasons, including structural and technological constraints, misguided national policies and an unfavorable external economic environment, the potential of these two sectors has been ignored. The implementation of an intelligent farming system makes it possible to cope effectively with both productivity and low income issues and those related to climate change. The Food and Agriculture Organization (FAO), a specialized agency of United Nations, estimates that food production must increase by at least 60% to meet the demand of the 9 billion people expected to populate the world in 2050. It states that one people between eight is currently food insecure [3]. It is therefore urgent to find sustainable solutions to ensure global food security in the coming decades. As for the livestock sector, the use of technologies makes it possible, for example, to monitor animals, to know in real-time the state of their health and well-being, to acquire information on livestock, to improve the management of herds and to better guide them during transhumance through predefined corridors [4], etc.

The remaining of this paper is organized as follows. Section 2 presents the context and the motivation. Section 3 describes our multi-layered IoT architecture. Finally, Sect. 4 presents the related work and Sect. 5 concludes our work.

2   Context and Motivation

Transhumance is a phenomenon that involves migrating livestock from one place to another by traveling several kilometers and crossing fields of crops. The goal is to allow livestock to feed properly and reproduce. Generally, the non-respect of the passages planned for the animals called corridors can lead to a destruction of the harvests and lead to deadly clashes. This can have a negative impact on the development and economy of a country, especially in developing countries. In addition, it is noticed that the phenomenon of flood, can cause very serious damages and have significant impacts on the quality of life of the people living in rural areas. The damages can be both material and human. These two factors led us to think of the establishment in Benin, particularly in the Ouémé valley (second largest valley in the world) [5], of a project that we named THINGALIVE (**TH**e **I**nternet of thi**N**gs for intelli**G**ent **A**griculture and **L**ivestock

In the Valley of ouEme) that aims to introduce the Internet of Things [1] in agriculture and livestock, including the transhumance of animals.

This work will allow us, in addition to getting the usual information on a given crop field (soil condition, growth level, humidity, temperature), to provide reliable information about the imminent arrival of a flood so that the farmers can anticipate and save the harvest by sheltering more crops and also to reduce the risks of frequent drowning.

On the other hand, researches conducted in the course of this project will enable pastoralists in transhumance to effectively monitor livestock by following the corridor defined for their passage from the South of Benin and reduce clashes with farmers. Those clashes include the slaugther of cattle, the destruction of the harvest and the loss of human life. So, breeders will be able to have real-time information if they deviate from the corridors and have frequent information on the state of the grazing along the corridor.

THINGALIVE project will therefore lead to a more intelligent agriculture that will allow the farmer to be fulfilled and better enjoy the fruits of his toils. On the other hand, farmers will benefit from a transhumance that is both peaceful and intelligent in the predefined corridor by also providing useful information on the areas of the corridor where the pasture is well provided throughout the displacement or position of the water bodies.

Thus, THINGALIVE project will allow the use of technologies related to the IoT to achieve the following objectives:

- Better inform farmers and breeders to ensure peaceful relationships
- Make profitable the activities of farmers and breeders for a better development impact
- Reduce or eradicate the deadly clashes between farmers and breeders
- Create smart villages that are better organized to face the flood and avoid the destruction of the crops
- Preserve the security and privacy of the information.

The THINGALIVE project is still in its earlier stage and is divided into several phases, given its scale. Thus, this paper will only focus on the proposal of the architecture that will gradually lead to the achievement of the objectives mentioned above.

Thus, the proposed architecture is intended to allow:

- breeders to keep their herds as much as possible during transhumance in the corridors provided for this purpose.
- farmers to intervene in time to prevent the total destruction of their crops in case of negligence on the part of a breeder.
- the collection, storage and processing of data necessary for rapid decision-making.

3   High Level IoT Architecture for THINGALIVE

This section presents a short overview on IoT reference model, describes the architecture proposed for THINGALIVE project and compares the two architectures to show how our architecture fulfils the IoT basic requirements.

3.1   Reference IoT Model

Due to the rapid growth of the IoT, to cope with the lack of standardization of IoT model, it is important to have a reference architecture. This model needs to give a common view of the different levels of devices, tools, standards and protocols needed to make IoT running from the data generation by the devices, their processing and transmission, to their use by applications. Many models and architectures have been proposed such as Lamda Architecture [6,7], Kappa Architecture [7], IoT World Forum reference model [2] and many others, depending of the covered domains. The authors of [2] proposed a multilevel model to give clear definitions and descriptions applicable to elements and functions of IoT systems and applications. Then, the reference model has been proposed to bring simplification, clarification, identification, standardization and organization into IoT system setting up. The reference model has seven levels which are shown in Fig. 1:

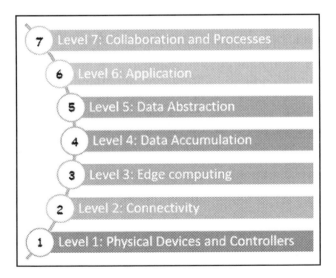

Fig. 1. IoT reference model

- Level 1: Physical Devices and Controllers. This level is composed by physical devices and controllers that might control many devices/endpoints which send and receive information and can give sometimes a first level of processing.

- Level 2: Connectivity. This level gives a reliable, timely information transmission between devices across networks on the one hand and between the network and the available functions at Level 3 on the other hand.
- Level 3: Edge Computing. This level ensures the conversion of the network data flows into information in order to serve the next level for storage and high level processing.
- Level 4: Data Accumulation. This level captures network data in movement from the previous levels and stores them, using different database technologies for non-real-time applications.
- Level 5: Data Abstraction. With IoT, data originate from many sources. This level aims at focusing on presenting data and its storage in such a way to enable easier implementation and provide powerful applications. This level processes the data to make them ready for the next level. Data protection with appropriate authentication and authorization is also provided.
- Level 6: Application. This level provides information interpretation. Different types of application can be developed depending of the nature of the data acquisition devices and business needs from data available at Level 5. This will allow getting better end-user experience for mobile users, business analysts and for monitoring purposes.
- Level 7: Collaboration and Processes. This level highlights the fact that many people need to collaborate to make working an overall IoT ecosystem through many processes that involve many data generated by IoT systems.

3.2 High Level Multi-layered Architecture for THINGALIVE

This section presents our proposed multi-layered architecture for smart agriculture and livestock based on IoT technologies.

We identified three main requirements for our architecture which are :

- Completeness: our architecture should meet the key properties of IoT reference model architecture.
- Flexibility: this gives our architecture the possibility to be independent from any technology and protocol constraints.
- Simplicity: this ensures our architecture to be clear and easy to understand.

Figure 2 shows the multi-layered architecture proposed for the THINGALIVE project. Our architecture is firstly composed of a stack of five main layers that highlight the required functionalities of an IoT-based architecture. Those layers are: Data Acquisition Layer, Connection Systems/Technologies Layer, Data Processing and Storage Layer, Service Layer and Notifications Layer.

Moreover, it integrates a lateral stack of two additional layers that show interaction with the other layers for monitoring and give access to the services provided to the different actors. Those are: Monitoring System and Stakeholders layers.

Following is the description of the proposed architecture.

Fig. 2. THINGALIVE multi-layered IoT architecture

– **Data Acquisition Layer**

This layer is composed of elements that produce information collected by IoT devices, sensors and actuators. The data can be produced by weather, flooding situation, the position of the green grass, rivers and cattle. Drones and IoT devices are used to collect data that are sent through the next layer using different communication technologies. The data transmitted can be processed in real-time or with delay depending of the usage.

– **Connection Systems/Technologies Layer**

This layer provides communication functions for IoT devices. It allows the transmission of the data flows from the sensors to the next level for storage, processing and use. There are many proprietary technologies and protocols in use, but the standardization increases quickly and allows more interoperability. IoT uses several well-known and emerging technologies, namely Wi-Fi, Bluetooth, ZigBee, Z-Wave, 6LowPAN, Tread, Neul, LoRaWAN, Near Field Communication (NFC), Sigfox, etc., in addition to 2G/3G/4G cellular technologies [2,8,9]. Depending of the purpose of the collected data, they could be sent either to the database for future use or directly to application for real-time exploitation. This layer is designed to be reliable and is able to deliver information in real-time between devices over the network by implementing various communication protocols. Both protocols in common use on the standard network and IoT-aware protocols will be used. For example, LoRaWAN or SigFox [8] technology can be used to transmit data from sensors to the place they will be analyzed in order to act and take decisions.

Among the common protocols available on TCP/IP stack, HTTP is used for some IoT devices. However, it does not support IoT devices environment constraints, such as low memory, low bandwidth, low power and others. Moreover, many web-derived protocols are also proposed but they have some limitations. In the literature, more suitable IoT protocols have been proposed to give better facilities for communication in IoT world. The most popular protocols are CoAP (Constrained Application Protocol) [10] and MQTT (Message Queuing Telemetry Transport) [11,12]. Depending of the IoT devices and the usage, our architecture will use one that suits a case.

– **Data Processing and Storage Layer**

This layer is the most important of our architecture, since it provides data processing and storage. Data processing is performed according to the target of utilization by converting network data flows into information. This layer tackles high-volume data analysis and transformation since IoT devices may generate a lot of samples of data that need to be analyzed in order to take decision and to be stored. The analysis can be performed in real-time or delayed based on stored data. The existing analysis techniques and tools are based on common techniques such as machine learning, neural networks [13,14] and big data analytic techniques [15] used in cloud computing to process largest data. Emergency data are processed directly and sent to related service to serve for quick handling of events. Batch processing is based on stored raw data used to build analytic solution in order to act and perform prediction. This layer provides understandable information to the higher layer. Data are filtering, cleanup and aggregate for utilization by each service using data in motion and/or data at rest. For storage, streaming or continuous data may be stored on big data system such as Hadoop [16], MongoDB [17] and non-real-time data may be stored in relational database where data are always available. Real-time data is usually used to setup alert systems. This layer provides functionalities such as multiple data formats reconciliation, consistent semantics of data assurance across sources, transformation of data for higher level application, consolidation of data into one place using ETL (Extract, Transform and Load) or data replication, access to multiple data stored through data virtualization and data protection. Today, OLTP databases [18,19] and data warehouses are used to carry and manage the amount of data generated by multiple IoT devices.

- **Service Layer**
  This layer is the one that helps to make use of the amount of data provided by the IoT systems. The interpretation of information is performed by this layer from real-time data and/or non-real-time data. The applications developed on the stack of this layer are based on different requirements, such as monitoring, prediction and control. The data transformed from the previous layer are used here to provide various functionalities. For example, alert system can be setup using real-time data to provide quick response time in case of disaster. Furthermore, analytic applications is setup to interpret data for business decisions. This layer is the one that provides interactions between the different actors and the IoT systems setup for smart Agriculture. The services developed by our architecture can be based on restful web service and many protocols designed for IoT.

- **Notifications Layer**
  This layer provides interaction with users through their devices. The services provided by the IoT systems are reachable from the common communication devices (laptops, phones, tablets, etc.). Web services using SOAP or REST and restful API are used to provide services to the end user. Taking into account user's position, the information received will provide him with the possibility to make a decision. This layer provides a dashboard to follow different events from the devices and to manage the different devices available in the IoT system.

- **Monitoring System**
  The first additional layer provides an interface to manage the devices, the tools, the services and our architecture end-users. This layer can take into account the monitoring of the IoT devices, the users and services management, the cloud infrastructure and services management, the communication network management and the databases administration.

- **Stakeholders**
  The use of the services developed around the data generated by the devices allows many interaction between the people involved and the processes that will run behind the real-time or non-real-time data that move through the network.
  The second additional layer is composed of the main actors of our architecture. Five of them are formally identified. They are:
  - The Agricultural farmers. This actor is the farmer that has the land and performs agricultural activities on it.
  - The Transhumant breeders. This actor is the breeder who travels along the corridors to have green grass and rivers for the cows and other animals.
  - The Officers and Authorities. The officer or the authority is the actor that can be called or can receive a message notifying that something wrong is happening so that the security company tries to solve the issue.
  - The Transhumance Corridor Management Team. This team is composed by many people, from the government, geographers to the representatives

of farmers and breeders. This committee defines each year the corridor that will be followed by the breeders.

- The infrastructure managers. The infrastructure will be managed by our team and may be used by some farmers that will be equipped with our IoT devices and materials. Some breeders also may have the devices placed on some cows to visualize in real-time their position along the corridor in order to send an alert when they didn't follow the corridor.

Our architecture provides six main functions that are spread over the seven layers namely: Collection, Storage, Analysis, Prediction, Adaptation and Output (Application).

3.3 THINGALIVE Architecture vs IoT World Forum Reference Model

This section compares the IoT World Forum reference model [2] with our proposed architecture in order to show how our architecture is complete by taking into account all of the functionalities delivered by the seven layers of the reference model. Our architecture has two layers less than the reference model and aggregates many functions on each layer to reduce the complexity. Figure 3 shows a comparison between our architecture and the IoT World Forum reference model. The links from the reference model to our architecture show the correspondence between the layers on the both sides.

Our Data Acquisition Layer provides the functionalities delivered by the first layer of the reference model, Physical Devices and Controllers.

Our Connection Systems/Technologies Layer plays the role of the second layer which is Connectivity.

Our third layer, Data Processing and Storage Layer is the most important and aggregates the functionalities of the third, fourth and fifth layers of the

Fig. 3. Comparison between THINGALIVE architecture and IoT world reference model

reference model, Edge Computing, Data Accumulation and Data Abstraction. This layer is the core of our architecture.

The fourth proposed layer, named Service Layer tackles the functions given by the application layer of the reference model. The additional Monitoring System layer can also be associated for services delivery one.

The last layer named Notifications layer proposed the role played by the seventh layer of the reference model, Collaboration and Processes. The additional Stakeholders and Monitoring system layers can be associated to add more functionalities.

This comparison shows that our architecture fulfils the basic requirements of IoT systems.

4   Related Work

The Lambda Architecture presented in [6] is a robust system for massive amount of data collection and processing, but its core is centralized in the data centers or in the cloud. This architecture can limit the effectiveness of the analytics to quickly respond.

The authors of [2] proposed a layered IoT architectural reference model that provides a clean, simplified perspective on IoT and solutions that make easy the data collection, processing and service. This proposition splits the IoT problem into smaller parts and provides interoperability between devices in addition to security. This architecture needs to be adapted according to each application, in particular in african context where few communication technologies are available.

The authors of [20, 21] show that the problem between breeders and farmers is real, but they didn't provide any concrete IT solutions to overcome the situation.

The work in [4], proposed a solution that addresses the mapping of the corridors without showing a full applicable IT solution to reduce clashes between breeders and farmers.

Many existing IoT-based solutions [22–24] are partial whereas the solution we proposed in this paper, aims to provide an integrated architecture that is useful for both breeders, farmers and authorities. This architecture tries to handle many aspects which are common for breeders and farmers.

5   Conclusion

The IoT agricultural applications are making it possible for ranchers and farmers to collect meaningful data. Large landowners and small farmers must understand the potential of IoT market for agriculture by installing smart technologies to increase competitiveness and sustainability in their productions. With the rapid growth of the population, the demand can be successfully met if the ranchers, as well as small farmers, use agricultural IoT-based solutions in a prosperous manner. This is the reason why we wanted to propose an architecture whose main objectives were to allow both farmers and breeders to be alerted in case of deviation of herds during transhumance. This is only possible through the data collection, storage and processing system that can assist in reliable decision-making inherent in good herd management. The architectural solution proposed in this paper represents an important step that should create the hope of definitively solving the conflicts related to the destruction of crops due to the transhumance of animals on the one hand and issues related to crops destruction due to flooding occurrence on the other hand. Indeed, the Data Acquisition Layer allows the collection of information that is subsequently sent to the Data Processing and Storage Layer through the Connection system layer for processing and storage. The processed data are used to send alerts to different stakeholders through the Notification Layer by using services offered by the Service Layer.

In future work, our architecture will be improved to take into account all of the IoT ecosystem and new technologies, protocols and devices. We will provide full details on the implementation of each stack of our architecture.

References

1. Gubbi, J., Buyya, R., Maruslc, S., Palaniswami, M.: Internet of Things (IoT): a vision, architectural elements, and future directions. Future Gener. Comput. Syst. **29**(7), 1645–1660 (2013)
2. Hanes, D., Salgueiro, G., Grossetete, P., Barton, R., Henry, J.: IoT Fundamentals: Networking Technologies, Protocols, and use Cases for the Internet of Things. Cisco Press, Indianapolis (2017)
3. FAO, Exemples de réussites de la FAO en matière d'agriculture intelligente face au climat (2014). www.fao.org/climatechange/29830-0beb869615795a9960 ada6400c62b3783.pdf. Accessed Oct 2019
4. Kitchell, E., Turner, M.D., McPeak, J.G.: Mapping of pastoral corridors: practices and politics in eastern Senegal. Pastoralism **4**(1), 17 (2014)
5. AFDB, Bénin : La vallée de l'Ouémé se transforme grâce au PAIA-VO (2017). https://www.afdb.org/fr/projects-and-operations/selected-projects/benin-la-vallee-de-loueme-se-transforme-grace-au-paia-vo-23. Accessed Oct 2019
6. Marz, N., Warren, J.: Big Data: Principles and Best Practices of Scalable Realtime Data Systems. Manning, New York (2013)
7. Pawar, K., Attar, V.: A survey on data analytic platforms for Internet of Things, In: Proceedings of CAST, pp. 605–610 (2016)
8. Aloÿs, A., Jiazi, Y., Thomas, C., Townsley, W.: A study of LoRa: long range & low power networks for the Internet of Things. Sensors **16**(9), 1466 (2016)
9. Zanella, A., Bui, N., Castellani, A., Vangelista, L., Zorzi, M.: Internet of Things for smart cities. IEEE Internet Things J. **1**(1), 22–32 (2014)
10. Shelby, Z., Hartke, K., Bormann, C.: The constrained application protocol (CoAP). No. RFC 7252 (2014)
11. Locke, D.: MQ telemetry transport (MQTT) v3.1 protocol specification. IBM developerWorks Technical Library, p. 15 (2010)
12. Singh, M., Rajan, M.A., Shivraj, V.L., Balamuralidhar, P.: Secure MQTT for Internet of Things (IoT). In: Proceedings of Fifth CSNT, pp. 746–751 (2015)
13. Qiu, J., Wu, Q., Ding, G., Xu, Y., Feng, S.: A survey of machine learning for big data processing. EURASIP J. Adv. Signal Process. **2016**(1), 67 (2016)

14. Che, D., Safran, M., Peng, Z.: From big data to big data mining: challenges, issues, and opportunities. In: Hong, B., Meng, X., Chen, L., Winiwarter, W., Song, W. (eds.) DASFAA 2013. LNCS, vol. 7827, pp. 1–15. Springer, Heidelberg (2013). https://doi.org/10.1007/978-3-642-40270-8_1
15. Gandomi, A., Haider, M.: Beyond the hype: big data concepts, methods, and analytics. Int. J. Inf. Manage. **35**(2), 137–144 (2015)
16. Dittrich, J., Quiané-Ruiz, J.A.: Efficient big data processing in Hadoop MapReduce. In: Proceedings of VLDB Endowment **5**(12), 2014–2015 (2012)
17. Li, T., Liu, Y., Tian, Y., Shen, S., Mao, W.: A storage solution for massive IoT data based on NOSQL. In: Proceedings of IEEE GreenCom (2012)
18. Cai, H., Xu, B., Jiang, L., Vasilakos, A.V.: IoT-based big data storage systems in cloud computing: perspectives and challenges. IEEE Internet Things J. **4**(1), 75–87 (2017)
19. Arora, V., Nawab, F., Agrawal, D., El Abbadi, A.: Multi-representation based data processing architecture for IoT applications. In: Proceedings of 37th ICDCS, pp. 2234–2239 (2017)
20. Clanet, J.C., Ogilvie, A.: Farmer-herder conflicts and water governance in a semi-arid region of Africa. Water Int. **34**(1), 30–46 (2009)
21. Ange, M., Kinhou, B., Brice, S.: Transhumance and conflicts management on Agonlin plateau in Zou department (Benin). J. Biodivers. Environ. Sci. (JBES) **4**(5), 32–145 (2014)
22. Patil, K.A., Kale, N.R.: A model for smart agriculture using IoT. In: Proceedings of IEEE ICGTSPICC (2016)
23. Srinivasulu, P., Babu, M.S., Venkat, R., Rajesh, K.: Cloud service oriented architecture (CSoA) for agriculture through Internet of Things (IoT) and big data. In: Proceedings of ICEICE (2017)
24. Popović, T., Latinović, N., Pešić, A., Zečević, Ž., Krstajić, B., Djukanović, S.: Architecting an IoT-enabled platform for precision agriculture and ecological monitoring: a case study. Comput. Electron. Agric. **140**, 255–265 (2017)

Agrilogistics - A Genetic Programming Based Approach

Divya D. Kulkarni$^{(\boxtimes)}$ and Shivashankar B. Nair

Indian Institute of Technology Guwahati, Guwahati, India
{divyadk,sbnair}@iitg.ac.in

Abstract. The advent of technology in the agriculture sector, such as precision agriculture, the Internet of Things (IoT) and machine learning has dramatically improved the experience of farming scenario. Apart from improving the farming conditions, there is a need for focused effort to achieve a balanced ecosystem in the supply chain of agrilogistics. Inefficient price signals conveyed to the farmer, erratic price fluctuations and inflation of the agri-produce coupled with the presence of several intermediaries, tend to imbalance the system. In this work, we propose an IoT based agrilogistic system coupled with a genetic programming algorithm to ensure fair prices across all the participants within. The system evolves and generates a set of programs that, in turn, generates the selling rate for every participant in the supply chain in a manner that confers fairness.

Keywords: Internet of Things (IoT) · Genetic Programming · Agrilogistics · Supply chain

1 Introduction

The agriculture sector has seen enormous changes lately due to the advent of technology. An IoT plays a significant role in traditional precision agriculture, wherein the data is collected from a variety of connected devices and sensors, setup in the fields, thus improving both yield and productivity. IoT in agriculture mainly comprises setting up sensors across large tracts of fields, surveying and collating data mostly using either sensor networks or drones. Sensors used are varied in nature and include those that can sense temperature, humidity and soil-moisture [4]. Cameras have also been used as sensors to judge the quality of the plants [1]. Various solutions have been proposed to augment IoT with precision agriculture [3,9,11,14], but only a few have been actually implemented effectively [6,18]. Many have proposed the use of machine learning and data mining techniques for improving yield, controlling pests, managing soil, etc. [15,16] but actual implementations of only a few have shown decent results [5,7].

There are several other factors that need to be addressed in the making of a fair agriculture based ecosystem. For instance inefficient price signals, the

P. Pereira et al. (Eds.): SC4Life 2019, LNICST 318, pp. 83–96, 2020.
https://doi.org/10.1007/978-3-030-45293-3_7

presence of too many intermediaries and information asymmetries [2,12] can lead to a severe losses to a farmer.

In order to protect the producer from erratic price fluctuations and to handle the problem of inefficient price signals in agrarian countries like India, the government generally sets up a Minimum Support Price (MSP).

Though this may protect the farmers from incurring severe losses, it does not guarantee the best price for their produce mostly because they are not aware of the overall dynamics of the market. Presence of too many intermediaries such as middle-men, agents, and brokers between the point of production (farm) to the point of vending and consumption also causes erratic price fluctuations. The problem at times can cascade resulting in a gross wastage of the product due to high production and low demand. Governments also ensure to stock warehouses managed by them with the produce to control market trends. Such warehouses buy the produce from farmers at the MSP and endeavour to always maintain a buffer stock of the produce. It may happen that the quantum of produce stored exceeds the buffer stock. Under such conditions, the same is released to the market at a fair price. Such an increase or decrease in stock in the warehouse coupled with dynamically varying production and demands can create a large turbulence in profits made by the supply chain. Mau et al. [10] points out that the agriculture sector lacks efficient consumer response, which could guide the producer in the production of the goods based on the demands of the customer. It is reported in [17] that profits are mostly skewed away from the producers due to the presence of various intermediaries. In an agrilogistic system, ensuring a mechanism that profits all the participants is an uphill task. To handle this supply chain in agrilogistics (logistics system of the agriculture sector), this mechanism would need to be aware of all the connected dynamics of the market so as to advise each of the participants of the action to be taken by them.

One of the methods to solve the supply chain agrilogistics is to initially collect a huge amount data which naturally can be generated only over a large period of time, and then analyze it using various machine learning techniques including deep neural networks. This could mean huge losses (during the data collection interval) with hardly anything gained or learned. A mechanism wherein learning commences during the data collection phase itself would greatly ameliorate the problem. One of the ways this could be realized is by making programs evolve using Genetic Programming (GP) [8] based techniques during the course of data collection. Execution of such programs will help steer the system being controlled to a better level. In GP, the quality of a program is measured by a fitness score, which in an agrilogistic scenario could be the selling rate of the product at every stage. In addition, an IoT based agrilogistic supply chain system, data received from heterogeneous sensors could guide the evolution of such programs.

In this work, we propose a Genetic Programming (GP) [8] based strategy to learn to handle the dynamics of the supply chain and accordingly advise the participants on whom to sell their stock in a network of producers (farmers), warehouses and vendors so as to get the best price. The strategy takes into consideration the dynamically changing demand, the quantum of stock,

Fig. 1. The proposed model of supply chain management in agrilogistics

temperature, humidity and time elapsed after harvest and evolves programs over time which when run maximizes the selling rates across all the participants.

2   Methodology

The work herein describes a method to generate and evolve efficient programs for an IoT based supply chain of agrilogistics shown in Fig. 1. As illustrated the participants include sets of farmers, F = $\{F_1, F_2, F_3..., F_n\}$, warehouses, W = $\{W_1, W_2, W_3, ..., W_m\}$ and vendors, V = $\{V_1, V_2, V_3, ..., V_p\}$. A farmer F_i who generates the produce can either send them, part or whole, over to a warehouse W_j or a vendor V_k. Likewise W_j, which maintains a buffer stock of the produce, could channel excess amounts to any of the vendors based on demand. Eventually, the vendors sell the produce to the consumers. In addition, there are q number of number of autonomous vehicles (G) at a site x (where $x \in \{\{F_i\}, \{W_j\}, \{V_k\}\}$), G_{x_q}, at each of the locations or sites of the participants. A vehicle G is responsible for transporting a certain quantity of produce from one site to the other.

The IoT infrastructure is used to sense and record parameters, such as ambient temperature and humidity, age of the produce, its quantum and quality, at every site. The recorded data is then sent to the cloud which runs the proposed GP based algorithm to evolve programs, with the primary objective being to maximize the selling rates, while at the same time maintaining their consistency at the respective sites. The evolved program provides the destination where the produce has to be transported to and the selling rate at the destination.

Important Parameters. The main parameters and terms used in the system are explained below.

1. *Temperature (T) and Humidity (H):* Both temperature and humidity affect the quality of the produce. The measurements are done at the sites of every F_i, W_j and V_k using the temperature and humidity sensors at respective IoTs installed therein. Based on fixed predetermined ranges of values, temperature and humidity, are recorded as High (*hi*), Moderate (*mod*) and Low (*lo*).
2. *Quantum of Produce (Q):* It is the net quantity of a specific produce available at an instant of time at the site of a participant. Q also assumes values denoted as *hi*, *mod* and *lo*. It is measured using a load cell connected to the IoT at the respective sites.
3. *Age (τ):* The *age* of any produce is defined as the time elapsed from the time of harvest to the current time. The age of the produce increases irrespective of its location and is independent of all other parameters.
4. *Quality (φ):* The *quality* of the product affects its overall selling rate. Higher the *quality*, higher would be its selling rate. The quality of produce is assumed to degrade with increase in either T or H or τ. Just as temperature and humidity, ϕ of a produce takes values *hi*, *mod* and *lo*.
5. *Demand (δ):* It is one of the most significant terms and affects the dynamics of the system. δ increases when Q at the vendors is *lo* and decreases otherwise. Demand influences the production and outflux rates of the produce from a site, thereby affecting their selling rates at different sites that constitute the system. Demand also is expressed as *hi*, *mod* and *lo*.
6. *Distance (D) to the Destination (ψ):* It is the distance between the site from where the produce is to be shipped and the site where it is to be delivered (Destination site ψ).
7. *Outflux (O) of Produce:* Outflux is amount of produce a deliverer ships to the destination (ψ). It is calculated locally at the respective IoT site. In our work we assume the produce P to be *onions, tomatoes* and *cotton*.
   Outflux of the produce P from the site x to the site ψ is given by the formula below:

$$O_P^{x \to \psi} = \alpha * \delta_P * Q_P^x \tag{1}$$

   where α is a constant and δ_P^x and Q_P^x are the demand and the quantum of the produce P at the site x, respectively and x and $\psi \in \{\{F\}, \{W\}, \{V\}\}$.
8. *Selling Rate (ρ):* The selling rate per unit of a produce, ρ, is determined at every site x for every produce P in the supply chain. The selling rate is directly proportional to the quality, ϕ, of the produce, demand from the customer, δ, and the distance, D, to the destination where it needs to be transported. It is inversely proportional to the quantum, Q, and age, τ, of the produce.

Selling rate, ρ, is given by the Eq. (2):

$$\rho_P^x = \beta * \frac{\delta_P * \phi_P^x * D_P^x}{Q_P^x * \tau_P^x} \tag{2}$$

where β is a constant, P is the produce whose ρ is being calculated at site x respectively, $x \in \{\{F\}, \{W\}, \{V\}\}$.

The parameters T, H and Q are sensed using the associated sensors while those of τ, ϕ, and O are computed by the respective IoTs, locally. The rest wiz. δ and ρ are computed in the cloud as shown in the Fig. 1.

Evolution of Programs. The generic version of a program in a population of programs, used in this work, has three tuples corresponding to a *farmer*, *warehouse* and *vendor* respectively, as shown below.

$$S \equiv ((F^{(T,H,P,\delta_P,\phi_P,Q_P,\psi,\rho_P)^i}), (W^{(T,H,P,\delta_P,\phi_P,Q_P,\psi,\rho_P)^j}), (V^{(T,H,P,\delta_P,\phi_P,Q_P,\rho_P)^k}))^l \tag{3}$$

where T, H, δ, Q, η can take either of the values *hi,mod* or *lo* and S is set of all such programs evolved. Each tuple of the program refers to all the *farmers*, all the *warehouses* and all the *vendors* at that instant of time. This tuple denotes the rule that infers the selling rate and the destination to which the produce needs to be shipped from the corresponding site i.e. F^i, W^j or V^k based on the values of the parameters. At the site, V^k, the produce is sold to the customers. For instance, the portion of the first tuple ($i = 1$) related to the first farmer's site of the program is illustrated below.

$$((F^{(lo,lo,onions,hi,hi,mod,W_2,45)})^1), (F^{(hi,lo,onions,hi,mod,mod,W_1,30)})^1)$$

The above portion of the program that can be expressed as a rule below -

FOR{*the site of the farmer F_1*} **IF** {*the temperature and humidity are low, the produce is onions with high demand having high quality and moderate quantum*}, **THEN** {*the selling rate is 45 units and the destination to which it needs to be shipped is W_2*} **ELSE IF** {*the temperature is high and humidity is low, the produce is onions with high demand having moderate quality and moderate quantum*} **THEN** {*the selling rate is 30 units and the destination to which it needs to be shipped is W_1*}.

Programs such as these are stored in a repository in a cloud. In the current scenario, the selling rate, ρ, of a produce is considered as the fitness score of the associated program. The goal is to maximize ρ so that the concerned seller get the maximum profit. It may be noted that the selling rate is contained by the demand of the consumers (as seen in Eq. 2) and hence programs evolve in a manner that is congenial to all participants, including the consumers.

The Algorithm

In the GP approach, the initial programs are generated randomly. In the work reported herein, it is proposed that the sensed parameters T, H, Q *and* ϕ are obtained and calculated using the IoT infrastructure at each of the sites participating in the agrilogistics scenario, thereby greatly curtailing the otherwise random search space. The GP program is assumed to be hosted in a cloud.

When all these values from all the sites are initially sent to the cloud, the demand of each type of produce is computed. Based on the demand, the outflux (O) of the produce is calculated. Using a randomly selected destination (ψ), the selling rate (ρ) of the produce (P) is then computed. These values viz. P, O, ρ and ψ are sent to the concerned site. These computations are done for every P at every site at the cloud. The respective IoT at the sites, communicates with an autonomous vehicle or a transporter within its site, which in turn delivers the O units of the produce P to the concerned destination, ψ. A program, as discussed earlier, which includes all the sites is thus generated and stored in a repository within the cloud. The cloud always receives the data from all the IoTs and structures the incoming data, I in the form shown below as a three tuple:

$$I \equiv (F^{\{T,H,P,\phi_P,Q_P\}^i}, F^{\{T,H,P,\phi_P,Q_P\}^j}, V^{\{T,H,P,\phi_P,Q_P\}^k})^l \qquad (4)$$

The next time, the cloud receives and structures an I, the GP program first checks whether the first tuple for the first farmer, F_I^1, sent by the site matches with any one of the former portion of the first tuple F_S^1 in the set of stored programs S. If so, ψ_S^j (which could be either W_S^j or V_S^j) from the latter portion of F_S^1 is retrieved. Using this information, the GP program retrieves the tuple for the same in the second or third tuples, as the case maybe, in S. This retrieved tuple is compared with the corresponding tuple W_I^1 or V_I^1 (as the case maybe). The corresponding ψ_S^k (which could be either W_S^k or V_S^k) is retrieved. Using this information, the GP program retrieves the tuple for the same in the third tuples in S. This retrieved tuple is compared with the corresponding tuple W_I^1 or V_I^1 (as the case maybe). If all comparisons are true, then the three tuples from S namely F_S^1, W_S^j and V_S^k sent back to the IoT site of F_1. In case, no match is found, the GP evolves a new program using crossover and mutation as explained later.

The crossover operation is applied when the currently reported parameters match with at least one tuple in S stored in the repository. The operation of crossover involves two *parent programs* in S, the first *parent* is one whose former portion of the first tuple in S matches with the first tuple of I. The other parent in S could be one whose former portion of any of its two latter tuples matches with either of the second or third tuple of I. The crossover operation is illustrated in the Figs. 3, 4 and 5. If there are multiple candidates for the *parent programs*, then those *parents* are selected which infer the highest selling rates. The crossover operation results in two new programs are stored in the repository and retrieved as and when required in future. In this condition too, the three tuples from S namely F_S^1, W_S^j and V_S^k sent back to the IoT site of F_1.

If a few parameter values in F_I^1 do not match with the former portion of F_S^1, then those in F_I^1 are copied on to F_S^1 to achieve the mutated solution. Then, the corresponding selling rate is calculated and the solution is sent back to the IoT site of F_1. The mutation operation is illustrated in the Figs. 6 and 7.

Fig. 2. Two of the programs generated at the initial generations corresponding to the items - **onion** and **cotton**

The process of matching, crossover and mutation is done across all tuples in I so as to complete one generation of evolution.

If there are no matching programs to perform either of the crossover or mutation operations, then a new program is generated and routed to a randomly selected destination with the selling rate determined as per the Eq. 2.

3   Results

Generation of Initial Population of Programs. We simulated the GP cum IoT side algorithms while generating the appropriate values of the pertinent sensors. First, we generated the initial population of programs as described in the previous section, and stored them in the repository within the cloud. Figure 2 shows the illustration of two of the initial the programs generated as per Eq. 3 for the products (*onion*) and (*cotton*). There are three blocks in the program viz. the farmer, the warehouse, and the vendor blocks representing the three tuples in Eq. 3, each corresponding to the conditions observed at the respective sites. In Fig. 2, the ρ corresponds to the fitness of that particular program at that site for the associated produce. The selling rate is calculated as per the Eq. 2. We generated 50 such programs as the initial population and stored them in the repository in the cloud.

Evolving New Programs. After the initial programs were generated over time, when the sites report the next set of observed conditions to the cloud, the GP program searches the repository for the matching programs as explained in the previous section. If the matching program is found, the cloud reports the ϕ where the O_P^x has to be routed, and ρ_P^x, at which the produce has to be sold to the ϕ. If a match is not found, then either the operation of crossover or mutation is applied.

The Figs. 3, 4 and 5 depict the scenario, where crossover operation is applied. Parent 1 program in Fig. 3 represents *Parent* 1, where the tuple corresponding to the site of the farmer F_2 match with the currently reported parameters of F_2, whereas the remaining tuples corresponding to W_1 and V_2, do not match with the currently reported parameter values. Similarly, *Parent* 2 program in

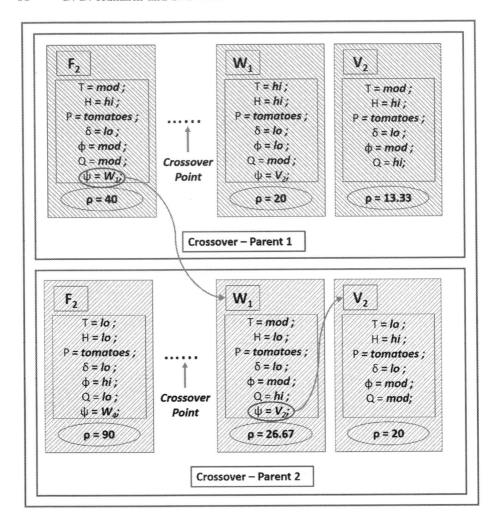

Fig. 3. Parent programs - crossover operation

the same Fig. 3 depicts *Parent 2* where the tuples corresponding to W_1 and V_2 match with the respective currently reported parameter values. The crossover mechanism is applied on the matched programs to obtain two new programs, one of them which can cater to the current parameters as shown in the Fig. 4 and the other one shown in Fig. 5 is saved in the repository for future use.

Mutation operation is depicted in Figs. 6 and 7. The *parent* program in Fig. 6, has the value of the parameter Q as *lo* for the site F_1, whereas the currently reported value of Q at F_1 is *mod*. This parameter is mutated as shown in the Fig. 7 and a new program is obtained. The selling rate (or the fitness) of this newly generated program is calculated and updated in the repository.

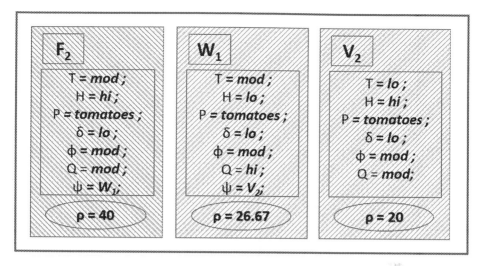

Fig. 4. Resultant program 1 - post crossover operation

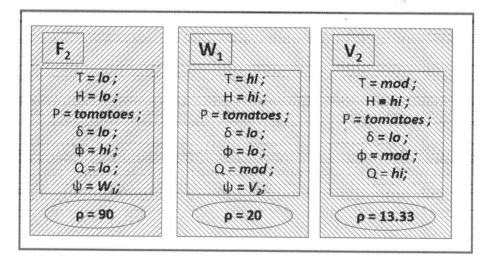

Fig. 5. Resultant program 2 - post crossover operation

As we generate and evolve the programs as per Eq. 3, the programs grow in dimension. The pseudocode in Pseudocode 1 and the Fig. 8, depicts the programs assembled for the site F_1 at an instant of time. As more and more programs are evolved, the conditions in the programs also increase, thereby resulting in a complex program. When we observe Figs. 2 and 8, we can observe the increasing conditions as more programs evolve.

Fig. 6. Parent program - mutation operation

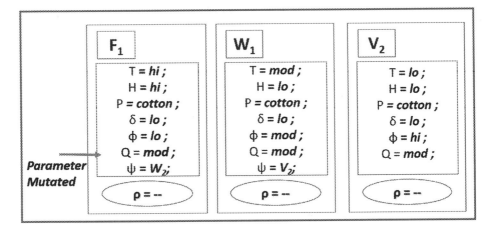

Fig. 7. Resultant program - post mutation operation

The graph of the selling rate of all the participants F, W and V plotted against the generations as the programs evolve is shown in the Fig. 9. The selling rates of all F, all W and all V is given by σ_F, σ_W and σ_V, respectively, as below:

$$\sigma_F = \sum_{i=1}^{m}\sum_{q=1}^{P} \rho_q^{F_i}$$

$$\sigma_W = \sum_{j=1}^{n}\sum_{q=1}^{P} \rho_q^{W_j} \tag{5}$$

$$\sigma_V = \sum_{k=1}^{o}\sum_{q=1}^{P} \rho_q^{V_k}$$

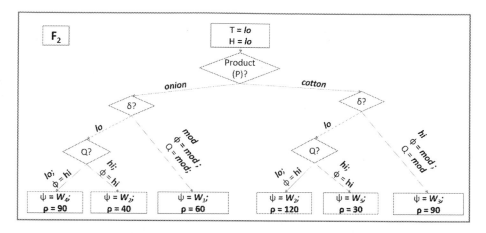

Fig. 8. A Snapshot of assembled programs

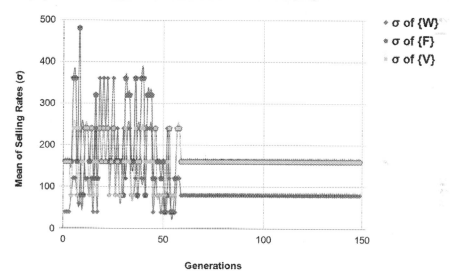

Fig. 9. Graph of the selling rates across generations

In the graph, shown in Fig. 9, the selling rates till 50th generation represent the initial population of programs generated. After which, the programs evolve as per the GP based algorithm. In the initial generations, we can observe fluctuations in the σ_F, σ_W and σ_V, wherein only one of the three sets of participants (F, W and V) seem to get high selling rates whereas others are getting lower values. However, as the programs evolve, all the σ converges to narrow bands. As can be seen, σ_F and σ_V converge to almost the same narrow band, while σ_W converges to a lower value. This is because, at each W_i there is certain amount of buffer stocked, causing an increase in the respective Q, consequently decreasing the ρ as per the Eq. 2. This lower value of σ_W conforms to the standard

Pseudocode 1 : Part of the pseudocode of one of the programs assembled

```
1  switch X do
2  │  case X ← F₂ do
3  │  │  if  T == lo && H == lo then
4  │  │  │  if P == onion then
5  │  │  │  │  if δ == lo then
6  │  │  │  │  │  if Q == lo && φ == hi then
7  │  │  │  │  │  │  ψ ← W₄
8  │  │  │  │  │  │  ρ ← 90
9  │  │  │  │  │  else if Q == hi && φ == hi then
10 │  │  │  │  │  │  ψ ← W₂
11 │  │  │  │  │  │  ρ ← 40
12 │  │  │  │  else if δ == mod then
13 │  │  │  │  │  if Q == mod && φ == mod then
14 │  │  │  │  │  │  ψ ← W₁
15 │  │  │  │  │  │  ρ ← 60
16 │  │  │  else if z == cotton then
17 │  │  │  │  if δ == lo then
18 │  │  │  │  │  if Q == lo && φ ← hi then
19 │  │  │  │  │  │  ψ ← W₂
20 │  │  │  │  │  │  ρ ← 120
21 │  │  │  │  │  else if Q == hi && φ == hi then
22 │  │  │  │  │  │  ψ ← W₅
23 │  │  │  │  │  │  ρ ← 30
24 │  │  │  │  else if δ == hi then
25 │  │  │  │  │  if  Q == mod && φ == mod
26 │  │  │  │  │  then
27 │  │  │  │  │  │  ψ ← W₃
28 │  │  │  │  │  │  ρ ← 90
```

warehousing practices [13]. It can thus be seen that each participant in the supply chain gets a fair rate for the produce.

4   Discussions and Conclusions

We have proposed a novel way of looking at the Supply Chain in the agriculture sector, to setup fair prices of commodities by taking into consideration the factors which affect the selling rate. This will eliminate the influence of middlemen on the prices, and possibly bring down erratic price fluctuations. The proposed work combines an IoT with supply chain management in agrilogistics and gives an indication to the farmer as to what products are in demand enabling him/her to concentrate on producing them. This insulates the farmer from producing excessively large quantities of a low demand produce or vice versa which may otherwise result in wastage and financial losses. Such an end to end system, provides for a win-win situation for all the participants involved in the supply chain. This can be clearly seen from the resulting graph wherein the selling rate for all participants seem to converge to a narrow band. While the IoT provides a clear and exact picture of the ground truth of the produce at various sites, the GP learns from what it has made the system do in the past using the programs in its repository. In some sense it learns from scratch and does not really require for one to wait for the collection of large amounts of data before arriving at a solution. Most of the current AI methods bank on the initial availability of a huge amount of relevant data which is then churned to produce some meaningful results using computationally heavy algorithms such as deep learning. Learning from what has been done so far during the data collection phase is grossly missing. The paradigm discussed herein could thus be well suited for learning during a data collection phase. It may even allow for better and more pertinent data to be generated thereby eventually increasing the efficacy of the traditionally used large-data driven algorithms. There are yet certain other aspects which need to be addressed to optimize the transport of goods from one site to another as also put the IoT in the real-world. Our future work will thus include the realization of an actual agent based IoT and cloud to comprehend the challenges of the paradigm when implemented in the real-world.

References

1. Bock, C.H., Nutter Jr., F.W.: Detection and measurement of plant disease symptoms using visible-wavelength photography and image analysis. Plant Sci. Rev. **6**, 73 (2012)
2. Chand, R.: Development policies and agricultural markets. Econ. Polit. Wkly. **47**(52), 53–63 (2012). http://www.jstor.org/stable/41720551
3. Gebbers, R., Adamchuk, V.I.: Precision agriculture and food security. Science **327**(5967), 828–831 (2010). https://doi.org/10.1126/science.1183899. https://science.sciencemag.org/content/327/5967/828
4. Gondchawar, N., Kawitkar, R.: IoT based smart agriculture. Int. J. Adv. Res. Comput. Commun. Eng. **5**(6), 838–842 (2016)
5. He, Y., Zeng, H., Fan, Y., Ji, S., Wu, J.: Application of deep learning in integrated pest management: a real-time system for detection and diagnosis of oilseed rape pests. Mob. Inf. Syst. (2019). https://doi.org/10.1155/2019/4570808
6. Kapetanovic, Z., Vasisht, D., Won, J., Chandra, R., Kimball, M.: Experiences deploying an always-on farm network. GetMobile Mob. Comp. Commun. **21**(2), 16–21 (2017). https://doi.org/10.1145/3131214.3131220
7. King, A.: Technology: the future of agriculture. Nature **544** (2017). https://doi.org/10.1038/544S21a
8. Koza, J.R., Koza, J.R.: Genetic Programming: On the Programming of Computers by Means of Natural Selection, vol. 1. MIT Press, Cambridge (1992)
9. Mat, I., Kassim, M.R.M., Harun, A.N., Yusoff, I.M.: IoT in precision agriculture applications using wireless moisture sensor network. In: 2016 IEEE Conference on Open Systems (ICOS), pp. 24–29. IEEE (2016)

10. Mau, M.: Supply chain management in agriculture - including economics aspects like responsibility and transparency. In: European Association of Agricultural Economists, 2002 International Congress, 28–31 August 2002, Zaragoza, Spain (2002)
11. Mekala, M.S., Viswanathan, P.: A survey: smart agriculture IoT with cloud computing. In: 2017 International Conference on Microelectronic Devices, Circuits and Systems (ICMDCS), pp. 1–7, August 2017. https://doi.org/10.1109/ICMDCS.2017.8211551
12. Negi, S., Anand, N.: Supply chain of fruits & vegetables' agribusiness in uttarakhand (India): major issues and challenges. J. Supply Chain Manag. Syst. 4(1), 43–57 (2015)
13. Ozsen, L., Coullard, C.R., Daskin, M.S.: Capacitated warehouse location model with risk pooling. Naval Res. Logistics (NRL) 55(4), 295–312 (2008)
14. Patil, K.A., Kale, N.R.: A model for smart agriculture using IoT. In: 2016 International Conference on Global Trends in Signal Processing, Information Computing and Communication (ICGTSPICC), pp. 543–545, December 2016. https://doi.org/10.1109/ICGTSPICC.2016.7955360
15. Patil, S.S., Thorat, S.A.: Early detection of grapes diseases using machine learning and IoT. In: 2016 Second International Conference on Cognitive Computing and Information Processing (CCIP), pp. 1–5. IEEE (2016)
16. Shekhar, Y., Dagur, E., Mishra, S., Sankaranarayanan, S.: Intelligent iot based automated irrigation system. Int. J. Appl. Eng. Res. 12(18), 7306–7320 (2017)
17. TeamYS: Agri-logistics in India: challenges and emerging solutions (2013). https://yourstory.com/2013/05/agri-logistics-in-india-challenges-and-emerging-solutions/
18. Vasisht, D., et al.: FarmBeats: an IoT platform for data-driven agriculture. In: 14th USENIX Symposium on Networked Systems Design and Implementation (NSDI 17), pp. 515–529 (2017)

Real World Third-Person with Multiple Point-of-Views for Immersive Mixed Reality

Zebo Yang$^{(\boxtimes)}$, Mingshu Zhang, Taili Zhang, Linhao Fu, and Tatuso Nakajima

Waseda University, Tokyo 169-8050, Japan
{zebo,momochi,ztl_eric,nogizakakazumi,
tatsuo}@dcl.cs.waseda.ac.jp

Abstract. Technologies of Virtual Reality (VR), Augmented Reality (AR) and Mixed Reality (MR) are increasingly applied in urban construction and smart cities. As one of the high fidelity revivification methods, the purpose of these applications is to provide a better immerse experience over the combination of realistic and virtual interactions. Numerous methods and models are adopted to simulate real life scenarios. Regularly, first-person perspective (1PP) is a spontaneous way to revive reality virtually, and this is also what most manufacturers do. In a different way, we tend to verify the feasibility of a new perspective for VR, AR or MR: a third-person perspective (3PP) with multiple Point of View (PoV) from different fixed cameras. We implemented an immersive AR environment for users to control or view themselves in a third person perspective. They are able to switch among different perspectives in different angles, including a first-person view. We developed a simple game based on this environment and conducted user study with this implementation. The result shows that people will generally be intrigued and willing to pay for a new MR experience (like 3PP) if the process is effortless and pleasurable. The most welcomed thing is the ability to switch perspectives during a VR or AR experience. This environment can be extended to real world services such as interviewing, dating and picnic, etc. or future smart cities services that use VR and AR, such as VR traffic management, VR communities empathetic planning and AR navigation, etc.

Keywords: Virtual Reality · Augmented Reality · Third person view · Future cities · Video games

1 Introduction

Today, the diversity of Virtual Reality (VR), Augmented Reality (AR) and Mixed Reality (MR) applications enters the field of urban settlements and smart cities [1, 2]. Prolificacy in similar patterns of AR and VR applications, coupled with constantly changed future possibilities produces a great demand of novel experiences. While AR and VR hardware are augmented from time to time, the design of Head-Mounted Display (HMD) spontaneously inspires the same pattern: first-person perspective (1PP) centered with the HMD. For example, Minecraft VR [3], an exploratory VR game with a low-poly aesthetic, Pokemon Go [4], an AR game for capturing Pokemon or battling gyms, Fragments

© ICST Institute for Computer Sciences, Social Informatics and Telecommunications Engineering 2020
Published by Springer Nature Switzerland AG 2020. All Rights Reserved
P. Pereira et al. (Eds.): SC4Life 2019, LNICST 318, pp. 97–108, 2020.
https://doi.org/10.1007/978-3-030-45293-3_8

[5], a mystery-solving MR game for Hololens, and researches like [6, 7], are all designed in the classic first-person view. However, first-person perspective sometimes cannot adequately tender horizon or information for virtual or augmented realities, especially in cases that require a macroscopic view, such as VR or AR tools for self-validation, rehabilitation, traffic detection, safety instruction or education [8–11]. We believe essential future smart cities services would be energized and consummated with these AR or VR enhancement.

With the question of perspective comparison [12] and the intention to explore potential AR/VR modes, we tend to probe into different applicable perspectives for MR users. Specifically, we verify the capability of fixed-camera third-person perspectives (3PP) for immersive AR applications and the ability to switch between different perspectives. In order to implement the fixed-camera third-person views for MR applications, we set up a rectangle room with cameras attached at different positions and use it as the experiment space. Each position of the cameras represents a different perspective for the user. The display of the VR HMD will show the live video footages from these cameras. When the user enters the room, he/she is able to see himself/herself from one of the perspectives created by these cameras. What the user does in the room represents what he/she operates to the virtual world and he/she is able to view all the actions from the HMD in real time. Moreover, we augment the video contents from the cameras, adding augmented and mixed realities to the environment. We set up action triggers in the room: when the user 'touches' one of these triggers, corresponding event will be operated. For example, when the user touches a locker, information of the locker owner will show up. Ultimately, content shown in the HMD will be automatically switched to another camera/perspective when the system detects the vision of the user may be blocked by his/her own body. It will be easier for the user to finish certain tasks in this way. In the case of Fig. 1, when the user steps through the trigger, the viewpoint will be switched to the right perspective from the left one.

This paper aims to create a third-person immersive environment for the upon features and verify the effectiveness of this perspective for AR, VR and MR. The prototype is built upon Unity 3D [13] and we use several webcams as the sources of different perspectives. Video stream of the right camera will be shown in HMD and serve as the current perspective. HTC VIVE [14] is used as the VR headset and TPCAST [15] is adopted to make the whole process wireless. TPCAST is a wireless adapter attached to the HMD, broadcasting the content from PC to the VR headset, removing the need for transmitting cables, which can also be done by the wireless adapter from VIVE [16].

Beyond entertainment, VR, AR and MR is likewise significant for many scenarios, especially for future smart cities services [10, 17]. Derivative applications of the third-person view environment can be of great help in these scenarios. For example, recent treatment approaches with virtual reality in stroke rehabilitation is rapidly adopted in clinical settings [18], and virtual reality researches on urban safety for preventing child pedestrian injury come into notice [10]. With the perspectives of multiple Point of View (PoV), in future cities, users may be able to observe themselves in a third-person view timely, anywhere and anytime, if the involved devices become perfectly wireless and portable, or the city gives the effort to open the CCTV (Closed-Circuit Television) for limitary public access.

Fig. 1. Perspective switching

In the following sections, Sect. 2 describes several related works. Section 3 introduces the prototype implementation. Section 4 proposes the design and results of the user study. Section 4 describes limitations and challenges. Lastly in Sect. 5, we give conclusion and future possibilities.

2 Background and Motivation

In terms of the great attention paid to the ability of VR to immerse people into another reality, it seems to imply that first-person perspective is the perfect option for VR. As more and more AR or MR headsets come into mass production, such as HoloLens 2 [19], the ability to augment reality is also attached to the first-person perspective. We believe it can be more than like that. Playing in multiple perspectives in mixed realities is not always a second rate experience. For example, Chronos [20] uses a third-person perspective in the VR game by following the protagonist in a third-person camera. In many cases, it is more comfortable for a user to keep distance from the action. In this way, the user may feel less of the VR Sickness [21]. Based on the products of first-person and third-person view with a virtual main character, we tend to research and verify the combination of multiple perspectives in AR/VR. Further, we make the virtual protagonist real by using real-time video feeds from a fixed-camera, creating an immersive mixed reality in a real world third-person perspective: the protagonist is you and you are in a third-person point of view. To verify this two aspects, we developed a prototype and conducted user study with it.

2.1 Related Work

Third-person perspective has appeared in video games and AR/VR applications for years. This perspective seems preferable in action games with a protagonist roaming in a virtual world [3]. There are roughly two types of third-person perspectives in video games: a following PoV behind the protagonist like GTA [27], or a fixed-camera PoV attached from a distance, containing the character and a range of the environment where the character operates in, such as Biohazard 2 [28]. All of these perspectives are important for video games, and in [4], the authors check whether the GTA kind third-person perspective in AR/VR could share a preference. We tend to verify the availability of fixed-camera PoV with a perspective switching strategy: third-person perspectives from different angles (as shown in Fig. 1) and a first-person perspective (the classic AR perspective like Hololens 2).

A research of vision-based wearable device proposes dynamic gestures to interact virtual objects in the scene, in order to create a pervasive and interactive AR experience [5]. It provides a new way to interact with objects in augmented reality, using technologies of image processing to recognize different gestures. It inspired us to adopt similar solutions to indoor localization and body gesture detection. Since we tend to verify the effectiveness of the new perspectives in this research, instead of interaction gestures at this moment, we did not implement gesture based interaction in our prototype. Instead, we use VIVE Tracker [22] to implement an approximate indoor localization and use Vuforia Engine in Unity [23] to recognize markers in the scene, which play the role of the perspective switching and action triggers.

In [8], authors mention the technological impact of third-person perspective on daily life and its adoption on therapy and rehabilitation, especially coupled with virtual reality. We share the same idea on the impact of VR, AR and MR on the case of medication. In our future works, we plan to adapt our implementation to the scenario of medication and rehabilitation and verify the effectiveness of fixed-camera third-person view in this way. The implementation of this research is compatible with most indoor situations with proprio-perception intention, such as self evaluation of dancing, exercising, doing work out or other behaviors. We believe multiple perspectives for VR and AR have incremental weight on diversifying people's daily lives in future smart cities.

2.2 Motivation

As more AR/VR applications and more gameplay modalities emerge due to the demanding market, people may suffer from the gap between themselves and the points of view in the virtual or augmented reality. For example, a fast action will be quite difficult to track on a standard first-person perspective or a classic following third-person view [4]. Manufacturers will probably need some extra effort before adding this category of virtual ingredients to the virtual or augment reality. On the other hand, when inventing a teleport characteristic for the protagonist, such as teleport between dimensions in Halo 5 [24], the suddenly switch of camera to a different context is easy to leave a sense of disorientation. A fixed camera third-person perspective does not have these problems. Within the current field of view, it is spontaneous to implement any fast action or teleport features. With a fast pace and fiercely competitive AR/VR market, one more effective choice is always safe to have. Thus, we want to verify the availability of this perspective and multiple PoV in VR, AR and MR implementations.

To tackle this, we create a mixed reality environment with multiple selectable PoV, including first-person perspective and fixed camera perspective from different angles. These points of view are implemented as camera footages streaming to a wireless VR HMD. With this environment, we tend to verify two things: the acceptance of fixed camera third-person perspective in virtual reality and the preference of the ability to change perspective in virtual reality.

3 Design and Implementation

In order to verify the availability of fixed camera third-person perspective and the ability of selectable PoV, we implemented a prototype based on Unity 3D and HTC VIVE, and invited people to try it and participate in the experiment. In this section, we introduce the settings of hardware and software configuration of our prototype.

(a) Camera Settings   (b) Hardware connection

Fig. 2. Space and hardware setup

3.1 Hardware Setup

We set up a rectangle room (As shown in Fig. 2a) as the experiment space, which is covered by the field of view of four cameras. Two of the four cameras are attached diagonally to the corner of the roof while one of the rest is attached to the middle of the longer wall and the last one is set on the ground of the shorter side. With these four cameras, we simulate four different PoV from different angles. As shown in Fig. 2b, all of these cameras are connected to a PC that runs the Unity project. Footage of the current camera selected by the user will be processed by Unity and eventually streamed to the HTC VIVE headset. We use Logitech Wide Angle Webcam and Broadcaster Wi-Fi Webcam [25] for these perspectives.

The selection of these four camera positions corresponds to the four angles that video games frequently used in fixed camera third-person perspective. The correlation between these four positions and perspectives is shown on Fig. 3. The two cameras at the corners of the roof are considered to have the widest range of FoV (Field of View) and contain the most information in the space. The one at the middle of the wall provides a horizontal view and the one at the ground looks up at the user and provides the information under any covers like the table top or upper side of the shelf, which is blocked when using the looking down cameras.

(a) Perspective of Camera 1   (b) Perspective of Camera 2

(c) Perspective of Camera 3   (d) Perspective of Camera 4

Fig. 3. Correlation between the four positions and perspectives

On the other hand, considering the flexibility of the experiment process, we need to allow the user to move freely in the room. This require the headset to be wirelessly connected, instead of letting it drag behind or probably trip over the user. In order to effectuate a wireless headset, we originally tried to process the Unity game or the PC desktop as video stream and project it to a smart phone and use Cardboard [26] to visualize the VR content. However, this process is laborious and turned out with bad performance because of the limited computing power of a smart phone. Instead, we use a third-party gadget called TPCAST to wirelessly transmit VR content to HTC VIVE headset with an integrated router, a transmitter and a receiver, substituting the cable transmission. Likewise, another option could be the wireless adapter from VIVE [16].

We set up markers in the room for mixed reality effects. The markers serve as the interactive objects in the game and are rendered as virtual objects like treasures, keys or any other necessary props in the virtual world. Users can interact with these objects with the VIVE controllers or directly touch them. Besides, there are some virtual triggers and objects in the game without physical markers for implementing virtual interactive objects, for example, a moving ghost. In future works, we may also use markers to set up some critical triggers in the room. Perspective will be automatically switched when one of these triggers is touched off. The positions of triggers and the way to touch off them should be selected and tested discreetly and deliberately because a wrong trigger would be a huge shock for the user.

3.2 Implementation

(a) 3PP mixed footage

(b) 1PP mixed footage

(c) 3PP with secondary 1PP

(d) 1PP with secondary 3PP

Fig. 4. The game scene mixed with camera footage

Based on the above hardware configuration, we developed a simple game with Unity 3D and run it with HTC VIVE. The game is designed simple for proof of concept. The user is supposed to avoid a moving skeleton and get to the treasure box in a limited time. As shown in Fig. 4, we reconstruct a rectangle space of our lab into a Unity scene and make some of the objects in the space appear with virtual effects. The skeleton is a trigger in game moving back and forward in front of the start point and the treasure box is a marker in game placed behind the skeleton. If the user collides with this skeleton or does not finish the game within the limited time (120 s), the game is over and shows a failure interface with a restart button. If the user goes through the skeleton and touches the treasure box with the VIVE controller, the game is completed successfully and a success interface shows up. The virtual effects to the reconstruction of the experiment space is raw and unripe, but it proofs the feasibility of virtual reconstruction and the availability of the augmented real life experience. To guide the user through the experiment, we let one of our researchers stand inside the FoV of the cameras. He shows up in the game scene and serve as a RPG (role-playing games) instructor.

By default, we provide the camera 1 (fixed camera third person perspective (3PP)) perspective in the experiment. To finish the task, the user can switch to first-person perspective (1PP) or other angles of the third-person perspectives manually. We encourage users to use all of these perspectives, and compare the feedback of different angles and views. Users can change the current perspective by clicking on the buttons listed at the left top side of the screen (Fig. 4a) with the VIVE controller.

4 Initial User Study

In order to conduct an evaluation and assessment to our approach, we have developed an experiment that measures user scores based on various indicators of our implementation. We asked participants to do questionnaires and interviews after the experiment and drew conclusion from the statistical result and feedback records. We aim to verify the approach in two respects: the fixed-camera third-person view for MR and the ability to switch perspectives in an immersive experience.

4.1 Participants and Procedure

We invited 12 college students (age m = 23.80, SD = 1.84, six men, six women) to participate in the user study. We set up the demonstration environment described in Sect. 3, and helped the participant to reset the experiment and wear the headset. We introduced the experiment, the perspectives and the objective task to the participants individually, and taught them how to interact with virtual objects. We showed them how to switch perspective and how to deal with triggers and markers. Participants are encouraged to use as many perspectives as possible before finishing the experiment and asked to successfully finish the task for at least one time. We observed the participants aside and stood by in case they have any problems. Users could actually see one observer in the game scene because the observer stood inside the FoV of the cameras. Users can turn to this 'RPG character' for instructions, just like interacting with virtual characters in classic role playing games, for example, GTA 5 [27]. Each participant was asked to fill out a questionnaire after the experiment, followed by a one-on-one interview.

4.2 Results and Feedback

We adopted the five-point Likert scale (1 - disagree/bad, 5 - agree/good) to develop ten rating queries. We asked the participants to complete the questionnaire right after the experiment. We observed that each experiment cost about 10 min averagely and the questioning and interview cost roughly 15 min for each participant. From the result of the questionnaire (as shown in Table 1), we know 91.7% of the participants have used VR devices before. The participants rated highest for the ability of changing perspectives in an immersive process (83.3% rated over 3 points).

From Table 1, we know P1 and P2 cameras (diagonal roof corners in Fig. 2) are the most welcomed perspectives among the four fixed camera third-person views in the

Table 1. Result of rating questions. (P1–P4 cameras are explained in Fig. 2)

	Average points	Standard deviation
Classic 1PP VR	3.83	0.58
Classic 1PP AR	3.92	0.67
Fixed camera 3PP (P1 + P2) in the demo	3.68	0.99
Fixed camera 3PP (P3) in the demo	3.61	0.90
Fixed camera 3PP (P4) in the demo	3.42	0.89
Fixed camera 3PP (Overall) in the demo	3.57	0.90
1PP AR in the demo	4.42	0.51
Able to switch perspectives	4.50	0.74
3PP with secondary 1PP (Fig. 4c)	3.87	0.63
1PP with secondary 3PP (Fig. 4d)	4.49	0.79
Generally about the experience	4.00	1.02
Willing to pay if well-developed	3.75	0.62

prototype, but collectively lower than the traditional first-person perspectives. However, when the fixed camera 3PP is combined with the classic 1PP, the ratings generally become higher. Specifically, rating of 1PP with secondary 3PP (Fig. 4d) is significantly increased and even surpass the classic VR and AR 1PP.

Moreover, P3 camera is rated slightly lower than P1 and P2 while P4 is the lowest. Overall, fixed camera third-person perspective is no better than the classic first-person perspective in AR/VR, but the P1 and P2 perspectives are generally accepted and could be a practical extra perspective for VR or AR applications. For example, use fixed-camera third-person views in indoor occasions and first-person in outdoor environments, having the secondary first-person and third-person attached correspondingly. Also, the rating for the ability of changing perspective during a gameplay is high. We speculate that people enjoy the freeness of selecting their own preferable perspective, instead of having what a system defines for them.

On the other hand, from the answers of multiple selection questions and interviews with the participants, we find that most participants (83.3%) consider the ability to switch perspectives is the best feature of this immersive MR environment and as a fresh experience, this third-person view is generally novel and acceptable to them. 66.6% of them are willing to pay for applications with such perspectives involved if the applications are fully developed. The most critical problem of this environment is the unnatural perspective. Users are worried that they may feel dizzy in this perspective if playing with it for long. 'Easy to block the vision' and 'hard to control' are ones of other concerns. We select the most typical ones and list them in Table 2.

Based on the result, we speculate that immersive third-person has incremental values to VR or AR applications, especially when it is combined with a natural perspective and serve as a supplementary perspective, providing more information and feedbacks for the users. The participants generally approve of the concept of this MR experience

Table 2. Pros and Cons.

Type	Description	Percentage
Pros	Be able to switch perspectives	83.3%
Pros	A fresh experience with AR/VR	41.7%
Pros	Be able to observe yourself	62.3%
Cons	May feel dizzy because of the unnatural perspective	58.3%
Cons	Easy to block the vision behind you	33.3%
Cons	Hard to control	33.3%

(4.00 points out of five in Table 1) and we believe the acceptability of such products is dependent on the experience, operability, how entertained the game is or how effective the application is, which demands reliable and fail-proof future implementations.

5   Current Limitations and Challenges

From the fixed camera 3PP demonstration, we see possibilities and limitations of this perspective and we summarize the challenges of similar kinds of implementation. The most critical problem of the fixed camera 3PP is the unnatural view of oneself. Users will hesitate to move at the beginning because they feel unreliable in an unnatural perspective. They are afraid to collide something unintentionally and feel hard to control themselves. A possible scenario is to use 1PP mainly and give a smaller rectangle view of the fixed camera 3PP at the corner as a secondary perspective (Fig. 4d). Users can use this extra perspective to obtain more information and don't have to stay in an unnatural perspective. They can switch the perspectives if they get used to the fixed camera 3PP and want to have a more macroscopic view.

On the other hand, fixed camera 3PP only provides one side view of objects or people in the room, so if you can see the front, you can not see the back, and vice versa. To overcome this constrain, users will have to switch between the diagonal perspectives to see the whole thing. The actions of switching between perspective can be automated and triggered at proper conditions such as when the user turn around, when the user's face is blocked by a table surface (when the user is trying to look below the table), or track the user's eyesight. This automation can be a challenge on development involved with image processing, face/motion detection, real time video processing and machine learning.

Compared with the following 3PP, fixed camera 3PP is more suitable for a complementary macroscopic view, instead of a sole perspective. Following 3PP is more spontaneous while multiple fixed camera 3PPs contain more information. Users will always prefer more customized options. Multiple fixed camera 3PPs will give incremental value to immersive experience when united with other perspectives, but they have difficulty serving as the only perspectives. Generally, people will get uncomfortable if using these perspectives for a long time. Solutions to avoid this uncomfortableness could be a challenge. One possible method is to combine these perspectives to a natural perspective like 1PP or following 3PP.

Moreover, this approach adopts commonly-used webcams to explore the efficacy of gaming perspectives for real world scenarios while leaving the camera variables out. The influence of camera variables in real life scenarios such as concave or convex viewpoints, mirroring effects and coverage issues, etc. could be explored accordingly.

6 Conclusion and Future Direction

We present a mixed reality indoor environment with multiple fixed camera third-person perspectives and a first person perspective for AR/VR applications, which can be extended to outdoor environments in future smart cities with ambient accessible intelligent cameras. We implement a prototype and conduct user study with this environment. Through the process, we speculate that immersive third-person has incremental values to VR, AR or MR applications. We consider the feasibility of such applications is up to their maneuverability, entertainment and effectiveness, which requires more fail-proof future researches. Basically, people will generally accept and be willing to pay for the new VR experience (fixed-camera third-person) when the process is effortless and pleasurable. We also conclude limitations and challenges of our implementation. A critical problem of this perspective is the unaccommodated view, which proof this perspective is not suitable for long-term use. Nonetheless, these perspectives provide a more macroscopic information of the environment and fresh angles for observing oneself. It is beneficial to combine fixed camera third-person view with classic first-person or following third-person perspectives. Additionally, the ability to choose a favorite perspective is generally a good option. In a such background of highly diverse immersive experiences, a novel perspective or angle will invariably be a fair alternative.

In the future, the interaction of perspective switch would be refined by motion detection such as detecting motions of raising head or pointing to the camera that provides the perspective you want to use. The game plot should be enriched and real people could show up and interact with users in the room, acting as interactive non-player characters (NPC). Beyond entertainment, we would verify the possibilities of multiple fixed camera 3PP usage in rehabilitation, education, self behavior analysis like dressing, dancing, etc., or smart cities services such as traffic management, urban safety instruction, etc. We want to adapt the 3PP environment to outdoor scenario with newly set-up or existing cameras (e.g. CCTV) and check on the potential derivatives.

References

1. Boris, P., Srdan, K., Maja, P.: Augmented reality based smart city services using secure IoT infrastructure. In: 28th International Conference on Advanced Information Networking and Applications Workshops, Victoria, BC, pp. 803–808 (2014). https://doi.org/10.1109/waina.2014.127
2. Zhihan, L., Tengfei, Y., Xiaolei, Z., Houbing, S., Ge, C.: Virtual reality smart city based on WebVRGIS. IEEE Internet Things J. 3(6), 1015–1024 (2016). https://doi.org/10.1109/JIOT.2016.2546307

3. Richard III, R.: What's your perspective? SIGGRAPH Comput. Graph. **33**(3), 9–12 (1999)
4. Patrick, S., Daniel, T., Frédéric, V.: The benefits of third-person perspective in virtual and augmented reality? In: VRST 2006 (2006)
5. Zhihan, L., Alaa, H., Shengzhong, F., Shafiq ur, R., Haibo, L.: Touch-less interactive augmented reality game on vision-based wearable device. Pers. Ubiquit. Comput. **19**, 551 (2015)
6. Slater, M., Spanlang, B., Sanchez-Vives, M.V., Blanke, O.: First person experience of body transfer in virtual reality. PLoS ONE **5**(5), e10564 (2010). https://doi.org/10.1371/journal.pone.0010564
7. Bergström, I., Kilteni, K., Slater, M.: First-person perspective virtual body posture influences stress: a virtual reality body ownership study. PLoS ONE **11**(2), e0148060 (2016). https://doi.org/10.1371/journal.pone.0148060
8. Patrick, S., Tej, T., Olaf, B., Frederic, V., Daniel, T.: Quantifying effects of exposure to the third and first-person perspectives in virtual-reality-based training. IEEE Trans. Learn. Technol. **3**(3), 272–276 (2010)
9. Barsom, E.Z., Graafland, M., Schijven, M.P.: Systematic review on the effectiveness of augmented reality applications in medical training. Surg. Endosc. **30**(10), 4174–4183 (2016). https://doi.org/10.1007/s00464-016-4800-6
10. David, C.S., Joanna, G., Joan, S.: Validation of virtual reality as a tool to understand and prevent child pedestrian injury. Accid. Anal. Prev. **40**(4), 1394–1400 (2008)
11. Jeremy, B., Kayur, P., Alexia, N., Ruzena, B., Sang-Hack, J., Gregorij, K.: The effect of interactivity on learning physical actions in virtual reality. Media Psychology **11**(3), 354–376 (2008)
12. Denisova, A., Cairns, P.: First person vs. third person perspective in digital games: do player preferences affect immersion? (2015). https://doi.org/10.1145/2702123.2702256
13. Unity 3D. https://unity.com. Accessed 20 June 2019
14. HTC VIVE. https://vive.com. Accessed 20 June 2019
15. TPCAST Wireless Adaptor. https://www.tpcastvr.com. Accessed 20 June 2019
16. HTC VIVE Wireless Adapter - Virtual Reality. https://www.vive.com/eu/wireless-adapter/. Accessed 20 Juen 2019
17. Lotfi, A., Faten Ben, A., Aref, M.: In-vehicle augmented reality traffic information system: a new type of communication between driver and vehicle. Procedia Comput. Sci. **73**(2015), 242–249 (2015)
18. Laver, K.E., Lange, B., George, S., Deutsch, J.E., Saposnik, G., Crotty, M.: Virtual reality for stroke rehabilitation. Cochrane Database Syst. Rev. **11**, CD008349 (2017)
19. Microsoft Hololens 2. https://www.microsoft.com/en-us/hololens. Accessed 20 June 2019
20. Gunfire Games, Chronos. https://www.oculus.com/experiences/rift/929508627125435/. Accessed 20 June 2019
21. Lee, J., Kim, M., Kim, J.: A study on immersion and VR sickness in walking interaction for immersive virtual reality applications. Symmetry **9**, 78 (2017)
22. HTC VIVE Tracker. https://www.vive.com/eu/vive-tracker/. Accessed 20 June 2019
23. Vuforia Engine for Augmented Reality. https://developer.vuforia.com/. Accessed 20 June 2019
24. Microsoft Studios, Halo 5: Guardians. https://www.microsoft.com/en-us/p/halo-5-guardians/brrc2bp0g9p0. Accessed 20 June 2019
25. Logitech Webcam. https://www.logitech.com/en-us/video/webcams. Accessed 20 June 2019
26. Google Cardboard - Virtual Reality. https://vr.google.com/intl/en_us/cardboard/. Accessed 20 June 2019
27. Rockstar Games, Grand Theft Auto V. https://www.rockstargames.com/V/. Accessed 20 June 2019
28. Capcom, Resident Evil 2. https://www.imdb.com/title/tt0161941. Accessed 20 June 2019

Internet of Things for Enhanced Smart Cities: A Review, Roadmap and Case Study on Air Quality Sensing

Gonçalo Marques[1,2(✉)] 🆔 and Rui Pitarma[1]

[1] Polytechnic Institute of Guarda, Guarda, Portugal
goncalosantosmarques@gmail.com, rpitarma@ipg.pt
[2] Instituto de Telecomunicações, Universidade da Beira Interior, Covilhã, Portugal

Abstract. The smart city concept is a strategy to face relevant open issues regarding the socio-economic development requirements that promote people health and well-being. Smart homes are a fundamental element of smart cities and are intended to meet several applications for enhanced living environments and occupational health. Most individuals stay most of their time indoors, and therefore, smart homes are unquestionably an essential place to monitor. Indoor air quality has a meaningful negative influence on occupational health and well-being. Moreover, cities are responsible for a relevant portion of greenhouse emissions, and the outdoor air quality monitoring is relevant to detect adverse air quality situations and design interventions to promote public health. Air quality sensing is a fundamental element of people's daily routine and must be incorporated in smart homes and smart cities to promote health and well-being. Furthermore, this data can be evaluated by health professionals for diagnostics support and to correlate patient symptoms with their living environment but also to support city managers in the intervention planning for enhanced living environments. This paper presents a review and roadmap on air quality sensing and proposes an Internet of Things architecture for air quality supervision. The outcomes are encouraging as the presented system can be used to provide a correct and cost-effective air quality assessment. The proposed method can be used to support city managers to detect possible unhealthy scenarios in smart cities in useful time.

Keywords: Air quality sensing · Ambient assisted living · Enhanced living environments · Indoor environment quality · Internet of Things · Occupational health · Smart cities

1 Introduction

The Internet of Things (IoT) is a ubiquitous behaviour of a variety of entities with intelligence and sensing abilities which can collaborate to achieve shared objectives [1, 2]. IoT technologies offer numerous advantages to several domains such as smart cities, smart homes, healthcare and ambient assisted living (AAL) [3, 4].

Published by Springer Nature Switzerland AG 2020. All Rights Reserved
P. Pereira et al. (Eds.): SC4Life 2019, LNICST 318, pp. 109–121, 2020.
https://doi.org/10.1007/978-3-030-45293-3_9

The smart city can be assumed as an approach to embrace modern urban productivity requirements in a general framework and to focus on the role of information and communication technologies (ICTs) on the creation of enhanced living environments [5]. Cities face relevant open issues regarding the socio-economic development requirements to promote people health and well-being [6]. Moreover, the smart city aims to moderate the obstacles caused by the urban population increase and accelerated urbanisation [7]. One of the most consistent open issues regarding smart cities is the no operability between different systems. IoT can present the interoperability to develop a centralised urban-scale ICT framework for enhanced living environments [8]. Is relevant to mention that smart cities will cause several meaningful effects at distinct layers on science, productivity and technology. The smart city will lead to complex challenges in society regarding the ethical and moral context. The smart city must provide correct information access to the right individuals. The security and privacy of that information must be established because that data is accessible at a distinct spatial scale where people can be distinguished [9].

Furthermore, IoT brings numerous opportunities regarding the development of modern daily routine applications and services for smart cities [10]. Several technologies closely related to the smart city context connected with IoT architecture will improve our daily routine and promote health and well-being [11].

Most individuals stay most of their time indoors, and therefore, smart homes are unquestionably an essential domain regarding the smart city context. IoT architectures can provide ubiquitous and pervasive methods for environmental data acquisition and provides wireless communication technologies for enhanced connectivity. Particularly, indoor air quality (IAQ) has a material adverse impact on occupational health and well-being. Therefore, the IAQ supervision is determinant for enhanced living environments and should be a requirement of all buildings and consequently, an integral part of the smart city context. The Environmental Protection Agency (EPA) recognises that IAQ values can be one hundred times higher than outdoor pollutant levels and established air quality on the top five environmental hazards to well-being [12].

Moreover, IAQ affects the most underprivileged people worldwide that remain exposed and therefore, can be compared with other public health problems such as sexually transmitted infections [13]. IAQ supervision must be seen as an effective method for the study and assessment of occupational health and well-being. The IAQ data can be used to detect patterns on the indoor quality and to design interventions plans to promote health. The proliferation of IoT devices and systems makes it possible to create automatic machines with sensing, connection and processing capabilities for enhanced living environments.

Air quality sensing must be an essential element of smart cities and smart homes. On the one hand, the IAQ can be estimated by providing CO_2 supervision system for enhanced public health and well-being. The CO_2 indoor levels can not only be used to evaluate the necessity of fresh air in a room but also can be used as a secondary sign of unusual concentrations of other indoor air pollutants. On the other hand, cities are responsible for a relevant portion of greenhouse emissions. Therefore, CO_2 monitoring must be provided on both indoors and outdoors environments. The concentrations of CO_2 are growing to 400 ppm, achieving further records every time after they started to be analyzed in 1984 [14]. The outdoor CO_2 monitoring can be relevant to plan interventions on traffic and to detect the emission of abnormal amounts of CO_2 in real-time. Moreover, real-time monitoring of CO_2 levels in smart cities at different locations allows the identification of points of interest to plan interventions to decrease the greenhouse gases.

This paper presents not only a review and a roadmap on the development of new methods and architectures for the implementation of air quality monitoring systems but also a case study regarding the development of a CO_2 monitoring system based in IoT architecture named **MoniCO$_2$** for enhanced living environments and public health in smart cities. This solution provides a mobile application for CO_2 data analytics and visualisation.

The rest of the document is written as follows: Sect. 2 presents a review on air quality monitoring systems; Sect. 3 is concerned to the application of air quality sensing in the smart city context; Sect. 4 presents the design of a cost-effective monitoring system for air quality assessment; Sect. 5 describes the discussion, and the conclusion is presented in Sect. 6.

2 A Review on Air Quality Monitoring Systems

Several IAQ management systems are presented in state of the art, a review summary is presented in this section. Numerous low-cost IoT methods for air quality management that supports open-source and wireless communication for data collection and transmission but also allow different places supervision at the same time through mobile computing technologies are proposed by [15–22].

An IAQ supervision system based on IoT, which incorporates temperature, humidity and CO2 sensing features developed for the smart city context is proposed by [23]. The data is collected and transmitted from the receiver node and is recorded on a personal computer. The data can be accessed through a LabVIEW and Android application.

An Air quality observation system based on the Arduino UNO microcontroller and low-cost sensors for CO_2 monitoring was proposed by [15]. The nodes receive and send data using ZigBee communication technology. However, this solution does not incorporate mobile computing technologies for data consulting.

The development of a wireless sensor network (WSN) for IAQ management is presented in [24]. This method incorporates temperature, humidity, gas and particulate matter (PM) sensors to determine the environmental health of monitored space. The collected data is used as feedback to control heating, ventilation and air conditioning systems in a smart building.

An IoT method to implement an IAQ management is presented in [25]. The proposed architecture incorporates portable sensors for data collection and implements a low power area network. The collected data is analysed using the cloud. The results presented states the reliability of the air quality sensing data to change behaviour patterns to promote health and well-being.

A cost-effective urban $PM_{2.5}$ supervision system which incorporates mobile sensing features is proposed by [26]. The proposed method incorporates a humidity and temperature sensor, GPS, a dust sensor and a noise sensor. The tests conducted are favourable and can ensure the ability to supervisor air quality at low-cost with reasonable precision.

Air quality sensing is an essential requirement for smart cities and further for global public health. Consequently, the design of cost-effective supervision solutions is a trending and relevant research field. Concerning the quality and appropriate contribution of various actual monitoring solutions [15, 23–26], a shortened comparison study is presented in Table 1.

Table 1. Summarised comparison review table of air quality sensing solutions.

MCU	Architecture	Sensors	Connectivity	Data consulting	Notifications	Ref.
PIC 24F16KA102	IoT	Temperature, humidity and CO_2	nRF24L01	Desktop and mobile	×	[23]
Arduino UNO	WSN	CO_2	ZigBee	×	×	[15]
Waspmote	WSN	CO, CO2, PM, temperature and relative humidity	ZigBee	Desktop	×	[24]
STM 32F103RC	IoT	PM, temperature and humidity	IEEE 802.15.4 k	Web and mobile	×	[25]
Mosaic-Node	StandAlone	GPS, PM2.5, noise, humidity and temperature	×	×	×	[26]

After the review of Table 1, the authors assume that the presented solutions incorporate different microcontroller units based on PIC, Arduino, Waspmote and STMicroelectronics. Moreover, various architectures are used in the development and design of air quality monitoring solutions. The proposed systems can be based on IoT, WSN or be standalone solutions. The most sensors for air quality monitoring are used to measure CO_2. One of the best indicators for air quality is the CO_2 concentration as it is emitted in high amounts and is comparatively effortless measured.

Regarding connectivity, the numerous communication technologies are used, and they are typically wireless. Several methods for data consulting are available such desktop, mobile and web applications. However, the solutions available in the literature does not incorporate notifications and easy installation methods. Notifications can be essential to advise the building or city manager to project arbitrations to improve the air quality on time.

In sum, the literature review presents several automatic systems and projects for air quality sensing, which support the relevance of the IoT architecture and mobile computing technologies as having a significant role in promoting health and well-being.

3   Air Quality Sensing for Enhanced Smart Cities

Smart homes are an essential and integral part of smart cities which had been studied for decades [27]. Smart homes are intended to meet several main applications such as the occupant's activity recognition to promote health and well-being, the use of multimedia technologies for monitoring, wherever the information obtained in the context is managed to trigger a notification for the occupant's protection. Additionally, the smart homes which the main propose is to improve energy efficiency using electric devices automation [28]. Numerous technological enhancements had decreased the cost of the implementation and design of smart homes. However, the development of automatic and intelligent systems for smart homes remains a significant challenge. Likewise, it is imperative to develop a system which can be easily installed and configured both in smart and traditional buildings. In the recent past, the number of sensors and actuators on the smart city context has increased, which lead to the creation of rich datasets for further investigation and data analytics. Smart homes present an effective method for enhanced living environments and improve numerous daily routine activities and provide the digitalisation of people's everyday activities [29]. In general, smart homes are developed for older adults to provide reliable healthcare systems and adequate real-time supervision of the occupant's health and well-being and to deliver feedback to the caregiver. An essential challenge for the smart city and smart home context is the security and privacy of the collected data. Therefore, high-quality research regarding the creation of secure methods to handle sensitive data is demanded [30, 31]. Air quality sensing must be assumed as significant in the smart city context, considering the air quality effects on people's health and well-being. Furthermore, indoor and outdoor air quality must be provided to improve people's health anytime and everywhere.

Nowadays, smartphones support excellent capabilities for data communication and processing, which can be assumed to consult the air quality data in real-time as people carry them in their daily lives. Moreover, buildings support numerous communication technologies and incorporate automation features. The vehicles are also crucial for the mobility of people in smart cities and are an essential source of air pollution. After combining air quality sensing for indoor and outdoor pollution monitoring, the city manager can achieve several benefits for public health and well-being. The gathered data can be used to project arbitrations on the traffic to decrease the pollution levels in the most critical locations of the city.

Additionally, the smart homes must incorporate air quality sensing to detect in useful time unhealthy situations and plan interventions to avoid them to occur. The air quality data must be validated before been stored and should be accessible anytime, anywhere. Furthermore, the data consulting method should be pervasive and ubiquitous and provide enhanced visualisation tools for data analytics. Specialists can analyse this information to assistance patient diagnostics and associate well-being complications with exposure conditions.

Air quality sensing includes several different stages such as data collection, data processing, data imputation, data storage and data analytics to deliver real-time notifications and alerts for enhanced public health (Fig. 1).

Moreover, the air quality data analysis can trigger critical alarms and notifications for the city and building managers using middleware services. The data collected by

Fig. 1. Schema of an air quality sensing roadmap for enhanced living environments on smart cities.

the air quality monitoring systems are examined before storage. If this data surpasses the established thresholds, a warning should be triggered to support the occupants and city managers to act on time to promote air quality by applying proper air purifying methods inside buildings or by providing different strategies for traffic flow. These real-time alerts offer numerous advantages to achieve various and effective changes because these notifications not only provide measures to improve air quality but also allow the recognition of air quality patterns while repeated harmful situations are identified and to plan interventions to stop them from occurring.

In sum, for all the stated reasons in this section, air quality sensing must be seen as an essential element of people's everyday routine and be incorporated in smart cities to promote health and well-being. This data can be evaluated by professionals to achieve several health benefits that in another way, are impossible to address. Air quality monitoring allows the creation of rich datasets with spatiotemporal behaviour data, which will enable data consulting for city administrators to facilitate accelerated and effective arbitrations to promote public health.

4   Internet of Things Architecture for CO_2 Monitoring System: A Case Study

Taking into account all the requirements of air quality sensing, the authors develop the *MoniCO₂* solution. In this section, the detailed materials and methods used in the design of the proposed system are presented.

The *MoniCO₂* is an air quality supervision solution, which incorporates easy installation and configuration. The proposed system uses an ESP8266 which provides built-in wireless networking technologies capabilities and includes an SGP30 Multi-Pixel Gas sensor as a sensing unit. The central goal of the recommended method is to promote health and well-being in smart cities. The proposed method wishes to deliver a mobile computing solution for air quality management to improve public health and safety (Fig. 2). The authors develop a cyber-physical system based on the ESP8266 module, which supports the IEEE 802.11 b/g/n protocol. The data collected is stored in a Microsoft SQL Server database using ASP.NET web services. Mobile computing software has been developed for data consulting using the Swift programming language.

Web Services

ESP8266   SGP30

Acquisition Module

**Mobile
Application**

**SQL SERVER
Database**

Fig. 2. *MoniCO$_2$* system architecture.

Furthermore, the proposed data acquisition module has been developed using on open-source frameworks, and is a cos-effective system, with numerous benefits when associated with actual methods. The acquisition module uses a FireBeetle ESP8266 (*DFRobot*) as a microcontroller, and the SGP30 gas sensor module (*Adafruit*) is connected using the I2C interface. Figure 3 presents the prototype designed by the authors.

The FireBeetle ESP8266 is a wireless board with unified antenna switches, power and low noise amplifiers which is compatible with 802.11 b/g/n protocols. Additionally, this board is WPA/WPA2 compatible and includes a 32-bit MCU and 10-bit ADC. The selected board includes a 16 MB SPI flash memory.

The sensing unit is composed by the SGP30 Multi-Pixel Gas sensor, a metal-oxide gas sensor developed at Sensirion. This sensor provides a calibrated output with 15% of accuracy and provides an I2C connection for data communication [32]. The sensor range for eCO$_2$ and TVOC concentration is 400–60,000 ppm and 0 to 60,000 ppb, respectively. The eCO$_2$ output is based on a hydrogen measurement. The sensor sampling rate is 1 s, and the average current consumption is 48 mA.

The proposed method offers a history of the variations of the indoor situation to support the home or city administrator to deliver an accurate examination of the environment. The data collected can likewise to be employed to assist decision-making on potential arbitrations for enhanced public health and well-being. The acquisition module firmware is executed employing the Arduino Core, which is an open-source framework

Fig. 3. Acquisition module connection diagram.

that intends to facilitate the use of regular Arduino libraries on the ESP8266 board without an external Arduino board. The proposed system cost is presented in Table 2. The choice of the sensor unit has been made according to the cost of the module as the principal intention was to study the functional design of the proposed method. The *MoniCO₂* is a low-cost system for air quality management, which costs an estimated 38.04 USD (Table 1).

Table 2. Amount value of the components used to design the proposed method.

Component	Amount (USD)
FireBeetle ESP8266	7.50
Adafruit SGP30 module	19.95
Cables and box	10.59
Overall cost	38.04

The proposed system offers a relevant function that delivers an easy configuration of the wireless network. The system is configured as a Wi-Fi client however if it is incapable of connecting to the wireless network or if no Wi-Fi networks are ready, the proposed system turn to hotspot mode and start a wireless network. At this time, this hotspot can be used to configure the Wi-Fi network to which the system will be connected through the introduction of the network access credentials.

The iOS application, denominated *MoniCO₂Mobile*, has been established using Swift in Xcode. The developed application has iOS 12 as minimum application requirements (Fig. 4). This mobile application includes numerous essential features, such as real-time data consulting using numeric tables and charts. Using the mobile application, people can inquire about the environmental data after authentication. Consequently, people can hold the parameters of chronicle records for additional examination. The introduced method is a decision-making tool to project arbitrations sustained by the data obtained for enhanced public health.

Fig. 4. *MoniCO$_2$Mobile* application: last collected data.

5   Current Status and Discussion

The proposed system was installed and tested inside a controlled laboratory environment. The system was tested continually for two months, and several experiments had been conducted with induced simulations. The module is powered using a 230 V-5 V AC-DC 2A power supply. The experiments indicate that the proposed air quality monitoring system can be used to detect unhealthy scenarios based on the CO_2 and TVOC data at low-cost. The data is collected every 30 s, but this value can be changed according to the needs of the installation. The *MoniCO$_2$Mobile* offers information checking as graphical or statistical modes. An example of the data gathered by the system is represented in Fig. 5. The graphs present the results gathered in the physical environment, including provoked simulations of smoke. The results are promising the proposed IoT architecture can provide accurate CO_2 monitoring in real-time and demonstrate a fast response on significative CO_2 variation.

The chart view available on the mobile application provides an improved inspection of observed parameters behaviours when compared with the statistical presentation. First, mobile software presents quick and straightforward access to the obtained data and allows further accurate investigation of air quality progression. Consequently, this method is a relevant instrument for air quality surveillance and to assist decision making on potential interventions to improve performance but also to detect exposure risk scenarios. Second, this IoT architecture offers chronological data evolution for improved air quality assessment, which is particularly appropriate to identify unhealthy scenarios and project interferences to improve health and well-being. Moreover, the mobile application provides a configuration are for the alerts, and the user can easily change that values according to the requirement of the monitored space.

Fig. 5. *MoniCO₂Mobile* application: settings and chart view.

The mobile software provides fast and intuitive access to the collected data as mobile phones have today high performance and storage capacities, and most people use them every day. In this way, the building or city manager can transport the air quality data of their environment for further analysis.

Currently, most air quality monitoring systems are high-priced and are established on random sampling. Therefore, these methods are limited by offering data associated with a particular sample without temporal association. Right to be told, the professional systems available on the market are accurate and developed for industrial activities. Further, some solutions are portable and compact. However, these solutions do not support real-time information accessibility for city authorities or build managers. These real-time alerts are essential to facilitate accelerated and decisive interference to promote health and safety. The existing industrial products offer data history constricted to the system memory and required special software for data downloading and administration. The design and development of innovative air quality sensing systems based on the literature which support real-time data consulting for examination and visualisation must be assumed as an essential enhancement regarding the smart city objectives.

Compared with the systems presented in Table 1, the proposed solution provides adaptability and precision of analysis in real-time, providing a meaningful progression of the actual air quality monitoring systems. The results are promising as the proposed system can be used to provide a correct air quality assessment at low-cost. The proposed method can be used to support city managers to detect possible unhealthy scenarios in smart cities in useful time. Another essential benefit of the presented method is the scalability related with the modularity of the solution. The installation can be done through one module, but other modules can be added in the future regarding the requirements of the environment.

IoT is a standard that intends to increase the quality of personal experience. IoT architectures and AAL will reciprocally provide systematic improvements leading to the design of automated and intelligent systems to promote health and well-being. IoT is as a meaningful concept to improve daily routine actions in numerous fields such as buildings, manufacturing, healthcare, smart homes and smart cities. Shortly, innovative methods will improve the number of intelligent solutions established in traditional people houses.

The authors consider that soon, most of the residences will be controlled in real-time and implement warnings to inform the homeowner in the occurrence of inadequate ambient quality. Our living environments will support monitoring features, and the data gathered will be distributed with the therapeutic specialist to compare wellness complications among inadequate practices of the patients and assist clinical assessment.

6   Conclusion

The smart city concept is an approach to embrace current urban production in a mutual context as cities face relevant open issues regarding the socio-economic development requirements and to improve people well-being. IoT will be able to offer the operability between different systems to develop a centralised urban-scale framework for enhanced smart cities.

Smart homes are an essential and integral part of smart cities and are intended to meet several applications to promote health and well-being. Most individuals stay most of their time indoors, and therefore, smart homes are unquestionably an extraordinary place to monitor. Moreover, IoT architectures can provide ubiquitous and pervasive methods for environmental data acquisition and provide connectivity for data transmission. Particularly, IAQ has a material adverse impact on occupational health and well-being. Therefore, air quality sensing must be seen as an integral part of society's everyday activities and must be incorporated in smart cities to promote health and well-being.

Moreover, this data can be evaluated by health professionals for diagnostics support and to correlate patient problems with their living environment. Nevertheless, the air monitoring solutions available in the literature does not incorporate notifications and easy installation methods. Notifications can be essential to advise the building or city manager in real-time to design mediations to promote the air quality in useful time. Therefore, this manuscript had performed a review and roadmap for air quality sensing and proposed an IoT architecture for air quality supervision. The results are encouraging as the suggested system can be used to provide proper air quality assessment. The proposed method can be used to support city managers to detect possible unhealthy scenarios in smart cities early. Furthermore, mobile software provides fast and intuitive access to the collected data, as actually, most people use mobile phones.

References

1. Giusto, D. (ed.): The Internet of Things: 20th Tyrrhenian Workshop on Digital Communications. Springer, New York (2010). https://doi.org/10.1007/978-1-4419-1674-7
2. Marques, G., Pitarma, R., Garcia, N.M., Pombo, N.: Things architectures, technologies, applications, challenges, and future directions for enhanced living environments and healthcare systems: a review. Electronics **8**, 1081 (2019). https://doi.org/10.3390/electronics8101081
3. Atzori, L., Iera, A., Morabito, G.: The Internet of Things: a survey. Comput. Netw. **54**, 2787–2805 (2010). https://doi.org/10.1016/j.comnet.2010.05.010
4. Marques, G.: Ambient assisted living and Internet of Things. In: Cardoso, P.J.S., Monteiro, J., Semião, J., Rodrigues, J.M.F. (eds.) Harnessing the Internet of Everything (IoE) for Accelerated Innovation Opportunities, pp. 100–115. IGI Global, Hershey (2019). https://doi.org/10.4018/978-1-5225-7332-6.ch005
5. Caragliu, A., Del Bo, C., Nijkamp, P.: Smart cities in Europe. J. Urban Technol. **18**, 65–82 (2011). https://doi.org/10.1080/10630732.2011.601117
6. Schaffers, H., Komninos, N., Pallot, M., Trousse, B., Nilsson, M., Oliveira, A.: Smart cities and the future internet: towards cooperation frameworks for open innovation. In: Domingue, J., et al. (eds.) FIA 2011. LNCS, vol. 6656, pp. 431–446. Springer, Heidelberg (2011). https://doi.org/10.1007/978-3-642-20898-0_31
7. Chourabi, H., et al.: Understanding Smart Cities: An Integrative Framework. Presented at the January (2012). https://doi.org/10.1109/HICSS.2012.615
8. Zanella, A., Bui, N., Castellani, A., Vangelista, L., Zorzi, M.: Internet of Things for smart cities. IEEE Internet Things J. **1**, 22–32 (2014). https://doi.org/10.1109/JIOT.2014.2306328
9. Batty, M., et al.: Smart cities of the future. Eur. Phys. J. Spec. Top. **214**, 481–518 (2012). https://doi.org/10.1140/epjst/e2012-01703-3
10. Hernández-Muñoz, J.M., et al.: Smart cities at the forefront of the future internet. In: Domingue, J., et al. (eds.) FIA 2011. LNCS, vol. 6656, pp. 447–462. Springer, Heidelberg (2011). https://doi.org/10.1007/978-3-642-20898-0_32
11. Rashidi, P., Mihailidis, A.: A survey on ambient-assisted living tools for older adults. Biomed. Health Inform. IEEE J. Of. **17**, 579–590 (2013). https://doi.org/10.1109/JBHI.2012.2234129
12. Seguel, J.M., Merrill, R., Seguel, D., Campagna, A.C.: Indoor air quality. Am. J. Lifestyle Med. (2016). https://doi.org/10.1177/1559827616653343
13. Bruce, N., Perez-Padilla, R., Albalak, R.: Indoor air pollution in developing countries: a major environmental and public health challenge. Bull. World Health Organ. **78**, 1078–1092 (2000)
14. Myers, S.S., et al.: Increasing CO_2 threatens human nutrition. Nature **510**, 139–142 (2014)
15. Salamone, F., Belussi, L., Danza, L., Galanos, T., Ghellere, M., Meroni, I.: Design and development of a nearable wireless system to control indoor air quality and indoor lighting quality. Sensors **17**, 1021 (2017). https://doi.org/10.3390/s17051021
16. Akkaya, K., Guvenc, I., Aygun, R., Pala, N., Kadri, A.: IoT-based occupancy monitoring techniques for energy-efficient smart buildings. In: 2015 IEEE Wireless Communications and Networking Conference Workshops (WCNCW), pp. 58–63. IEEE, New Orleans (2015). https://doi.org/10.1109/WCNCW.2015.7122529
17. Marques, G., Pitarma, R.: A cost-effective air quality supervision solution for enhanced living environments through the Internet of Things. Electronics **8**, 170 (2019). https://doi.org/10.3390/electronics8020170

18. Marques, G., Ferreira, C.R., Pitarma, R.: Indoor air quality assessment using a CO_2 monitoring system based on Internet of Things. J. Med. Syst. **43** (2019). https://doi.org/10.1007/s10916-019-1184-x

19. Marques, G.M.S., Pitarma, R.: Smartphone application for enhanced indoor health environments. J. Inf. Syst. Eng. Manag. **1** (2016). https://doi.org/10.20897/lectito.201649

20. Marques, G., Pitarma, R.: Monitoring and control of the indoor environment. In: 2017 12th Iberian Conference on Information Systems and Technologies (CISTI), pp. 1–6. IEEE, Lisbon, Portugal (2017). https://doi.org/10.23919/CISTI.2017.7975737

21. Marques, G., Pitarma, R.: IAQ evaluation using an IoT CO_2 monitoring system for enhanced living environments. In: Rocha, Á., Adeli, H., Reis, L.P., Costanzo, S. (eds.) WorldCIST 2018. AISC, vol. 746, pp. 1169–1177. Springer, Cham (2018). https://doi.org/10.1007/978-3-319-77712-2_112

22. Marques, G., Pitarma, R.: An indoor monitoring system for ambient assisted living based on Internet of Things architecture. Int. J. Environ. Res. Public. Health. **13**, 1152 (2016). https://doi.org/10.3390/ijerph13111152

23. Shah, J., Mishra, B.: IoT enabled environmental monitoring system for smart cities. In: 2016 International Conference on Internet of Things and Applications (IOTA). pp. 383–388. IEEE, Pune, India (2016). https://doi.org/10.1109/IOTA.2016.7562757

24. Bhattacharya, S., Sridevi, S., Pitchiah, R.: Indoor air quality monitoring using wireless sensor network. Presented at the December (2012). https://doi.org/10.1109/ICSensT.2012.6461713

25. Zheng, K., Zhao, S., Yang, Z., Xiong, X., Xiang, W.: Design and implementation of LPWA-based air quality monitoring system. IEEE Access **4**, 3238–3245 (2016). https://doi.org/10.1109/ACCESS.2016.2582153

26. Gao, Y., et al.: Mosaic: a low-cost mobile sensing system for urban air quality monitoring. In: IEEE INFOCOM 2016 - The 35th Annual IEEE International Conference on Computer Communications, pp. 1–9. IEEE, San Francisco, CA, USA (2016). https://doi.org/10.1109/INFOCOM.2016.7524478

27. Moukas, A., Zacharia, G., Guttman, R., Maes, P.: Agent-mediated electronic commerce: an MIT media laboratory perspective. Int. J. Electron. Commer. **4**, 5–21 (2000)

28. De Silva, L.C., Morikawa, C., Petra, I.M.: State of the art of smart homes. Eng. Appl. Artif. Intell. **25**, 1313–1321 (2012). https://doi.org/10.1016/j.engappai.2012.05.002

29. Wilson, C., Hargreaves, T., Hauxwell-Baldwin, R.: Smart homes and their users: a systematic analysis and key challenges. Pers. Ubiquit. Comput. **19**, 463–476 (2015)

30. Shen, J., Wang, C., Li, T., Chen, X., Huang, X., Zhan, Z.-H.: Secure data uploading scheme for a smart home system. Inf. Sci. **453**, 186–197 (2018). https://doi.org/10.1016/j.ins.2018.04.048

31. Dorri, A., Kanhere, S.S., Jurdak, R., Gauravaram, P.: Blockchain for IoT security and privacy: the case study of a smart home. In: 2017 IEEE International Conference on Pervasive Computing and Communications Workshops (PerCom Workshops), pp. 618–623. IEEE, Kona, Big Island, HI, USA (2017). https://doi.org/10.1109/PERCOMW.2017.7917634

32. Rüffer, D., Hoehne, F., Bühler, J.: New digital Metal-Oxide (MOx) sensor platform. Sensors **18**, 1052 (2018). https://doi.org/10.3390/s18041052

Citizen-Centre Needs

Smart Pedestrian Network: An Integrated Conceptual Model for Improving Walkability

Fernando Fonseca[1(✉)] ⓘ, Paulo Ribeiro[1] ⓘ, Mona Jabbari[1] ⓘ, Elena Petrova[2] ⓘ,
George Papageorgiou[3] ⓘ, Elisa Conticelli[4] ⓘ, Simona Tondelli[4] ⓘ, and Rui Ramos[1] ⓘ

[1] Centre for Territory Environment and Construction (CTAC),
University of Minho, Guimarães, Portugal
ffonseka@gmail.com
[2] Association for Sustainable Innovative Development in Economics, Environment and Society
(ASIDEES), Vienna, Austria
[3] European University Cyprus, E.U.C. Research Centre, Nicosia, Cyprus
[4] Alma Mater Studiorum, University of Bologna, Bologna, Italy

Abstract. Smart and sustainable mobility have recently emerged as a solution to the problems incurred by the intensive use of motorised transport modes. For many decades, cities have been planned based on the needs of vehicle traffic, neglecting basic human needs for active mobility and the adverse effects of motorised traffic on the natural environment. However, walking is an environmentally friendly transport mode and a healthy form of making physical activity. Thus, walking becomes an essential component of the transport and urban policies for achieving a more sustainable development process. This paper presents the research project Smart Pedestrian Network (SPN) that aims at promoting walkability as one of the critical dimensions of smart and sustainable mobility in cities. The paper analyses the various components linked to SPN that can make a pedestrian network "smart" and, therefore, a feasible alternative to motorised transport modes. Three integrated components are analysed: (i) an urban planning component supported in a GIS-based multi-criteria model to assess the conditions provided to pedestrians and to support the adoption of planning policies; (ii) a smartphone app for pedestrian navigation, displaying optional routes according to the pedestrian preferences and needs; and (iii) a business component to estimate and disseminate the multiple benefits of walking as well as the market potential of SPN. By promoting an innovative linkage of these three components, SPN has a great potential for improving walkability and, therefore, for creating more sustainable and liveable urban spaces.

Keywords: Smart Pedestrian Network · Walkability · Urban planning · Smartphone app · Walking benefits

1 Introduction

It can certainly be said that the last century was the century of cars. Private motorised vehicles nurtured the sense of individual freedom and radically changed the way cities

© ICST Institute for Computer Sciences, Social Informatics and Telecommunications Engineering 2020
Published by Springer Nature Switzerland AG 2020. All Rights Reserved
P. Pereira et al. (Eds.): SC4Life 2019, LNICST 318, pp. 125–142, 2020.
https://doi.org/10.1007/978-3-030-45293-3_10

have been designed and conceived. Throughout the past century, cars colonised the spaces of everyday life, generating visible effects in cities around the world such as public spaces invaded by parked vehicles, large streets serving huge suburbs, giving birth to an uncontrolled urban expansion that consequently generated situations of social isolation and segregation. As highlighted by Jacobs [1] cities are no longer conceived as a set of spaces and buildings, but only as individual buildings. High motorisation rates in conjunction with functionalism theories increased the separation of urban activities and spaces, turning the cities more fragmented and car-dependent. Nowadays, in the European cities, the private car is intensively used including for short urban trips: about 30% of the car trips are lower than 3 km, while 50% are lower than 5 km [2]. The intensive use of the car on urban trips is not only a matter of space and distance. It also produces environmental and health impacts. In European cities, 40% of CO_2 emissions and up to 70% of other pollutants are related within the intensive use of cars [3]. Noise pollution, consumption of non-renewable resources are other environmental consequences related to the use of the car. In the health domain, the use of car contributes to physical inactivity, which is a leading risk factor for premature mortality and various health problems associated to sedentary lifestyles, such as obesity, diabetes and depression [4].

In Europe, 73% of the population lives in cities, and it is expected that this number will rise to 80% by 2050 [5]. The concentration of the population in cities is causing several environmental, spatial, economic and social problems. One of the main problems is related to the intensive use of private cars, namely for short urban trips. In Europe, about 30% of the urban car trips are lower than 3 km, while 50% are lower than 5 km [2]. Note that a viable alternative transport mode for such short distances could simply be walking.

The intensive use of motorised vehicles causes several well-known problems, including pollution, traffic congestion, energy consumption, accidents and sedentary lifestyles [6]. In European cities, 40% of CO_2 emissions and up to 70% of other pollutants are related within the intensive use of cars [3]. By 2050, the EU has the goal of cutting transport emissions to 60% below 1990 levels to make cities more sustainable and liveable [7]. It is recognised that effective urban and transport planning policies should mitigate these problems namely by developing disruptive mobility solutions [8] so that the United Nations' Sustainable Development Goals can be achieved [9]. To make the transition to a low-carbon society, a new mobility paradigm, less supported on private car, is necessary [10]. The concepts of smart mobility and smart city have recently emerged to overcome these problems. To be considered smart, mobility must be sustainable [11]. The sustainable mobility concept encourages a modal shift towards more sustainable forms of transport namely by increasing the use of active modes such as cycling and walking [12]. The benefits of adopting more sustainable modes of transport are generally appreciated by people, but the various approaches to shift mobility paradigm failed due to the complex factors that prevent people for adopting behavioural change [13].

Walking is an environmentally friendly transport mode and a viable alternative mode of transport for short urban trips. Walking has many advantages when compared with car trips. In the environmental domain, walking consumes less non-renewable resources, reduces the emission of air pollutants, CO_2, and noise [14, 15]. In the economic domain, walking is costing far less than motorised transports, both in direct user costs and public infrastructure costs. Walking reduces health care costs, improves work productivity and has high accessibility and low complexity [14]. As the only energy required is provided by the traveller, walking also presents several health outcomes in terms of reducing obesity, cardiovascular diseases, diabetes, stress, among others [13, 15]. For all these benefits, walking gained enormous popularity for its potential to promote more sustainable mobility and healthier lifestyles.

In this context, the goal of this paper is to present the research project "SPN - Smart Pedestrian Net". SPN is a pilot innovative European research project to assess and improve the walkable conditions provided to pedestrians. The overall goal is to develop a model to support European cities to become people-oriented by improving walkability as one of the important dimensions of smart, sustainable and inclusive cities. The paper explains the concept of the Smart Pedestrian Network and how the multiple dimensions attached to it in the planning, technological and business domains were considered.

2 Literature Review

Pedestrian studies can be divided into two main groups: (i) studies focused on assessing the conditions provided to pedestrians; and (ii) studies focused on analysing pedestrians behaviours and preferences. The first group integrates the studies on walkability, a concept widely used that reflects the quality of the walking conditions or, in other words, the extent to which the built environment supports and encourages walking safety [16]. Walkability is a multidimensional concept that combines several attributes or criteria with an impact on walking [17]. These criteria traditionally rely on 3Ds (density, diversity, and design) features of the built environment proposed by Cervero and Kockelman [18] plus the 2Ds (distance to transit and destination accessibility) added later by Cervero et al. [19]. Thus, physical environment mesoscale attributes such as land use mix, proximity to destinations, density and connectivity have been widely used in walkability studies [20, 21]. Microscale walkability approaches at the level of streetscapes have also been developed for evaluating walkability [22–24]. Objective measures have been predominantly used in walkability research by developing walkability audits [25, 26] and indexes [27–29] that evaluate and score the conditions provided to pedestrians. Such objective measures have been supported in Geographic Information Systems [30, 31], multi-criteria analysis [25, 32], virtual technologies [29, 33], Web-based services, such as WalkScore, among others. Subjective measures have been supported on qualitative assessments based on stated preferences and individual perceptions usually collected through questionnaires or by consulting expert panels [34].

Walkability has been analysed by assessing different criteria. Such criteria can be grouped in the following dimensions: accessibility, safety/security, pedestrian facilities, and land use. Accessibility is in the first level of walking needs [35] and can be described as the ability to reach desired destinations, making an acceptable effort [26]. Accessibility has been often quantified as the distance to public transport [36] and key amenities, such as schools , shops and urban parks [37]. It is widely recognised that 400 and 800 m are the referential walking distance to get bus stops and train stations, respectively [38]. In turn, safety refers to pedestrians being protected from traffic. Traffic safety is critical for making walkable environments and plays a significant role in the decision to walk [39], particularly for children and seniors. The characteristics of traffic (speed, volume), the characteristics of roads (lanes and directions) and the facilities for protecting pedestrians from traffic are factors with impact on walking. Public security is also a criterion with some impact on walking, mainly in cities characterised by urban violence [32]. Pedestrian facilities are infrastructure provided to enhance the pedestrian environment, to improve pedestrian mobility, safety, access, and comfort. For that reason, pedestrian facilities have been one of the most analysed factors, namely by considering the following criteria: the characteristics, maintenance and continuity of sidewalks [28], the presence of obstacles on sidewalks that creates discomfort and affects pedestrian safety [40]; slopes, as small positive increments in slopes decrease travel speeds and increase the energy and the effort required for walking [41, 42]; the presence of trees and greenery that bring several environmental, safety and aesthetic benefits and encourage people to walk and the walking experience [25]; and street furniture that helps in creating a more pleasant and attractive walkable environment [43]. Finally, the characteristics of land use have been found to affect mode choice and walking [44]. Land use is often operationalised using density, diversity and design measures. Areas with high densities (population, residential, commercial) usually generate more people walking, by decreasing the appeal of driving through congested areas where parking is often scarce [25, 45]. Densities are usually analysed by developing ratios and indexes. Diversity expresses the degree to which there is a mix of land uses within an area [46]. Mixed land use is found to be one of the most correlated characteristics with utilitarian walking [42, 45]. Entropy and dissimilarity indexes have been adopted to evaluate the level of diversity [26]. Urban design and planning practices also have a determinant impact on walking [22, 24, 39]. Some authors, such as Ewing and Handy [47] and Ewing et al. [22], developed tools and specific methods for measure urban design.

On the other hand, behavioural researches have been mostly focused on pedestrian choices and preferences [48]. As pedestrians move more slowly than vehicles, they are more sensitive to their surroundings, and numerous aspects affect the experience and behaviour of pedestrians [49]. These include aspect related to the neighbourhood environment (the meso and microscale criteria mentioned above), as well as individual factors, including demographic, socioeconomic and psychological aspects, such as the age, gender, and income. In this topic, some authors have studied how the individual characteristics of pedestrians and their physical condition influence their preferences and behaviours. For example, Bernhoft and Carstensen [50] demonstrated that older pedestrians prefer routes with crossings and signalised intersections more than young pedestrians. Giles-Corti et al. [39] also found that crossing major streets and areas with high intersection density were negatively associated with child's active travel to school. Walking behaviours are also affected by gender. Many studies on trips to school have found that girls are less likely to walk than boys [51]. Among university students, Delmelle and Delmelle [52] also found that females are less like to walk (and bike) to university than male students . Female students tend to be more cautious to the risk of active travelling on streets shared with traffic [52] and are also generally more concerned with security especially after dark [53]. Male students are found to be more likely to switch commuting modes throughout the year, while females are generally more likely to drive [52]. In turn, Moniruzzaman and Farber [54] also found that students from families with higher incomes are less available to use active modes and prefer to drive instead of walk. These walking behavioural approaches have been mostly carried through questionnaires and surveys [39, 51, 52] but also by using advanced spatial simulation tools [55] and mobile devices [24].

In sum, the literature shows that the option to walk and the choice of a specific route depend on a variety of different criteria. Individuals' decisions about where and whether to walk are highly complex and typically entail considering multiple factors, including internal factors related to the personal characteristics of individuals, as well as external factors related to the characteristics of the environment [38]. Distance and time to walk, perceived ease, comfort, safety, security, convenience, proximity and attractiveness of the route, as well as age, gender, ethnicity, income, household size, car ownership, among others are factors that influence the decision to walk and which route to take.

3   Method for a Smart Pedestrian Network

The concept of a Smart Pedestrian Network (SPN) aims at developing more walkable cities and increase the number of people who walk. The goal of SPN consists in developing an integrated concept to analyse the various aspects that can make a pedestrian network "smart" and therefore, a feasible alternative to motorised transport modes. SPN sustains that a "smart pedestrian network" is not reduced to a sustainable dimension resulting from replacing the car by walking, neither to the concept of an interconnected set of appropriate sidewalks covering a given urban area. The project sustains that implementing a Smart Pedestrian Network requires a broader and multi-linked integrated approach to support not only the adoption of efficient planning initiatives but also to provide data to pedestrians about the environmental, economic and health benefits of walking, by using the potential given by digital services and devices. Approaches only focused on specific issues can have a much-limited impact. For instance, the development of navigation tools for pedestrians only makes sense if the city provides minimum conditions for walking. Otherwise, people will not feel comfortable and safe and will prefer to drive instead of walk. Thus, a smart approach requires the development of innovative technological tools to help pedestrians in selecting routes according to their preferences as well as the dissemination of the benefits (externalities) of walking. Both components are vital for changing the paradigm of mobility, and for supporting policies and investments that could have a real impact on modal choice. In the following subsections, the roadmap to the smart pedestrian network is shown in Fig. 1, considering three dimensions: urban planning, smartphone app and externalities/business model.

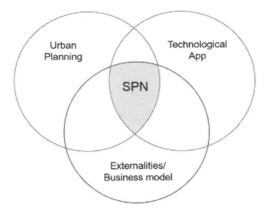

Fig. 1. Proposed roadmap for a Smart Pedestrian Network.

3.1 Roadmap for a Smart Pedestrian Network: Urban Planning

In the urban planning domain, the goal of SPN is to provide a tool to evaluate the conditions provided to pedestrians, to identify the areas more and less walkable and, therefore, to provide urban and transport guidelines for improving walkability and sustainable mobility. The core of the proposed tool is a GIS-based multi-criteria model, combining supply and demand-based walking fundamentals. The structure of the SPN model is presented in Fig. 2. Subsequent paragraphs, however, are indented.

Fig. 2. Structure of the SPN GIS-based multicriteria model.

As shown in the literature review, walkability is related to multiple interconnected criteria. Multi-criteria analysis is considered an appropriate tool for dealing with a wide range of criteria, for solving complex problems by assessing multiple solutions, yielding results that are more effective, clear and logical than single-criteria approaches, for helping decision-makers in finding solutions [56]. For that reason, multi-criteria analysis becomes a widely used decision-making technique in the urban and transport domains [57].

On the supply side and for developing the multi-criteria analysis, the first step consists in defining an extensive list of interdependent criteria with an impact on walking. As emphasised by Lin and Wei [58], many authors have based their assessments on a limited and subjective number of criteria. To overcome this debility, SPN was supported in an extensive list of 23 micro and mesoscale criteria, divided by the following four dimensions: accessibility, safety and security, pedestrian facilities, land use and urban design. The list of criteria is presented in Table 1.

Table 1. Dimensions and criteria included in the SPN model.

Dimensions	Criteria
Accessibility	Distance to bus stop Distance to light rail stations Distance to train stations Distance to public amenities Distance to car parking
Street connectivity	Intersection density Street integration
Safety and security	Traffic speed (km/h) Traffic lanes (number) Pedestrian crossings Public security (street light, graffiti, abandoned buildings)
Pedestrian facilities	Width of sidewalks Condition of sidewalks Obstacles on sidewalks Street furniture Slopes (%) Trees and greenery
Land use	Population density Residential density Non-residential density Land use mix
Urban design	Human scale/enclosure Complexity Transparency

For each criterion shown in Table 1, the model specifies the respective indicators and how each criterion should be assessed. Indicators were depicted from literature review specifying, for instance, the distance from which transport stations are within a walkable distance, defining ratios for analysing densities, describing which slopes are more comfortable for pedestrians, minimum sidewalks width, etc. The assessment involves both quantitative and qualitative assessment that requires detailed spatial data, such as disaggregated census data at the tract level, street and traffic data, digital models of the terrain, among others. This data is also required for developing the GIS-based model, where each criterion should be represented by a specific shapefile (GIS file). In a GIS environment is possible to visualise, analyse and map the performance of each criterion within a specific study area, as well as to make broader walkable analyses by overlapping several criteria.

After defining the criteria and developing the GIS model, the next step consists in integrating the demand side on the model by performing an extensive questionnaire to pedestrians. The goal of the pedestrian questionnaire is to include the pedestrians' perception on the model (a people-oriented model), namely to (i) define the relative importance of criteria (weighting process); and (ii) to collect additional mobility data (routing preferences, use of mobile devices, pedestrian behaviour, etc.). Converting the pedestrians' evaluation into values require operations of fuzzy logic, linear normalisation and analytic hierarchy process. The result is an assessment reflecting not only the walkable conditions objectively assessed in the city but also the evaluation made by pedestrians. The assessment can be focused on a specific criterion or in a specific part of the network (microscale approach), as can be extended to analyse the conditions provided by multiple/interdependent criteria or to the city level (macroscale approach). Based on the overall walkable levels assessed by the model, several planning measures can be proposed to improve the conditions provided to pedestrians. Planning guidelines should be discussed in close collaboration with city planners, decision-makers and other experts considering the pedestrians' needs and the problems identified.

3.2 Roadmap for a Smart Pedestrian Network: Smart Pedestrian Assistant Mobile Application as IT Solution

The concept of smart city is usually linked to the use of technological tools, which allow modern cities to enhance the quality of the services provided to citizens [59]. A wide range of public services can be deployed as part of smart city initiatives, including in the transport domain. For that reason, the project sustains that implementing a Smart Pedestrian Network also requires developing technological tools, such as pedestrian navigation tools, to aid people to walk and to show the benefits of walking. There are many navigations systems in the market but they mainly address the needs of vehicle users and do not take into account the conditions provided to pedestrians [60]. Thus, a pedestrian navigation system running on mobile devices, such as smartphones, are particularly useful for providing navigational aid to users at unfamiliar places and additional data related to their trips (tracing the routes, obtaining health data, etc.).

The mobile app Smart Pedestrian Assistant (SPA) developed in SPN introduced an innovative design and multiple new functions realising the key project concepts as follows:

- Identifying optional pedestrian routes between one specific origin and destination according to the pedestrian preferences and interests, including typical walks with kids, dogs, friends, invalids, in green areas, etc.;
- Providing three types of routes corresponding to the selected criteria (Fig. 3);
- Changing the offered route options over time avoid always the same routes and offer to pedestrians novel walking impressions;
- Taking into consideration passed route evaluations and statistics by pedestrians;
- Proving optional selection of flat routes, green routes, and safe routes (e.g. including benches, avoiding high traffic noisy streets, etc.);
- Inserting pedestrian data (age, gender, disability) during the routing process. For instance, elderly or disable pedestrians may prefer flat routes because they require less physical effort;
- Allowing pedestrians to express their physical and psychological satisfaction (visual aspects, comfort, security, tranquility) to improve the linkage between the urban and technological components of SPN;
- Allowing pedestrians to define preferences regarding total route time, distance, points of interest to be visited (e.g. 1 park, 2 museums, 1 restaurant, 2 shops, etc.) and obtain recommended optional routes that allow the walk within the defined restrictions (e.g. be back at home by 17:00 or in 4 h);
- Considering only circle route staring from home or hotel that shall satisfy multiple conditions in timing, points of interests, number of steps, type of streets, etc.;
- Having the route monitored during the walk to review it ongoing status such as current duration of the walk, places visited and those which are left to be visited;
- Being promptly informed by real-time notifications during the route and specific current location of the pedestrian regarding optional events such as accidents, gas and water leaks, terror acts, etc.;
- Obtaining the municipality recommendations to change the route if necessary;
- Interrupting the route at any time by some reason and get assistance in finding the shortest routes to necessary city services (toilet, hospital, police, etc.);
- Providing feedback to the municipality regarding the quality of routes, streets and walkability conditions.

Fig. 3. Smart Pedestrian Assistant prototype support for SPN routing.

The structure of the novel SPN technological solution enabling these functionalities is presented in Fig. 4. It consists of the latest innovation cloud web platform SCM - Smart City Monitor (https://smartcity.pharosnavigator.com) that continuously collects various urban static and dynamic (real-time) data from different urban sources and systems and transforms it into rich set of information services for the municipality management including city/districts/streets status for pedestrians, transportation, waste, energy, pollution, among others. As powerful new AI-driven digital transformation technology, the SCM allows applying all the relevant criteria that impact on walking: street network, topography, transport stations, location of amenities, and the overall data necessary for using the selected criteria. SCM works with multiple SPA of the pedestrians walking the city and supports them by providing real-time walkability data linked to Open-StreetMap (used as standard mapping service and database) as well as static geographic data provided in GIS format (from the SPN urban planning component).

The integrated real-time urban information system consisting of SCM and multiple SPAs used by pedestrians walking in the city can support the variety of services for the urban community (street temperature, local pollution, air quality, weather and traffic variability) and provide updates regarding various local events. The services, however, depend on the availability of relevant urban data, city sensor networks and connectivity between SPA and SCM (Wi-Fi, cellular 4G, 5G) as well as the city information operational centre, which can support such complex urban processes monitoring and events management.

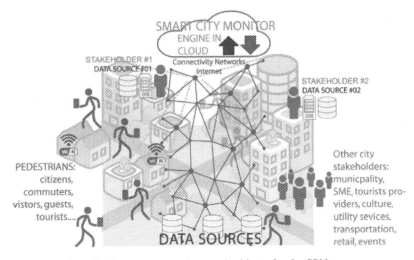

Fig. 4. Data sources and network objects for the SPN app.

3.3   Roadmap for a Smart Pedestrian Network: Externalities and Business Model

SPN provides information to pedestrians about the environmental, economic and health benefits of walking. The use of digital services and devices, such as SPA, has the potential for encouraging people to walk, including by providing data about the benefits of walking. Estimating the positive externalities of active travelling is a field not often analysed in the literature [61]. However, for SPN, a smart approach requires that providing data to people about the benefits of walking is vital for creating a paradigm shift in mobility, and for supporting policies and investments that could have a real impact on modal shift.

In this context, SPN also intends to estimate the benefits (externalities) of replacing the car by walking. Direct benefits for pedestrians include personal savings with fuel and car maintenance, travel time savings in short urban trips, health benefits resulting from walking, as well as benefits more difficult to quantify such as those resulting from social interaction with friends and family during group walks. Walking more and drive less also produce environmental benefits, namely in terms of reducing harmful emissions (CO_2, NOx, PMs, SO_2, noise) and reducing the consumption of non-renewable resources. Average travel distances, average speed and car emissions are variables that can be used for estimating these externalities. Some of these benefits are provided by the app namely those related to health (number of steps, calories burnt). The app can also be recalibrated for health recommendations namely for increasing the number of steps/day. The collaboration with some stakeholders is vital for estimating the many benefits that could potentially arise from SPN. For instance, in the case of the health benefits, working with insurance companies is critical to collect the necessary data to estimate the reduced healthcare costs incurred by insurance companies, governments and people.

A second component is related to the development of the business model for the SPN app. A business model is often described as the rationale of how an organisation creates, delivers and captures value [59]. Thus, a business model provides a coherent way to consider their options in uncertain, fast-moving and unpredictable environments. The SPN business plan [62] and model [63] is supported in a cost-benefit analysis for different scenarios related to the app. As shown in Fig. 5, the business model is divided into two phases. The first is related to the technological development of the tool and includes the following steps:

- Funding: secure funding and commitment for implementing SPA. Consult governments, municipalities other stakeholders, etc.;
- Research and design: attain the necessary tools, equipment and technology to begin the implementation of SPA;
- Testing and adapting: test the SPA with the participation of municipal authorities and end-users;
- Feedback: collect feedback from participants including pros and cons from their experience with SPN;
- Adjustments: make any necessary changes and adjustments to SPN to maximise its potential.

The second is more linked to marketing issues and includes the following steps:

- Marketing: with the expertise of the marketing team of SPN, the cities with the highest potential benefit of walking can be targeted.
- Launch: implement SPN in various European municipalities.

- Observe: collect data on SPN implementation, performance and feedback. Feedback will be collected continuously.
- Adjustments: make any necessary additional changes to SPN depending on user needs, geographical location, demographics etc.
- Global markets: once the team have enough experience with the European Market, the next target is the global market.

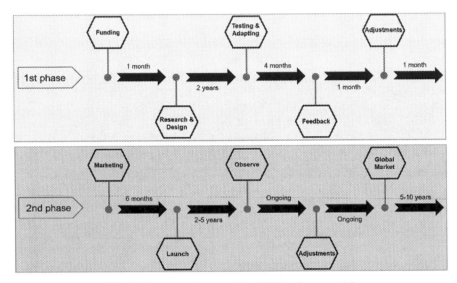

Fig. 5. Phases and steps of the SPN business model.

For each city of SPN prototype implementation, the SPN business model considers three scenarios: a Worst Case (1% users), an Average case (3% users), and a Best case (5% users). For each scenario, the business model takes into account incomes, as well as direct and indirect expenses for the premium version of SPA. Considering the multiple benefits of walking, there is an enormous potential for creating a truly disruptive innovative revenue model by buying and selling steps. Thus, the SPA can create measurable value for multiple stakeholders, including not only the SPA users (segmented customers) but also municipalities, governments, companies, among many others. As the navigation systems already available in the market do not include the quality of the pedestrian network and do not allow to communicate directly with local authorities, the business model estimates that there are many benefits of implementing SPN and that far outweigh the costs.

4   Prototype Implementation

SPN was developed, applied and tested considering the central areas of two medium-sized European cities: Porto and Bologna (Fig. 6). Porto is the second largest city in

Portugal and has a population of about 250 thousand inhabitants. Bologna is the capital of the Emilia-Romagna region in Italy and has about 390 thousand inhabitants. Both Porto and Bologna were walled cities with a long and rich history and culture. Based on the outstanding universal value of the urban fabric and its many historic buildings bearing remarkable testimony to the development over the past thousand years, the historic centre of Porto was classified by UNESCO as a World Heritage Site. Bologna is also an old city and contains an immense wealth of significant medieval, renaissance, and baroque artistic monuments. The city is particularly famous by the monuments and by the extensive porticoes and arcades that covered part of the city centre. The conditions provided to pedestrians in both cities are quite different, but both cities are engaged in improving walkability, particularly in the central areas. The prototype implementation of SPN includes SCM cloud engines for Bologna and Porto and their integration with SPA mobile applications. Thus, it is expected that SPN can improve walkability in both cities.

Fig. 6. Street network and central areas of Bologna and Porto.

5 Conclusions

Walking is one of the least expensive and most broadly accessible and sustainable mode of transport. Therefore and, as highlighted by Jabbari et al. [64], the quality of life in cities depends on the existence of suitable conditions to walk. The main goal of this paper was to enhance the concept of walkability in cities developed in the context of the undergoing project SPN - Smart Pedestrian Net. More particularly, the paper explains the concept of Smart Pedestrian Network and the multiple dimensions attached to it to improve walkability. Actions to promote walkability have mainly concentrated on making this sustainable form of travel easy and attractive by improving the general quality of built environments [65]. SPN argues that improving walkability and developing smart pedestrian networks requires a broader and multi-linked integrated approach. The proposed multi-linked approach is complementary supported on three components: urban planning, technological development and business case.

In the planning domain, SPN is supported on a GIS-based multi-criteria model. This model was built to assess the walkable conditions provided to pedestrians and to support the adoption of planning guidelines for improving walkability. The model can be distinguished by the existing multi-criteria assessment methods for the number of criteria involved (23) at both micro and mesoscales, by defining how each criterion should be evaluated and by involving the pedestrians in weighting each criterion. The goal is to make an assessment as much objective as possible and adopt a people-oriented approach: in each city, the model is adjustable according to the pedestrian's perceptions, because criteria with impact on walking are changeable from city to city. Moreover, the urban component is innovative because the criteria more valued were used as routing options in the SPN app. By identifying the streets more and less walkable and the respective causes, the model can be helpful for guiding planning policies to improve walkability and to provide an interconnected (network) set of sidewalks providing good conditions to pedestrians.

To strengthen the smart component of SPN, the project is also supported on the development of a new mobile app (Smart Pedestrian Assistant) to improve the walkability of citizens and tourists. In relation to the existing tools, the SPA is an innovative tool. As emphasised by Papageorgiou et al. [66], many of the existing routing systems were developed for driving or just for monitoring physical activity. However, common concepts used in car navigation tools are inappropriate for pedestrians, mainly because the complexity of human spatiotemporal behaviour requires other route functions than the shortest path. The designed SPA navigation tool has great potential to fill the gap between pedestrian needs and the existing navigation tools due to its useful and innovative features. The app is solely focused on pedestrian use and will enable routing based on the users' preferences and needs. Depending on the pedestrian evaluation (urban planning component), routing options can include, for instance, flat routes, green routes, safe routes, among other possible options. The app will support adjustable functions that can be used according to the characteristics of each user, their preferences in terms of the type of walk, its duration, distance, visits of various points of interests and quick changing of the route to address specific situations. Moreover, the tool is designed to have the ability to communicate directly with the information systems of the city administration to accumulate statistics and to provide information about the pedestrian conditions and urgent or planned events.

Finally, the business component has two goals. Firstly, to disseminate the several benefits (externalities) of walking. The goal is to estimate the benefits of walking instead of driving a car in daily urban trips. Positive externalities include travel time, fuel costs, harmful emissions and health benefits. The dissemination of the benefits of walking is vital for creating a paradigm shift in urban mobility, by promoting a walking mindset and supporting policies and investments to improve the conditions provided to pedestrians. Secondly, a business model was also developed for the SPA app. Preliminary results show that public would be interested in using the app, that could create value for multiple stakeholders namely for users (economic and health benefits), municipalities/public entities (less pollution, healthcare and cleaning costs), and insurance companies (fewer healthcare costs). Promoting the SPA app and involving key stakeholders, particularly those interested in promoting health, increased quality of life, sustainability and urban development is vital for disseminating the tool, attracting funds and increasing market share. In sum, SPN intends to improve walkability by considering three interlinked components that include quantitative and qualitative multiscale assessment, technological development and business components. In the future, the authors expect to present in detail the main findings resulting from the prototype implementation of SPN in Porto and Bologna.

Acknowledgments. FCT co-financing (ENSUF/0004/2016) - The authors gratefully acknowledge ERA-NET Cofund Smart Urban Futures for funding the research project SPN - Smart Pedestrian Net. The authors also acknowledge the national agencies for science, research and technology from Portugal, Italy, Austria and Cyprus for co-funding the project.

https://jpi-urbaneurope.eu/project/smart-pedestrian-net.

References

1. Jacobs, J.: The Death and Life of Great American Cities. Randome House, New York (1961)
2. Hooftman, N., Messagie, M., Mierlo, J., Coosemans, T.: A review of the European passenger car regulations – real driving emissions vs local air quality. Renew. Sustain. Energy Rev. **86**, 1–21 (2018)
3. Nanaki, E., et al.: Environmental assessment of 9 European public bus transportation systems. Sustain. Cities Soc. **28**, 42–52 (2017)
4. Berke, E., Koepsell, T., Moudon, A., Hoskins, R., Larson, E.: Association of the built environment with physical activity and obesity in older persons. Am. J. Public Health **97**(3), 486–492 (2007)
5. UN-United Nations: World Urbanization Prospects, the 2014 Revision Highlights. Department of Economic and Social Affairs, New York (2015)
6. Motoaki, Y., Daziano, R.: A hybrid-choice latent-class model for the analysis of the effects of weather on cycling demand. Transp. Res. Part A **75**, 217–230 (2015)
7. EC - European Commission: White paper: roadmap to Single European Transport Area, Report 144. EC, Brussels (2011)
8. Scarinci, R., Markov, I., Bierlaire, M.: Network design of a transport system based on accelerating moving walkways. Transp. Res. Part C **80**, 310–328 (2017)
9. Sachs, J.: From millennium development goals to sustainable development goals. Lancet **379**, 2206–2211 (2012)
10. Sopjani, L., Stier, J., Ritzén, S., Hesselgren, M., Georén, P.: Involving users and user roles in the transition to sustainable mobility systems: the case of light electric vehicle sharing in Sweden. Transp. Res. Part **71**, 207–221 (2019)
11. Garau, C., Masala, F., Pinna, F.: Cagliari and smart urban mobility: analysis and comparison. Cities **56**, 35–46 (2016)
12. Winters, M., Brauer, M., Setton, E.M., Teschke, K.: Mapping bikeability: a spatial tool to support sustainable travel. Environ. Plan. B Plan. Des. **40**, 865–883 (2013)
13. Pooley, C., et al.: Policies for promoting walking and cycling in England: a view from the street. Transp. Policy **27**, 66–72 (2013)
14. Pucher, J., Buehler, R.: Making cycling irresistible: lessons from The Netherlands, Denmark and Germany. Transp. Rev. **28**(4), 495–528 (2008)

15. Marqués, R., Hernández-Herrador, V., Calvo-Salazar, M., García-Cebrián, J.: How infrastructure can promote cycling in cities: lessons from Seville. Res. Transp. Econ. **53**, 31–44 (2015)
16. Southworth, M.: Designing the walkable city. J. Urban Plan. Dev. **131**(4), 246–257 (2005)
17. Shafray, E., Kim, S.: A study of walkable spaces with natural elements for urban regeneration: a focus on cases in Seoul, South Korea. Sustainability **9**, 587 (2017)
18. Cervero, R., Kockelman, K.: Travel demand and the 3Ds: density, diversity, and design. Transp. Res. Part D Transp. Environ. **2**(3), 199–219 (1997)
19. Cervero, R., Sarmiento, O., Jacoby, E., Gomez, L., Neiman, A.: Influences of built environments on walking and cycling: lessons from Bogotá. Int. J. Sustain. Transp. **3**(4), 203–226 (2009)
20. Frank, L., et al.: The development of a walkability index: application to the neighbourhood quality of life study. Br. J. Sports Med. **44**, 924–933 (2010)
21. Su, S., Pi, J., Xie, H., Cai, Z., Weng, M.: Community deprivation, walkability, and public health: highlighting the social inequalities in land use planning for health promotion. Land Use Policy **67**, 315–326 (2017)
22. Ewing, R., Hajrasouliha, A., Neckerman, K., Purciel-Hill, M., Greene, W.: Streetscape features related to pedestrian activity. J. Plan. Educ. Res. **36**(1), 5–15 (2016)
23. Yin, L.: Street level urban design qualities for walkability: combining 2D and 3D GIS measures. Comput. Environ. Urban Syst. **64**, 288–296 (2017)
24. Galpern, P., Ladle, A., Uribe, F., Sandalack, B., Doyle-Baker, P.: Assessing urban connectivity using volunteered mobile phone GPS locations. Appl. Geogr. **93**, 37–46 (2018)
25. Taleai, M., Amiri, E.: Spatial multi-criteria and multi-scale evaluation of walkability potential at street segment level: a case study of Tehran. Sustain. Cities Soc. **31**, 37–50 (2017)
26. Habibian, M., Hosseinzadeh, A.: Walkability index across trip purposes. Sustain. Cities Soc. **42**, 216–225 (2018)
27. Cain, K., et al.: Developing and validating an abbreviated version of the Microscale Audit for Pedestrian Streetscapes (MAPS-Abbreviated). J. Transp. Health **5**, 84–96 (2017)
28. Aghaabbasi, M., Moeinaddini, M., Shah, M., Asadi-Shekari, Z., Kermani, M.: Evaluating the capability of walkability audit tools for assessing sidewalks. Sustain. Cities Soc. **37**, 475–484 (2018)
29. Shatu, F., Yigitcanlar, T.: Development and validity of a virtual street walkability audit tool for pedestrian route choice analysis—SWATCH. J. Transp. Geogr. **70**, 148–160 (2018)
30. Stewart, O., et al.: Secondary GIS built environment data for health research: guidance for data development. J. Transp. Health **3**, 529–539 (2016)
31. Rigolon, A.: Parks and young people: an environmental justice study of park proximity, acreage, and quality in Denver, Colorado. Landsc. Urban Plan. **165**, 73–83 (2017)
32. Ruiz-Padillo, A., Pasqual, F., Uriarte, A., Cybis, H.: Application of multi-criteria decision analysis methods for assessing walkability: a case study in Porto Alegre, Brazil. Transp. Res. Part D **63**, 855–871 (2018)
33. Nasar, J., Holloman, C., Abdulkarim, D.: Street characteristics to encourage children to walk. Transp. Res. Part A **72**, 62–70 (2015)
34. Sanders, R., Cooper, J.: Do all roadway users want the same things? Transp. Res. Rec. J. Transp. Res. Board **2393**, 155–163 (2013)
35. Hall, M., Ram, Y.: Measuring the relationship between tourism and walkability? Walk Score and English tourist attractions. J. Sustain. Tour. **27**(2), 223–240 (2019)
36. Park, S., Choi, K., Lee, J.: To walk or not to walk: testing the effect of path walkability on transit users' access mode choices to the station. Int. J. Sustain. Transp. **9**(8), 529–541 (2015)
37. Battista, G., Manaugh, K.: Stores and mores: toward socializing walkability. J. Transp. Geogr. **67**, 53–60 (2018)

38. Jabbari, M., Fonseca, F., Ramos, R.: Combining multi-criteria and space syntax analysis to assess a pedestrian network: the case of Oporto. J. Urban Des. **23**(1), 23–41 (2018)
39. Giles-Corti, B., et al.: School site and the potential to walk to school: the impact of street connectivity and traffic exposure in school neighborhoods. Health Place **17**, 545–550 (2011)
40. Blecic, I., Canu, D., Cecchini, A., Congiu, T., Fancello, G.: Walkability and street intersections in rural-urban fringes: a decision aiding evaluation procedure. Sustainability **9**, 883 (2017)
41. Bahrainy, H., Khosravi, H.: The impact of urban design features and qualities on walkability and health in under-construction environments: the case of Hashtgerd New Town in Iran. Cities **31**, 17–28 (2013)
42. Lee, J., Zegras, C., Ben-Joseph, E.: Safely active mobility for urban baby boomers: the role of neighborhood design. Accid. Anal. Prev. **61**, 153–166 (2013)
43. Galanis, A., Eliou, N.: Evaluation of the pedestrian infrastructure using walkability indicators. WSEAS Trans. Environ. Dev. **12**(7), 385–394 (2011)
44. Dhanani, A., Tarkhanyan, L., Vaughan, L.: Estimating pedestrian demand for active transport evaluation and planning. Transp. Res. Part A **103**, 54–69 (2017)
45. Wei, Y., Xiao, W., Wen, M., Wei, R.: Walkability, land use and physical activity. Sustainability **8**, 65 (2016)
46. Conticelli, E., Maimaris, A., Papageorgiou, G., Tondelli, S.: Planning and designing walkable cities: a smart approach. In: Papa, R., Fistola, R., Gargiulo, C. (eds.) Smart Planning: Sustainability and Mobility in the Age of Change. GET, pp. 251–269. Springer, Cham (2018). https://doi.org/10.1007/978-3-319-77682-8_15
47. Ewing, R., Handy, S.: Measuring the unmeasurable: urban design qualities related to walkability. J. Urban Des. **14**(1), 65–84 (2009)
48. Koh, P., Wong, Y.: Comparing pedestrians' needs and behaviours in different land use environments. J. Transp. Geogr. **26**, 43–50 (2013)
49. Guo, Z., Loo, B.: Pedestrian environment and route choice: evidence from New York City and Hong Kong. J. Transp. Geogr. **28**, 124–136 (2013)
50. Bernhoft, I., Carstensen, G.: Preferences and behaviour of pedestrians and cyclists by age and gender. Transp. Res. Part F **11**, 83–95 (2008)
51. Hatamzadeh, Y., Habibian, M., Khodaii, A.: Walking behavior across genders in school trips, a case study of Rasht, Iran. J. Transp. Health **5**, 42–54 (2017)
52. Delmelle, E., Delmelle, E.: Exploring spatio-temporal commuting patterns in a university environment. Transp. Policy **21**, 1–9 (2012)
53. Lois, D., Monzón, A., Hernández, S.: Analysis of satisfaction factors at urban transport interchanges: measuring travellers' attitudes to information, security and waiting. Transp. Policy **67**, 49–56 (2018)
54. Moniruzzaman, M., Farber, S.: What drives sustainable student travel? Mode choice determinants in the Greater Toronto Area. Int. J. Sustain. Transp. **12**(5), 367–379 (2018)
55. Fu, L., Cao, S., Shi, Y., Chen, S., Yang, P., Fang, J.: Walking behavior of pedestrian social groups on stairs: a field study. Saf. Sci. **117**, 447–457 (2019)
56. Oses, U., Rojí, E., Gurrutxaga, I., Larrauri, M.: A multidisciplinary sustainability index to assess transport in urban areas: a case study of Donostia-San Sebastian, Spain. J. Environ. Planning Manage. **60**(11), 1891–1922 (2017)
57. Ribeiro, P., Fonseca, F., Santos, P.: Sustainability assessment of a bus system in a mid-sized municipality. J. Environ. Planning Manage. (2019). https://doi.org/10.1080/09640568.2019.1577224
58. Lin, J., Wei, Y.: Assessing area-wide bikeability: a grey analytic network process. Transp. Res. Part A **113**, 381–396 (2018)
59. Díaz, R., Muñoz, L., González, D.: The business model evaluation tool for smart cities: application to SmartSantander use cases. Energies **10**, 262 (2017)

60. Papageorgiou, G., Maimaris, A.: Towards the development of Intelligent Pedestrian Mobility Systems (IPMS). In: ICELTICs 2017 International Conference on Electrical Engineering and Informatics, Banda Aceh, Indonesia, 18–20 October (2017)

61. Qiu, L., He, L.: Bike sharing and the economy, the environment, and health-related externalities. Sustainability **10**, 1145 (2018)

62. Papageorgiou, G., Petrakis, C., Ioannou, N., Zagarelou, D.: Effective business planning for sustainable urban development: the case of active mobility. In: 14th European Conference on Innovation and Entrepreneurship, Kalamata, Greece, 19–20 September (2019)

63. Papageorgiou, G., Efstathiadou, T., Efstathiades, A., Maimaris, A.: Promoting active transportation via information and communication technologies. In: 18th IEEE International Conference on Smart Technologies, Novi Sad, Serbia, 1–4 July (2019)

64. Jabbari, M., da Fonseca, F.P., Ramos, R.A.R.: Assessing the pedestrian network conditions in two cities: the cases of Qazvin and Porto. In: Arefian, F.F., Moeini, S.H.I. (eds.) Urban Heritage Along the Silk Roads. TUBS, pp. 229–245. Springer, Cham (2020). https://doi.org/10.1007/978-3-030-22762-3_15

65. Kim, S., Park, S., Lee, S.: Meso or micro-scale? Environmental factors influencing pedestrian satisfaction. Transp. Res. Part D **30**, 10–20 (2014)

66. Papageorgiou, G., Demetriou, D., Balamou, E., Maimaris, A.: Market Research and concept study for a smart pedestrian network application. In: PETRA 2018 Conference, Corfu, Greece, 26–29 June (2018)

Building Future Societies? A Brief Analysis of Braga's School Bus Project

Emília Araújo[1]([⊠]) [iD], Márcia Silva[1] [iD], Rita Ribeiro[1] [iD], and Filipa Corais[2] [iD]

[1] Communication and Society Research Centre, University of Minho, Braga, Portugal
emiliararaujo@gmail.com
[2] Municipality of Braga, Braga, Portugal

Abstract. This paper seeks to demonstrate the importance of implementing transport policies that meet home to school (and vice versa) mobility needs of children and young people. Over the last few years families' mobility has been given increasing attention. One of the most investigated aspects is home to work mobility. Nowadays there is an urgent need to study and propose intervention measures regarding children's mobility to school. In fact, studies show that the car is the preferred mode of transportation in Portugal. This trend has undoubtedly negative social, environmental and health consequences. Based on an evaluation study on the School Bus project in Braga (a research- intervention activity of BUILD-Braga Urban Innovation Laboratory Demonstrator), this paper discusses the difficulties in implementing sustainable mobility initiatives, pointing out anticipatory measures that can be taken in medium-sized cities in order to stop the expansion of children's transportation by car, and give them back spaces in the cities.

Keywords: Urban mobility · Future · City · Children · School bus · BUILD

1 Introduction

This paper aims to show the importance of implementing transport policies for children and young people that meet the needs of families and, at the same time, actively contribute to the much urgent change to more sustainable transport practices, particularly in cities with high population density and where circulation has become progressively chaotic due to the increase in vehicle circulation. It is based on the analysis of the available literature on school transport and the implementation of sustainable mobility for children and young people, and addresses the School Bus project, implemented in the city of Braga, in the North of Portugal.

There are several reasons for thinking about transportation of children and young people to school as a social and sociological problem. Among those reasons, the following ought to be stressed: (i) the regular and growing use of cars and the consequent rush-hour traffic chaos in the cities, which are the cause of accidents, and endless congestions, as well as considerable delays, which expose children and families to stress and anxiety; (ii) the weak provision of public transport and the non- adequacy of these to the mobility needs of families with school-age children and young people, as regards routes

© ICST Institute for Computer Sciences, Social Informatics and Telecommunications Engineering 2020
Published by Springer Nature Switzerland AG 2020. All Rights Reserved
P. Pereira et al. (Eds.): SC4Life 2019, LNICST 318, pp. 143–153, 2020.
https://doi.org/10.1007/978-3-030-45293-3_11

and schedules, among others; (iii) the distance between schools and the families' place of residence and their motivation to add their rides to work with the ones to school and; (iv) the low or total absence of participation of populations, schools, children and young people in the definition of transport policies aimed at quality of life and development of sustainable cities.

In this paper, we find it crucial that the transport of children and young people to and from school becomes a subject of collective and political concern, which involves rethinking and planning urban mobility holistically, not leaving decisions only up to families or schools. Accordingly, we propose the use of transdisciplinary approaches to children and young people's mobility, by suggesting there is a need to help practitioners develop innovation and entrepreneurial actions that are responsible and sustainable, in order to safeguard an alternative and better future for urban areas.

This paper is structured as follows. First, there is a brief introduction to the way social sciences, and particularly sociology, have been working on the phenomenon of children's mobility to and from school, considering that children's transport is a major issue in modern societies. Then, we describe the methodological steps developed during a research and evaluation project on the implementation of the school bus in the city of Braga. Afterwards we describe how families and children joined the school bus initiative and analyze its main positive and negative points. Finally, we discuss some practical considerations about the way children's mobility can be managed in order to reduce existing traffic congestion due to the massive use of cars in the city.

2   Urban Mobility: From Difficulties to Opportunities

Society's car dependency is difficult to revert [1–3] and entails several implications for children's lives [4]. In fact, children miss out on the opportunity to gain skills and autonomy, as well as the opportunity for social interactions, when circulating almost exclusively in cars. Furthermore, families waste time that could be used in more stimulating and fruitful activities. Besides health problems related to high levels of air pollution, and other diseases brought about by the increasing accelerated pace of life, cars are also related to the abovementioned increase in traffic congestion. It is a fact that the problem of traffic in cities, particularly in southern European countries, has been addressed by putting a great emphasis on the need to transition to electric and autonomous cars. However, this transition does not solve any major effects caused by cars. Instead, it only reshapes urban spaces' current challenges.

Actually, it is urgent to integrate school mobility and mobility of families in urban policies, by promoting means of movement and transport which, at the same time, empower children and allow them to enjoy public space and ensure a safe circulation between school, home and other places (for example, extracurricular activities) in a more sustainable way. This can be achieved in several ways, including by implementing the use of public transport, or by encouraging safe walking routes for children in their way to school. In any case, families and children needs must always be met. Most importantly, giving them back public space and teaching them how to reuse the time and space of transportation and travel, is a key factor for quality of life in the cities of the future.

2.1 The Problem of Mobility in Braga

From the citizen's point of view, assessed through field observation, the circulation in Braga has been getting increasingly more difficult for these last couple of years. People complain about the fact that there is traffic everywhere, circulation is very slow and parking is scarce and expensive.

Braga has currently about 181,000 inhabitants, with 57.8% of the population aged between 25–64, while the population under 25 is about 26%. The city centre is where most of the services, such as schools, health care services, public services, sports centres, among others, are. Braga attracts many people every day (about 48.020 movements) mostly from neighbouring counties: Vila Verde (11.502), Guimarães (10.638) and Barcelos (9.415) [5]. About 27.285 people move from Braga every day. The use of cars in Braga has been growing since 2010 (+17.5%). This is a trend that follows what is happening all over the country [6] (Fig. 1).

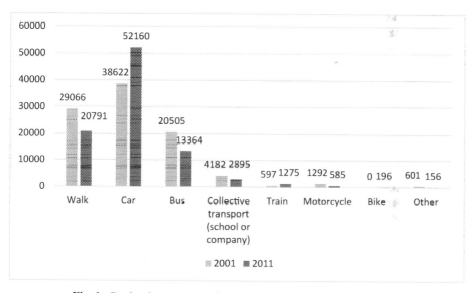

Fig. 1. Predominant means of transportation in Braga Source: [7, 8]

According to Teles [5], cars are used in about 67.3% of the movements within the county, and 79.8% outside the county. The average time spent in commuting home to work or schools is about 15 min (58.6%), with 30.5% of commuters spending 16 to 30 min. Rush hours occur between 8 and 9 am, and between 6 and 7 pm. There are about 499 cars per 1 000 inhabitants in Braga – a value equivalent to the national average. According to the same study [5], and because there are numerous schools in the city centre, car transportation to schools between 2001 and 2011 has grown more than 33%. These numbers clearly confirm the massive use of cars in day-to-day journeys, including home-school movement, and corroborate citizens' perception about mobility in Braga being "chaotic", "slow", "difficult" and "dangerous" (Fig. 2).

Fig. 2. Children crossing a street near school, in Braga (a car prevents them from crossing in the right place)

3   School Buses as a Key Answer to Sustainable Mobility

Nowadays, school buses are seen as an innovative, sustainable alternative in urban mobility. They are used worldwide for transporting students to and from school. Some of their most relevant effects relate to an increase in air quality by reducing CO_2 and other pollutant emissions, a decrease in traffic flow to schools, an increase in children's safety in their way to school and time families spend together. Besides being in tune with current environmental concerns, the fact is that the School Bus goes back a long way.

The first School Bus dates back to 1827, when George Shillibeer, inspired by buses in Paris, took the initiative to London. Despite its Parisian origin, it was in the United States of America that the school transport spread when Wayne Works built horse-drawn carriages - *school hacks* or *kid hacks* - in Indiana. Before having this means of transport, children went to school on foot, by wagon or sled. As car industry developed, Wayne Works took the opportunity to motorize these carriages, shortening travel time to schools. In 1936, the company developed a set of school buses and introduced the first design of school buses in steel. They are traditionally painted in yellow because this color is more visible in the morning and at night. Although the project was not very well accepted by parents, due to some safety issues, it was eventually considered one of the safest modes of school transport in the USA [9–11].

More recently, some cities have implemented school bus services, both on a permanent basis or as pilot initiatives. Some of the projects carried out mainly in Europe are mentioned below. At the Deutsche Schule, in London, the School Bus service has four routes. This service is available in the morning and afternoon. Costs associated with the service are incurred by the parents [12]. According to the newspaper *The Guardian* [13], some schools in London, Manchester and Edinburgh are taking steps to prohibit automobile traffic nearby schools. The Scottish government is committed to encouraging active transportation to and from school and reducing car dependence. In Scotland, during the "rush hour" - in the morning and in the afternoon- it is estimated that one in five cars on the road are busy transporting children to school. The government is interested in reducing the use of cars as a way to improve the health and well-being of children and young people, while reducing congestion and decreasing CO2 emissions. In 2009, the city of Lisbon carried out a mobility project aimed at implementing a bus system for public schools. This project aimed to reduce student mobility costs. The municipality traced some specific circuits (home-school and school-home), for students living more than 6 min' walk from school. Routes were established so that children would not have to walk long to get to the bus. The buses "Alfacinhas" had the capacity for 24 children, with average travel time of 15 min. Each bus had someone who was responsible for picking up and delivering each child to their parents, at the previously designated 'bus stop' [14]. In Canada, the Red Deer Catholic Regional Schools have implemented the School Bus service. Service costs are incurred by the families. Regarded as an extension of the school facilities, students cannot eat, drink, or stand when inside the buses. This service includes a mobile application that allows parents to know if the school bus is delayed or if, for some reason, it has been cancelled [15]

In general, studies about school buses show that they can be an effective alternative to using the car, or to walking to school. Besides the positive effects in terms of families' spent time and money, air quality and urban traffic, there are also some advantages associated to the well-being of children, such as: (1) the strengthening of personal contact, thus favoring sociability, as children have the possibility of interacting with colleagues of different ages and conditions, fostering feelings of trust and self-esteem; (2) the development of children's autonomy; (3) the safety of children, as public transportation is safer than cars, and school buses have low accident rates, most of which do not imply lethal injuries [16–20]. The more children are on buses, the fewer cars are on the roads.

4   The School Bus Project in Braga

The School Bus Project in Braga aims at reducing traffic both in the city centre and in the main entrances of the city, especially during morning rush hour. It has been designed and implemented by the Municipality of Braga in a partnership with a wider project – Braga Urban Innovation Laboratory Demonstrator[1] (BUILD). The project encompasses six schools: Colégio Leonardo Da Vinci, Colégio D. Diogo de Sousa, Colégio Teresiano, EB 2.3 Francisco Sanches, EB 2.3 André Soares and Conservatório de Música Calouste Gulbenkian. After the first experience in 2017, the school bus has been steadily operating since September 2018, with 413 children enrolled. Parents leave their children at one of the four interfaces (Municipal Stadium, Maximinos, Minho Center, Tenões) and they are, then, transported by bus to the schools' facilities. Being an important measure of the urban mobility policy, the Municipality undertakes all the costs of this program, so all families may benefit from free transportation, regardless of social and economic status (Fig. 3).

---

[1] Braga Urban Innovation Laboratory Demonstrator (BUILD) is a project of the Municipality of Braga with the following scientific partners: University of Minho, International Iberian Nanotechnology Laboratory and Centre for Computer Graphics; funded by the Fundo Ambiental - Ministry of the Environment.

Fig. 3. School bus interfaces and routes in Braga Source: Municipality of Braga

5   Methodological Note

This paper is based on bibliographic research on the use and history of the school bus and the results of a study conducted in the city of Braga on the School Bus project. The methodological choices allowed us to assess the project, as well as to analyse families' mobility practices and major concerns presented by some important stakeholders around thinking and reframing school mobility. A mixed method was followed, using qualitative and quantitative research techniques. Methodology encompassed systematic observation, focus groups, interviews and a survey.

The interviews involved some important players including school principals, parents and representatives of other entities, such as the police, the parish and the county council. The semi structured interviews were done according to a guide integrating the agents' concerns, personal experience and the identification of measures they suggested to solve problems related to school mobility. The interviews were recorded. After the transcription they were analysed according to content analysis procedures using MaxQda software.

The focus groups were conducted with children. Part of them were school bus users, others were not. These sessions with the children lasted for a maximum of 90 min. Children were asked to draw their main mean of transportation and then challenged to speak about it and share some ideas about the type of things they would change in their daily habits linked to mobility. Following data collection and systematization in a database, content analysis was used to extract information about three dimensions: the most frequent means of transportation to and from school, desire and intention of changing something in the trip.

The survey was applied to parents of children registered to use the School Bus. The questionnaire consisted of 27 questions, about sociodemographic information, safety perception on the areas surrounding schools, school mobility practices and satisfaction with the use of School Bus. The questionnaires were handed out to children in order to be filled in by their parents.

96 (out of the 130 delivered surveys) responses were received, involving 127 children, which represents a high response rate, ensuring considerable reliability of the conclusions. SPSS software was used to analyse the data.

6 Project Evaluation

6.1 School Directors

Mostly, school directors highlight the fact that the project contributes to creating new mobility habits, because "children who use public transport now will also use it later in life" (director of Colégio Leonardo da Vinci). In the interviews, directors stressed three main positive achievements: (1) student's punctuality, as children who use the School Bus do not arrive late to school. According to the director of Colégio D. Diogo de Sousa, the initiative "disciplines and helps students stick to schedules"; (2) pedagogical advantage for participating children as they arrive to school more willing and motivated for pedagogical activities than children who come by car. Children who take the school bus "arrive in a happier mood, more motivated to take classes. Children who arrive late with their parents, after working through the rush hour, directly into the classroom do not have the same healthy disposition" (Director of Colégio Leonardo da Vinci); (3) a significant decrease of traffic in the area nearby school, making it a more pleasant place for users (security, air quality, and calmness). However, directors also mention some negative aspects, namely the fact that the School Bus is not available for children of all ages, families are not yet aware of its advantages and struggle with the change in behaviour regarding the use and parking of cars near schools.

6.2 Parents

Even if they evaluate the School Bus very positively (82% rate it as excellent or very good and 98% intend to continue using the service in the future), parents seem to have some mixed feelings concerning the need to leave the children at the bus stop or taking them by car. According to the data gathered in the parents' evaluation survey, these contradictions are due to subjective representations and evaluation about children's safety, as well as their instinct to protect kids and a wish to spend as much time as they can with them, even if in traffic jams. The evaluation survey results show that parents are highly satisfied with the project as they feel children are more "independent, autonomous, and safe", they meet (new) friends, "they like to go with their mates, it is comfortable and makes them feel free and they are able to arrive earlier to school", which is almost impossible when traveling by car.

Parents also say that the School Bus helps them saving time in traffic as they are able to avoid the usual jams near schools and go directly to the workplace. Punctuality and quality of life are also mentioned. The table below sums up the most positive aspects mentioned by the parents (Table 1).

Table 1. Positive and negative aspects mentioned by parents in their evaluation of the school bus project in Braga

Positive aspects	Negative aspects
• Decrease in traffic and pollution	• The school bus should also ensure the bus ride home
• Strengthening of friendship ties with neighbors, both for children and their families	• Schedules should be more adequate, so that children should not have to get up so early in the morning
• Punctuality	• More routes and schedules should be available, for more flexibility
• Time saving for the family	

Overall, parents are very critical of the efficiency, availability and organization of public and school transportation in the city of Braga, not to mention the need for a service tailored to their daily routines. Besides, parents strongly claim that the spaces surrounding schools should be more secure and car-free, and users (especially parents) should avoid inappropriate behaviour such as parking in the middle of the street, or outside the parking spaces.

6.3 Children

Despite being very young (6 to 15), most of the School Bus users have strong opinions about this type of home-to-school transport. Because of their age, qualitative data gathering was an obvious choice. Focus groups took place in schools and sessions encompassed debating, writing and drawing about mobility. Participants were both School Bus users and non-users. Interestingly, 60% of the latter said they would like to join it. For those already using this service, positive opinions are over 95% and the main reasons for that are the urge to protect the environment, socializing with friends and arriving to classes on time (Fig. 4).

7   Children's Right to the City: What Still Needs to be Done

Somewhat unexpectedly, and contrary to the current environmental challenges and recent problems in urban areas, families seem to be increasingly dependent on cars. The pace of life, the need to respond to various demands located in different spaces, the distances between home and the workplace, the inefficiency of the public transportation network, the ever-increasing supply of cars are some of the reasons used to justify the increase in car users [21]. One of the factors that contribute greatly to the use of cars is also

Fig. 4. Child's drawing depicting the school bus ("Less mobile phones, more friends, less cars")

the number of after school activities children are involved in every day, which implies traveling both from home and from school. These activities include sports, music classes, foreign languages classes, among others [21, 22].

The analysis of the existing literature and the qualitative research conducted in the context of the School Bus project in Braga shows that the transportation of children and young people is a major issue in "smart cities" agenda, not only because of decarbonisation and quality of life in city centres, but also because short daily home- school-work commuting is deeply connected to societal challenges such as territorial and social cohesion, citizenship and participation, and bottom-up strategies for urban ecosystems [23–25].

To this end, measures that bring children and young people to the centre of the analysis contribute to thinking about the public space from the perspective and experience of those who will shape the future of our cities [26, 27]. For this purpose, social research ought to focus on the appropriation of spaces and commuting patterns of different social groups. Additionally, attention should be drawn to the risks and dangers associated with urban

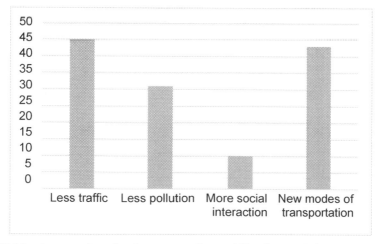

Fig. 5. Children's suggestions for change regarding mobility Source: Information provided by children's focus groups

circulation, intervention measures that favour the participation of children in the design of the city (see Fig. 5) and the routes to be carried out daily.

8 Concluding Remarks

In this text, we intended to present the main advantages of using the school bus on the routes to school, considering the importance of including children's mobility as a priority in the planning and design of cities in the future.

Transporting children to schools is a matter of great relevance in the analysis of mobility patterns of families [28] and has a significant impact not only on families' daily lives, but also on the organization of the territory because home to school commuting represents a weighty part of traffic congestion in the cities, especially during rush hours, both in the morning and by the end of the day [29].

However, using the car has a number of consequences, including for the health and well-being of children. Some are visible (for example, public spaces overcrowded with cars and the insecurity it entails). Others are more implicit, such as hindrances to children's autonomy or lack of physical activity.

Given the School Bus project's results, we may conclude that the objectives have been partially achieved, by having demonstrated the relevance of children and families' support for social and environmental sustainability regarding circulation in urban areas.

Funding. Funded by FCT - Fundação para a Ciência e Tecnologia, within the UID/CCI/00736/2019 project scope. Funded by Fundo Ambiental, project BUILD-Braga Urban Innovation Laboratory Demonstrator.

References

1. Banister, D.: The sustainable mobility paradigma. Transp. Policy **15**, 73–80 (2008)
2. Meaton, J., Kingham, S.: Children's perceptions of transport modes: car culture in the classroom? World Transp. Policy Pract. **4**(2), 12–16 (1998)
3. O'Brien C.: Children: a critical link for changing driving behaviour. York Centre for applied sustainability. York University, Toronto, Canada (2000). http://www.bikewalk.org/pdfs/childrendrivingbehavior.pdf. Accessed 21 June 2019
4. Mackett, R.: Increasing car dependency of children: should we be worried? Munic. Eng. **151**(1), 29–38 (2002)
5. Teles, P. (coord.): Estudo de mobilidade e gestão de tráfego. Câmara Municipal de Braga (2018)
6. INE - Instituto Nacional de Estatística: Inquérito à Mobilidade nas Áreas Metropolitanas do Porto e de Lisboa (2018). https://www.ine.pt/xportal/xmain?xpid=INE&xpgid=ine_publicacoes&PUBLICACOESpub_boui=349495406&PUBLICACOESmodo=2&&fbclid=IwAR2QzUZK0mUSEdKySZe1HqmObblKWR62vIyVhtVAAxrQhyNllna-DDfp2bk&xlang=pt. Accessed 25 June 2019
7. INE - Instituto Nacional de Estatística, Meio de transporte mais utilizado nos movimentos pendulares (2001). https://www.ine.pt/xportal/xmain?xpid=INE&xpgid=ine_indicadores&indOcorrCod=0000684&contexto=bd&selTab=tab2. Accessed 25 June 2019

8. INE - Instituto Nacional de Estatística, Meio de transporte mais utilizado nos movimentos pendulares (2011). https://www.ine.pt/xportal/xmain?xpid=INE&xpgid=ine_indicadores&indOcorrCod=0007093&contexto=bd&selTab=tab2. Accessed 25 June 2019

9. The Newswhell. History of the School Bus. (Blog post). https://thenewswheel.com/history-of-the-school-bus/. Accessed 11 June 2019

10. Transportation and Scholl Busing. The School Bus, History of Pupil Transportation, Issues in Pupil Transportation: https://education.stateuniversity.com/pages/2512/Transportation-School-Busing.html. Accessed 11 June 2019

11. Wagons, Hacks, and Sledges: History of the School Bus. https://www.edgarsnyder.com/blog/2015/08/history-of-school-bus.html. Accessed 11 June 2019

12. Deutsche Shule London, School Bus. https://www.dslondon.org.uk/admissions/school-bus. Accessed 08 June 2019

13. The Guardian, UK schools banning school run to protect pupils from air pollution. https://www.theguardian.com/environment/2018/jul/13/uk-schools-move-to-ban-the-school-run-to-protect-pupils-from-air-pollution. Accessed 08 June 2019

14. Martíneza, L., Viegasa, J.: Design and deployment of an innovative school bus service in Lisboa. Procedia Soc. Behav. Sci. **20**, 120–130 (2011)

15. Red Deer Catholic Regional Schools, School Bus Information. https://www.rdcrs.ca/schools/school-bus-information. Accessed 08 June 2019

16. Tamanaha, S.: Design para sistema de transporte de estudantes. Dissertação de final de curso, Universidade de São Paulo, Brasil (2014). http://www.fau.usp.br/fauforma/2015/assets/sergio_tamanaha.pdf. Accessed 18 May 2019

17. Yang, J., Peek-Asa, C., Cheng, G., Heiden, E., Falb, S., Ramirez, M.: Incidence and characteristics of school bus crashes and injuries. Accid. Anal. Prev. **41**, 336–341 (2009)

18. Desai, M., Takkalaki, P., Bhapri, M., Marshanalli, A., Malage, G.: Students tracking system for school bus. Int. Res. J. Eng. Technol, **4**(6), 2554–2557 (2017)

19. Kotoulaa, K., Botzoris, G., Morfoulaki, M., Aifandopoulou, G.: The existing school transportation framework in Greece – barriers and problems comparing to other European countries. Transp. Res. **24**, 385–392 (2017)

20. Tenniz, Z., Yilmaz, S.: Attention! school bus. Eur. J. Educ. Stud. **4**(2), 276–288 (2018)

21. Dowling, R.: Cultures of mothering and car use in suburban Sydney: a preliminary investigation. Geoforum **31**, 345–353 (2000)

22. Hjorthol, R., Fyhri, A.: Do organized leisure activities for children encourage car-use? Transp. Res. **43**, 209–218 (2009)

23. Moodie, M., Haby, M., Galvin, L., Swinburn, B., Carter, R.: Cost-effectiveness of active transport for primary school children - walking school bus program. Int. J. Behav. Nutr. Phys. Act. **6**, 1–11 (2009). https://doi.org/10.1186/1479-5868-6-63

24. Nasrudin, N., Nor, A.: Travelling to school: transportation selection by parents and awareness towards sustainable transportation. Procedia Environ. Sci. **17**, 392–400 (2013)

25. Lopes, F., Cordovil, R., Neto, C.: Children's independent mobility in Portugal: effects of urbanization degree and motorized modes of travel. J. Transp. Geogr. **41**, 210–219 (2014)

26. Pojani, D., Stead, D.: Sustainable urban transport in the developing world: beyond megacities. Sustainability **7**, 7784–7805 (2015)

27. Baslington, H.: Travel socialization: a social theory of travel mode behavior. Int. J. Sustain. Transp. **2**, 91–114 (2008)

28. Oliveira, C.S., Cruz, M.: Urban mobility patterns and the use of public transports in Portugal. In: Proceedings Clima 2008. Universidade de Aveiro (2008)

29. Ristell, J., Enoch, M., Quddus, M., Hardy, P.: Expert perspectives on the role of the bus in school travel. Munic. Eng. **166**(1), 53–58 (2013)

City Rankings and the Citizens: Exposing Representational and Participatory Gaps

Ana Duarte Melo[✉] [iD]

Communication and Society Research Centre, University of Minho, Braga, Portugal
anamelo@ics.uminho.pt

Abstract. A critical reflection on the purposes, role and performance of city rankings through an holistic communicational approach is at the core of this article. Grounded on a conceptual framework that highlights the contemporary idea of the city—beyond the smart city and more as a co-intelligent, collaborative and co-creative entity, and on the performance outputs of city rankings as territorial and strategic communication tools that actually represent the state of cities, we address the citizens' presence or contribute—as main city stakeholders—to city rankings. In order to make research tangible with a practical component, an exploratory comparative content analysis of three recognized city rankings: the CBI – City Brands Index 2017, the GCR – 2018 Global Cities Report, and the Global Liveability Index 2018—was carried out.

Conclusive notes argue that in order to effectively represent cities, as they are lived, thought and built by their citizens in their everyday, city rankings must rely in more real-time, updated, people's perception centred data, and embed more citizen participation and insights. Moreover, methodology transparency and accountability should be promoted in order to add trust value to city rankings.

Keywords: City rankings · Communication · Citizenship · Participation

1 Introduction

A communicational approach to territories is in order when we address the process of building "smart and liveable cities". The main insight of this article intends to reflect on how territories, particularly cities, engage in communication and on how communication—namely through city rankings, contributes (or not) to better cities. We will focus our attention in particular on city rankings as tools for gauging what is relevant in a city, but also as central communication tools in building the city's image, reputation and representation, that is, in adding symbolic and narrative value to the city. Our perspective draws on the idea of the city made by and for the citizens, a city as the communal capital and knowledge, a smart city that serves, includes and drives the collective. Therefore, the main question we intend to address could be summarized in a straightforward interrogation: do city rankings take the citizens into account through participatory practices?

P. Pereira et al. (Eds.): SC4Life 2019, LNICST 318, pp. 154–169, 2020.
https://doi.org/10.1007/978-3-030-45293-3_12

To assess this, we will analyse a number of city rankings and map some of its constitutive criteria that allegedly include citizens' inputs, whether through direct or indirect participatory practices. Furthermore, we will reflect critically on the use of city rankings as territorial communication management tools, namely on their strategic and managerial value. To set a framework to this research a diversity of notions is summoned, namely, the ideas of city, citizens and participation as constitutive parts of the city, the concepts of smart city, co-intelligent territory, territorial communication management, city brands, image and reputation. We consider them nuclear to understand the subject of city rankings.

What is a city and what does it mean? And how do city rankings contribute to construct that meaning and add value to the city?

2   A Conceptual Framework

2.1   From the *Smart City* to the *Co-intelligent Territory*

The smart city concept emerged in the 1990s, associated with the application of information and communication technologies to cities, therefore embedded within an intelligence framework, whether technology, human, institutional, energy, or data management centred just to name a few. Two main approaches can be found related to smart cities: (1) a management approach, focused on efficiency, resources and flows, crossing a number of areas: energy, mobility, transport, consumption, waste disposal, environmental impact, etc.; and (2) a social innovation approach, in which smart cities improve the lives of citizens and visitors: a smart city collects data from citizens, devices and assets to interact directly with both the community and the city infrastructure; optimize city operations and performance, services and interaction with citizens.

"There is a range of definitions of a smart city, but the consensus is that smart cities utilize IoT sensors, actuators, and technology to connect components across the city. This connects every layer of a city, from the air to the street to underground. It's when you can derive data from everything that is connected and utilize it to improve the lives of citizens and improve communication between citizens and the government that a city becomes a smart city" (Maddox 2018).

As recent as it is, the smart city is a work-in-progress concept, prone to discussion and criticism (Cardullo and Kitchin 2019; Hollands 2008; Rizzon et al. 2017). Hollands (2008) proposes a "preliminary critical polemic" in an effort to clear "[smart cities] definitional impreciseness, numerous unspoken assumptions and a rather self-congratulatory tendency (what city does not want to be smart or intelligent?)" (Hollands 2008, p. 304). The smart city concept involves both an operational, managerial insight and a philosophical and holistic approach to the city (Vanolo 2014).

Several designations emerged that point towards a general definition of what a smart city is: "Intelligent (…) Digital (…) Sustainable (…) Technocity (…) Well-being city" (Dameri 2013, p. 2546); or, in a more dynamic perspective, integrating the notion of change and transformation: "In today's modern urban context, we appear to be constantly bombarded with a wide range of new city discourses like smart, intelligent,

innovative, wired, digital, creative, and cultural, which often link together technological informational transformations with economic, political and socio-cultural change"
(Hollands 2008, p. 305).

According to Marsal-Llacuna, Colomer-Llinàs and Meléndez-Frigola, "Smart Cities
have evolved out of livable, creative, digital and knowledge cities, drawing heavily on the
concept of the Sustainable City and having in common a large technological component"
(Marsal-Llacuna et al. 2015, pp. 617–618).

Smart cities' critique frequently deals with opposing perspectives, namely techno
centred *vs* citizen centred or the private interest *vs* public interest; or long term effects
and objectives, namely sustainability (Martin et al. 2018); ethical issues such as privacy
(Zhang et al. 2019), big data; freedom (Vanolo 2014) or participation (Cardullo and
Kitchin 2019). Many of these critical perspectives converge on an essential question:
what does it mean to be a citizen in a city, i.e. what does it mean to be a *smart citizen* in
a *smart city*?

Maddox (2018) highlights smart cities' progress and perspectives, "Smart cities are
more than a trend—they're the wave of the future because the world is becoming more
urban, with 60% of the population expected to live in cities by 2050" (Maddox 2018) and
proposes a comprehensive guide to what a smart city is, concluding with a provocative
statement: "A truly smart city improves the quality of life for citizens and visitors, and
while a smart city can be many things, just as with humans, some are smarter than others"
(Maddox 2018).

In a comprehensive proposal Dameri (2013) establishes structural elements, namely,
territory, technology, citizens and government as components, and environmental sustainability, quality of life and well being, participation, knowledge and intellectual
capital, as objectives of the smart city concept.

Chourabi et al. (2012) identified eight critical factors of smart city initiatives: management and organization, technology, governance, policy context, people and communities,
economy, built infrastructure, and natural environment.

In a previous research we proposed a broader insight (Melo 2019), inspired on
Tom Atlee's concept of co-intelligence (Atlee 2012, 2014, 2017), to approach territorial "smartness", one based on systematic communicative engagement within the city's
stakeholders: "There is no smart territory without smart communication. There is no
smart territory without smart citizens who share the vision, essence, projects and planning of territories." (Melo 2019, p. 247). In this article we will focus further on the
participation area of Dameri's and on Chourabi's fifth factor—people and communities—as constitutive structural elements of the smart city. This perspective coincides
with the conclusions of Hollands (2008) that, to a certain extend, expose the smart city
as an impediment in itself:

"In essence the smart progressive city needs and requires the input and contribution of these various groups of people, and cannot simply be labelled as smart by
adopting a sophisticated information technology infra-structure or through creating self-
promotional websites. Cities are more than just wires and cables, smart offices, trendy
bars and luxury hotels, and the vast number of people who live in cities deserve more
than just these things. Because the smart city label can work to ideologically mask the
nature of some of the underlying changes in cities, it may be a partial impediment toward

progressive urban change. Real smart cities will actually have to take much greater risks with technology, devolve power, tackle inequalities and redefine what they mean by smart itself, if they want to retain such a lofty title" (Hollands 2008, p. 316).

In fact, collective intelligence is not a new concept. It has been studied more consistently after the 1980's. Stremtan (2008) wrapped up a definition based on diverse theoretical perspectives: "Collective intelligence is intelligence that emerges from the collaboration and competition of many individuals (…) appears in a wide variety of forms of consensus decision making (…) is the intelligence of connections, of relations (…) These connections induce co-operations, which constitute materialization of collective intelligence (Stremtan 2008, p. 10)".

Furthermore, the author refers to collective intelligence as "the capacity of an organization, of a collective to ask questions and to seek the answers together" (Stremtan 2008, p. 10). Concurrently, Tom Atlee's proposes a holistic, inclusive perspective of what co-intelligence is: "intelligence that takes wholeness, interconnectedness, co-creativity and participation seriously. Co-intelligence is collective, collaborative, synergistic, wise, empathic, heartful, and connected to greater sources of intelligence. It is often marked by how creatively it uses dissonance and diversity." (Atlee 2017, pp. 80–81). Therefore, a co-intelligent city would be grounded on democratic participatory practices, oriented by public wisdom and citizen-led politics and driven by social activism.

These visions, based in interconnectedness and participation, seem crucial to frame both the managerial and the communicative approaches—inspired in participatory and community communication—to territories in the contemporary.

Moreover, discussions on the concept of the city and the right to the city point towards a similar direction: a smart city is a communicative city. And is mostly defined by its citizens.

"The terms global city, smart city, connected city, sustainable city, inclusive city, and green city all encapsulate the collective value placed on a location where many people live and work. All these terms are both descriptive and normative of a reality based upon a gathering of people located in close proximity. A city consists of structures and services, but a city without people is simply an inanimate shell—a dead space. People and their needs define a city" (Drucker and Gumpert 2016, p. 1366).

2.2 Territorial Communication and City Rankings

Braga has currently about 181,000 inhabitants, with 57.8% of the population aged Territorial communication is intrinsic to the city's definition. Through communication the city as to think, project and question it-self on what it wants to communicate, how it wants to be perceived, why and what it wants to communicate. This is essentially strategic thinking, transversal throughout the communication interaction in the construction of the city's brand, image, reputation and symbolic value (Kavaratzis 2019; Kavaratzis and Kalandides 2015; Melo 2018, 2019; Papp-Váry 2011), hence, in the construction of its own identity (Anholt 2007; Ingenhoff et al. 2019).

"Besides the material capabilities of cities, how well they are able to brand themselves plays a large part in their success. The number of tourists, investors, new inhabitants, or the products of the city depend on the success of this self-branding. It also affects the locals and their sense of pride and contentment living in the city. Fortunately for cities, more and more brand models and rankings are available to assess their standing among others in respect to image and to reveal their comparative shortcomings" (Papp-Váry 2011, p. 555).

Territory provides a rich field for research, summoning a diversity of perspectives, including geography, public diplomacy, business and management, social psychology, sociology, urbanism and planning, political communication and communication science, demanding a transdisciplinary approach (Buhmann et al. 2019).

Territorial communication models have been developed and refined to serve the strategic communication of places (Anholt 2007; Buhmann et al. 2019; Kavaratzis 2019; Papp-Váry 2011). The most popular and recognized territorial communication model is certainly Simon Anholt's hexagon. This seminal model created to frame nation-brand communication was later adapted to cities. Also known as de "P's model" is based on five categories: Presence, Place, Pre-requisites, People, Pulse and Potential (Kirchener 2018, p. 2). Such models serve as inspiration for the setting of territorial indexes although open to systematic improvement, as "the challenges of combining the appeal of a holistic approach (…) with the necessity of specific measurement tools have not as yet been solved" (Merkelsen and Rasmussen 2019, p. 81).

Territorial rankings have been established—and used—for a number of reasons, assessment and competiveness being the most obvious ones (Drucker and Gumpert 2016; Merkelsen and Rasmussen 2019; Newburry and Song 2019). They are part of the strategic ammunition territorial managers, communication experts, politicians, urban planners and decision makers in general use to promote, enhance and add value to their nations, regions and cities. They use it to assess territories attractiveness—both theirs and their competitors, thus promoting territorial competitiveness (Chourabi et al. 2012; Giffinger et al. 2010), motivating and rewarding their teams performance, and establishing tangible strategic objectives.

Referring to nation branding attraction conditions, Merkelsen and Rasmussen argue that indexes "serve as catalyst for creating these conditions" (Merkelsen and Rasmussen 2019, p. 77) and they specify three: "a reputational logic (…) a state of competition (…) a simple solution to a complex challenge" (Merkelsen and Rasmussen 2019, pp. 77–79). They conclude by noticing the paradox that what "renders the nation brands index inappropriate as a tool for governments is the exact same quality that makes these rankings attractive to them" (Merkelsen and Rasmussen 2019, p. 81). These paradoxical characteristics seem to fit also the case of city indexes.

There are all types of rankings highlighting economic features, assessing developing metrics, cultural drivers, wellbeing, happiness, participation, transparency, governance and sustainability (Cabannes 2019; McArthur and Robin 2019; Meijering et al. 2014; Okulicz-Kozaryn 2013; Yigitcanlar and Inkinen 2019).

"The proliferation of criteria has led to the propagation of rankings and award programs allowing cities to proudly advertise their recognition as: livable, clean, large, sustainable, green, healthy, and slow. Awards recognize projects, vision, design, and research" (Drucker and Gumpert 2016, p. 1369).

Giving a meaning to data seems to be one of the outcomes and objectives of territorial rankings. Although some criteria might be fairly clear and objective such as the existence of a public transport network or public health care, other criteria such as the level of censorship or corruption might be more difficult to grasp. If aggregating data might be useful to understand some metrics, disaggregating them is frequently the fastest track to understand how narratives around territories are directed, i.e., if a city ranks good in a public health network assessment, does not mean that there is actual access from the population to that resource. Thus, when assessing a ranking, is important to mine the sources, the methods and interpretations offered to that data.

Marsal-Llacuna, Colomer-Llinàs and Meléndez-Frigola focused their work on establishing a set of criteria assembled in "a synthetic indicator to summarize a city's "intelligence" or "smartness"" (Marsal-Llacuna et al. 2015, p. 612). They draw attention towards the need to have physical and non-physical urban data, as much real time as possible, and highlight the need to produce comparable indicators with other rankings. More specifically, the authors insist on the "the need for an "intelligent index" to monitor the Smart Cities initiative" (Marsal-Llacuna et al. 2015, p. 620).

Rankings themselves are object of rating. The Branding Institute CMR, set up a methodology to evaluate rankings based on four criteria: "Relevance & Impact of Ranking; Added Value & Insights of Ranking; Trustworthiness & Intention of Ranking provider and media outlet and Methodology of Ranking" (Casanova et al. 2018).

Nevertheless, being commonly accepted as communication tools central to reputation and image management, territorial rankings have been criticized for being prone to instrumentalization and manipulation. Indexes are "more rhetorical than scientific as they primarily serve purposes of legitimization and persuasion" (Merkelsen and Rasmussen 2019, p. 80). Critique draws mostly on the fact that rankings are both being data driven vs people driven, elitist vs communal—"City rankings are a window onto the projected tastes of a highly specific elite" (O' Sullivan 2019), promoting mainly private interests instead of territorial ones, thus not representing the real life of the city: "it seems mistaken to present all cities as simple clusters of amenities, not when access to them is being subtly discouraged by broader social trends or actively denied to certain groups" (O'Sullivan 2019).

With a provocative tittle—"The Top 6 Reasons to Be Wary of City Rankings, Ranked"—Aarian Marshall draws attention to the controversial and unavoidable issues surrounding the topic of territorial rankings: "Different rankings measure totally different things. (…) Not all cities were included. (…) Some rankings measure reputation—not reality. (…) Some data is hard to find … (…) … While some data is just silly. (…) They're probably trying to sell you something" (Marshall 2015). These factors seem to set a sound starting point to inspire further research.

3   Research and Methodological Approach

Nowadays, school buses are seen as an innovative, sustainable alternative in urban Following the above considerations, conceptual framing and state of the art on the subject of territorial rankings a concern emerged: Are citizens represented and participating in city rankings? What is their role in the construction of city rankings narratives?

To find possible answers to this main research question, we set the following objectives: **to map scoring and categories** in city rankings; to **identify eventual citizen representational and/or participatory criteria**; to **critically reflect on** city rankings **purposes, meanings and objectives**.

The methodology used is qualitative and relies on hermeneutical interpretation and content analysis of three recognised city rankings: **City Brands Index 2017 (CBI), 2018 Global Cities Report (GCR)**, and **Global Liveability Index 2018 (GLI).**

The choice of these rankings was determined by notoriety on the Google research engine, but also by updating, access, availability and relevance. CBI – City Brands Index 2017 is an iconic city ranking, heir of the first incursions in territorial communication models, GCR – 2018 Global Cities Report, was selected for its broad scope and Global Liveability Index 2018 in order to include liveability criteria to the research, in an effort to eventually better representing citizens' insights on the cities.

The content analysis focused on the explicit categories published by each ranking to frame the data collected. Methodological explanation and transparency was also taken into account.

4   Results and Discussion

The three selected city rankings content was scrutinized in order to comparatively assess: the scope and methodology used; the cities that reached the top 10 scores, the categories proposed by these rankings to assemble data in a meaning making narrative, and the representation/participation of citizens.

4.1   The Rankings: Scope and Methodology

The CBI – City Brands Index 2017 is also identified as the "Anholt-GfK City Brands IndexSM (CBISM)". This index inherits the knowledge work ground of Simon Anholt's—both the Nation Brands Index and the City Brands Index were pioneering in 2005, "is run once every two years and measures the image of 50 cities" (Kirchener 2018, p. 3) and is published by GfK – Growth from Knowledge, a consultancy and market research company. Data was collected from 20 September to 3 October 2017 through "5,057 interviews across 10 countries (Australia, Brazil, China, France, Germany, India, Russia, South Korea, UK, and USA), with at least 500 interviews per country (…) The achieved sample in each country is weighted to reflect key demographic characteristics including age, gender, and education of the online population in that country" (Kirchener 2018, p. 3).

Six key dimensions are taken into account to rank cities in this index: "Presence (the city's international status and standing); Place (its physical outdoors aspect and transport); Prerequisites (basic requirements, such as affordable accommodations and the standard of public amenities); People (friendliness, cultural diversity, how safe one feels); Pulse (interesting things to do); Potential (the economic and educational opportunities available)" (Kirchener 2018, p. 2).

Results indicate the following ranking for the first 10 places: Paris, London, Sydney, New York, Los Angeles, Rome, Melbourne, Amsterdam, San Francisco and Berlin (Table 2). Nevertheless, links were provided to further contacts and information about the CBI – City Brands Index 2017, the index itself was not available, and the information provided was public only through press releases (Kirchener, 2018). People's insights (from 10 countries) are taken into account.

The GCR – 2018 Global Cities Report, published by A.T. Kearny, an American consultancy firm, "highlights regional trends revealed over the past decade and examines what defines the world's most influential cities" (Peterson et al. 2018, p. 1). It was established in 2008 assessing the performance of 60 cities. Based on the accumulated experience it position itself as going "beyond ranking cities (…) reveals which global cities are primed for urban transformation and growth" (Peterson et al. 2018, p. 1), exposing trends that indicate that nevertheless business activity, economics, information exchange and governance remain important criteria to score some points in the ranking, "human capital and cultural experience are also significant drivers of growth" (Peterson et al. 2018, p. 2).

The results are divided in two comparative strengths reports: the Global Cities Index, based on performance, and the Global Cities Outlook, based on potential. For this research we will take into account exclusively the Global Cities Index, centred in the current performance of cities.

This index analyses 135 cities worldwide, covering Africa (13), Asia Pacific (44), Europe (24), Latin America (15), North America (16) and Middle East (13). 27 variables grouped into a set of 5 weighted categories are considered to narrow the ranking score: "Business activity (capital flow market dynamics and major companies present); Human capital (education levels); Information exchange (access to information through internet and other media sources); Cultural experience (access to major sport events, museums, and other expos); Political engagement (political events, think tanks, and embassies)" (Peterson et al. 2018, p. 12). The first 10 cities (Table 2) in this ranking are: New York, London, Paris, Tokyo, Hong Kong, Los Angeles, Singapore, Chicago, Beijing, Brussels (Peterson et al. 2018, p. 13).

Methodology is explained in rather brief traits, more centred on how information is assembled and organised than on how it is actually collected, stating that "sources are derived from publicly available data" (Peterson et al. 2018, p. 12) and eventually substituted by country data if city data is not available.

The Global Liveability Index 2018, published by The Economist Intelligence Unit, states: "The concept of liveability is simple: it assesses which locations around the world provide the best or the worst living conditions. Assessing liveability has a broad range of uses, from benchmarking perceptions of development levels to assigning a hardship allowance as part of expatriate relocation packages" (EIU 2018, p. 7).

To find the most liveable cities of the world The Economist team analysed a number of complex variables (30) of 140 cities and aggregated them in 5 major metrics: stability, healthcare, culture and environment, education, and infrastructure (Abadi 2018).

Methodological processes are available and an explanatory chapter exposes how the rating is calculated, "For quantitative variables, a rating is calculated based on the relative performance of a location using external data sources" (EIU 2018, p. 8). However, the fact that "For qualitative variables, an "EIU rating" is awarded based on the judgment of in-house expert country analysts and a field correspondent based in each city" (EIU 2018, p. 8) reveals that the qualitative insight of this index is subject to personal sensibilities, however informed they may be, which may rise some concern over the credibility and impartiality of this kind of value judgment.

According to this index, the 10 most liveable cities in 2018 were Vienna, Melbourne, Osaka, Calgary, Sidney, Vancouver, Toronto, Tokyo, Copenhagen and Adelaide (Table 2).

Not surprisingly, some conclusions of the report account for "a correlation between the types of cities that sit at the very top of the ranking. Those that score best tend to be mid-sized cities in wealthier countries. Several cities in the top ten also have relatively low population density (…) foster a range of recreational activities without leading to high crime levels or overburdened infrastructure" (EIU 2018, p. 4). In parallel the index draws attention to the victims of success, "The "big city buzz" that they enjoy can overstretch infrastructure and cause higher crime rates. New York (57th), London (48th) and Paris (19th) are all prestigious hubs with a wealth of recreational activities, but all suffer from higher levels of crime, congestion and public transport problems than are deemed comfortable" (EIU 2018, p. 4). Nevertheless they seem to keep their attraction factor. "The question is how much wages, the cost of living and personal taste for a location can offset liveability factors" (EIU 2018, p. 4).

Comparatively, GCR – Global Cities Report 2018 (GCR) and The Global Liveability Index 2018 (GLI) cover an approximate number of cities worldwide, while CBI – City Brands Index 2017 (CBI) covers only 50 cities (Table 1). However, CBI is based on a qualitative assessment through online interviews intended to assess "the image" of the cities, whether GCR is grounded on publicly available data on 27 metrics and GLI uses a mixed methodology, based on quantitative data and qualitative assessment of experts (Table 1).

Table 1. City rankings' scope/method comparative analysis.

Publisher	Scope	Method
CBI – City Brands Index 2017		
Anholt-GfK	50 cities	5,057 online interviews in 10 countries; sample to reflect demographic reality
GCR – Global Cities Report 2018		
ATKearny	135 cities	Publicly available city data; 27 metrics;
The Global Liveability Index 2018		
The Economist Intelligent Unit	140 cities	30 qualitative and quantitative metrics

4.2 The Cities

An overview of the cities ranked in the top 10 positions in the different rankings analysed in this research reflect a diversity of assessments, exposing that the best city images, the best city performances and the most liveable cities in the world do not necessarily match (Table 2).

Actually, there is not any city that occupies one of the 10 top positions in all the three rankings. The best possible match appears to be London (number 2 in two rankings); present in two rankings but in diverse positions stand six cities (Los Angeles,

Melbourne, New York, Paris, Sydney, Tokyo); and present in only one ranking are 16 cities (Adelaide, Amsterdam, Beijing, Berlin, Brussels, Calgary, Chicago, Copenhagen, Hong Kong, Osaka, Rome, San Francisco, Singapore, Toronto, Vancouver, Vienna).

There seems to be a prevalence of big cities, geographically concentrated in Europe (8), North America (7) and Asia-Pacific (7).

Table 2. City rankings' top 10 cities comparative analysis

2017 CBI – City Brands Index	2018 GCR – Global Cities Report	The Global Liveability Index 2018
1. Paris	1. New York	1. Vienna
2. London	2. London	2. Melbourne
3. Sydney	3. Paris	3. Osaka
4. New York	4. Tokyo	4. Calgary
5. Los Angeles	5. Hong Kong	5. Sidney
6. Rome	6. Los Angeles	6. Vancouver
7. Melbourne	7. Singapore	7. Toronto
8. Amsterdam	8. Chicago	8. Tokyo
9. San Francisco	9. Beijing	9. Copenhagen
10. Berlin	10. Brussels	10. Adelaide

Concerning city image (CBI), Europe gets the most (5), followed by North America (3) and Asia-Pacific (2). The most performative cities (GCR) are mainly in Asia-Pacific (4), followed ex-aequo by Europe (3) and North America (3). Regarding the best cities to live (GLI), Asia-Pacific seems to offer more (5), followed by North America (3) and Europe (2).

4.3   The Categories

Analysing comparatively the city rankings' content is an attempt to find patterns that might produce further knowledge. Therefore, in this case, we will try to categorise the city rankings' categories.

A general overview portrays an apparent mismatch of the three city rankings at stake, pulverized in a diversified set of categories (Table 3).

CBI presents data on the image of 50 cities aggregated in presence, place, prerequisites, people, pulse and potential. Since it is based on interviews it reflects the perceptions people have on cities, whether they live there, visited the cities or not. To a certain extend it is a ranking of impressions that were constructed by direct experience, by the media, by cultural acknowledgement of the place and forged through accumulated reputational capital.

GCR reflects a mix of business activity, human capital, information exchange, cultural experience, and political engagement, whereas GLI categorises cities over stability, healthcare, culture and environment, education, infrastructure.

The first layer of analysis exposes two sets of categories: tangible—such as "business activity", "infrastructure" or "information exchange"—and intangible—such as "pulse" or "potential".

In a second layer we can find some common concepts or words that might qualify as categories. For example: culture, education, economics, environment, health or politics. They all seem important factors to assess a city.

The analysis gets more complex when we try to understand more deeply the semantics of these categories. What does "stability", "pulse" or "political engagement" mean? A "steady job"? The "vibe of economic growth"? The "activist output" of a city? According to the research, stability is the "prevalence of petty and/or violent crime; threat of terror, military conflict and/or of civil unrest/conflict"(GLI); pulse are "interesting things to do" (CBI) on a city and political engagement includes "political events, think tanks, and embassies" (GCR).

The examples above, exploratory as they are, expose the assumption that although categories are useful to aggregate data and produce a narrative, they but might be misleading to understand data and, without proper contextualisation, may mean literally anything.

Categories are a form of simplification and aggregation of complex data in order to make it intelligible, usable and meaningful. From all parameters of the present research this is the one where the strategic intentions of the city ranking producers might be more evident, as setting categories is an immediate form of interpreting reality, and therefore an attempt to control it.

Categories and the selection of criteria they entail are also indexed to the agenda setting of city rankings production. The case of GLI is quite illustrative. Published by The Economist Intelligent Unit is promoted as a Global Liveability City Index but was designed as a tool "to help companies decide how much "hardship" allowance they would need to pay employees who relocate (...) focuses on things that matter to expats, not citizens" (Rozek et al. 2018). But this is not a hidden agenda. The GLI explains that "assessing liveability has a broad range of uses, from benchmarking perceptions of development levels to assigning a hardship allowance as part of expatriate relocation packages (...) quantifies the challenges that might be presented to an individual's lifestyle in any given location, and allows for direct comparison between locations" (EIU 2018, p. 7). Nevertheless, widespread short versions of the city index, namely as catchy titles in media about new winners and losers (McArthur and Robin 2019), frequently make this agenda invisible, adding up to other critics, on lack of transparency: "It appears that, beyond the well-designed league tables and flurry of media attention, The Economist's Global Liveability Index is a mostly subjective rating with opaque methods for comparing cities (Rozek et al. 2018).

Therefore, to fully understand what a city ranking stands for, it is crucial to go deep into strategic and methodological explanations (when and if they are available).

4.4 The Citizen Representation/Participation

The issue of citizen representation and participation poses methodological challenges. Not only due to the above-mentioned difficulties on tracking data collecting processes and sources, but also due to the fact that citizens are embedded in the notion of the city.

Table 3. City rankings' categories comparative analysis.

Categories

CBI – City Brands Index 2017

- Presence (the city's international status and standing);
- Place (its physical outdoors aspect and transport);
- Pre-requisites (basic requirements, such as affordable accommodations and the standard of public amenities);
- People (friendliness, cultural diversity, how safe one feels);
- Pulse (interesting things to do);
- Potential (the economic and educational opportunities available)

GCR – Global Cities Report 2018

- Business activity (capital flow market dynamics and major companies present)
- Human capital (education levels)
- Information exchange (access to information through internet and other media sources)
- Cultural experience (access to major sport events, museums, and other expos)
- Political engagement (political events, think tanks, and embassies)

The Global Liveability Index 2018

- Stability (prevalence of petty and/or violent crime; threat of terror, military conflict and/or of civil unrest/conflict)
- Healthcare (availability and quality of private/public healthcare; availability of over-the-counter drugs; general healthcare indicators)
- Culture and environment (humidity/temperature rating; discomfort of climate to travellers; level of corruption and censorship; social or religious restrictions; sporting and cultural availability; food & drink; consumer goods & services
- Education (availability and quality of private education; public education indicators)
- Infrastructure (quality of road network, public transport; international links; energy provision; energy and water provision; and telecommunications; availability of good quality housing)

In the comparative analysis of the three city indexes is possible to observe indirect and direct representation and participation of citizens.

We would consider indirect representation/participation are present in variables related with citizens' actions and behaviours that contribute to construct the state of the city, such as "prevalence of petty and/or violent crime" (GLI); "level of corruption and censorship" (GLI) or "friendliness" (CBI).

Direct citizen representation/participation can be observed in the instrumental contribution of interviewer's opinions in the construction of city rankings, as in the case of CBI – City Brands Index. However, this direct participation is an indirect representation, if representational at all, because in the case of CBI the interviews were applied in 10 countries to assess the image of 50 cities, that do not necessarily coincide with a direct, living experience of the cities included in the ranking.

5   Conclusion

Throughout this reflective exploratory research, we aimed at finding whether city rankings, as assessing and promoting territorial communication tools, take the citizens into account, embedded in the notion of a smart city made by and for the citizens, grounded on communal capital and collective knowledge.

Conclusions point out that, **as city representation, city rankings prove to be reductive, frequently misleading,** and—although based on citizen status statistics, often collected from publicly available data, **tend not to embed citizen participation and insights,** thus exposing a representational and participatory gap. We would argue that, in order to effectively represent cities, as they are lived, thought and built by their citizens in their everyday, city rankings must rely in more real-time, updated, people's perception centred data, and embed more citizen participation and insights.

Although generally accepted and widespread through the media as assessing reports of the state of cities, city ranking's value seems to be strategically communicational and enhanced by its news worthy value. City rankings are (and set) opportunity to communicate, therefore can be seen and used more because of their value as promotional tools rather than because of their scientific input relevance.

This does not necessarily question sound scientific procedures in data collection of reputed organisations that contribute to knowledge. Actually, methodological processes within this research were briefly explained but not fully disclosed. Nor was this the main focus of the investigation. Nevertheless, more transparency and accountability of city ranking promoters might add to trust and credibility and more trans-disciplinary teams might enrich the insight and scope of city rankings.

Rather paradoxically, it seems to be not mainly the methodological design, but the use that is made of city rankings that puts city rankings at stake.

It is commonly accepted that city rankings contribute to construct meaning and add value to the cities, enhancing performance and competition. Notwithstanding we found that incomparable, out-dated or poor data that is simplified for the sake of understanding, measuring and controlling territorial realities, serves frequently as ground for assessment, thus establishing a rhetorical construct that does not mirror reality but a propagated through the media and commonly accepted narrative. Categories are a form of simplification and aggregation of complex data in order to make it intelligible, usable and meaningful. From all parameters of the present research this is the one where the strategic intentions of the city ranking producers might be more evident, as setting categories is an immediate form of interpreting reality, and therefore an attempt to control it, not necessarily to assess it.

Furthermore, the political economy of city rankings must be considered when assessing city rankings. Studying data costs money and the three cases we studied are designed and promoted by private organizations, however reputed, with their own agenda. Therefore, as powerful medicines, city rankings should be used with care and critical insight.

A final note on the limitations of the present reflection, based on an exploratory research: we believe further and larger scope investigation might produce different results. Next steps in research would go through more specific rankings and criteria, eventually to direct citizen perceptions—such as liveability, sustainability or happiness—and participation—such as activism, political involvement, direct deliberation. Both directions might produce a city ranking that reflects a city as it is lived and idealised by the citizens.

References

Abadi, M.: The 10 most livable cities in the world in 2018, 25 August 2018. Business Insider. https://www.businessinsider.nl/most-livable-cities-in-the-world-2018-8/

Anholt, S.: Competitive Identity: The New Brand Management for Nations, Cities and Regions. Palgrave Macmillan, Basingstoke (2007)

Atlee, T.: Participatory Sustainability – Notes for an Emerging Field of Civilizational Engagement. CreateSpace, Co-Inteligence Institute, Eugene (2017)

Atlee, T.: The Tao of Democracy: Using Co-Intelligence to Create a World That Works for All. North Atlantic Books, Berkeley (2014)

Atlee, T.: Empowering Public Wisdom: A Practical Vision of Citizen-Led Politics, vol. 4. North Atlantic Books, Berkeley (2012)

Buhmann, A., Ingenhoff, D., White, C., Kiousis, S.: Charting the landscape in research on country image, reputation, brand, and identity. In: Ingenhoff, D., White, C., Buhmann, A., Kiousis, S. (eds.) Bridging Disciplinary Perspectives of Country Image, Reputation, Brand, and Identity, pp. 1–10. Routledge, New York (2019)

Cabannes, Y.: Another City is Possible with Participatory Budgeting. University of Chicago Press Economics Books, Chicago (2019)

https://placebrandobserver.com/smart-cities-how-ict-impacts-urban-development-representation/

Cardullo, P., Kitchin, R.: Being a 'citizen' in the smart city: up and down the scaffold of smart citizen participation in Dublin, Ireland. GeoJournal 84(1), 1–13 (2019). https://doi.org/10.1007/s10708-018-9845-8

Casanova, M., Renner, M., Bielenstein, T.: Ranking of the Rankings, Rating the Rankings, in Branding Institute CMR homepage (2018) https://www.branding-institute.com/rating-the-rankings/ranking-of-the-rankings. Accessed 30 July 2019

Chourabi, H., et al.: Understanding smart cities: an integrative framework. In: 45th Hawaii International Conference on System Sciences, 4–7 January 2012. IEEE (2012)

Dameri, R.P.: Searching for smart city definition: a comprehensive proposal. Int. J. Comput. Technol. 11(5), 2544–2551 (2013)

Drucker, S., Gumpert, G.: The communicative City Redux, international. J. Commun. 10(2016), 1366–1387 (2016)

EIU: The Global Liveability Index 2018 A free overview, Economist Intelligence Unit (2018). http://www.eiu.com/Handlers/WhitepaperHandler.ashx?fi=The_Global_Liveability_index_2018.pdf&mode=wp&campaignid=Liveability2018. Accessed 12 Aug 2019

Giffinger, R., Haindlmaier, G., Kramar, H.: The role of rankings in growing city competition. Urban Res. Pract. 3(3), 299–312 (2010)

Hollands, R.G.: Will the real smart city please stand up? Intelligent, progressive or entrepreneurial? City 12(3), 303–320 (2008). https://doi.org/10.1080/13604810802479126

Ingenhoff, D., White, C., Buhmann, A., Kiousis, S. (eds.): Bridging Disciplinary Perspectives of Country Image, Reputation, Brand, and Identity. Routledge, New York (2019)

Kavaratzis, M.: City Branding. In: The Wiley Blackwell Encyclopedia of Urban and Regional Studies, pp. 1–4 (2019)

Kavaratzis, M., Kalandides, A.: Rethinking the place brand: the interactive formation of place brands and the role of participatory place branding. Environ. Plan. A 47(6), 1368–1382 (2015)

Kirchener, C.: Paris continues its reign as highest-rated city, Press Release, 30 January 2018. Anholt-GfK (2018). https://www.gfk.com/fileadmin/user_upload/dyna_content/Global/documents/Press_Releases/2018/20180130_PM_CBI_2017_efin.pdf. Accessed 3 Aug 2019

Maddox, T.: Smart cities: a cheat sheet, TechRepublic, Innovation, 16 July 2018. https://www.techrepublic.com/article/smart-cities-the-smart-persons-guide/. Accessed 3 Aug 2019

Marsal-Llacuna, M.L., Colomer-Llinàs, J., Meléndez-Frigola J.: Lessons in urban monitoring taken from sustainable and livable cities to better address the Smart Cities initiative. Technol. Forecast. Soc. Chang. **90**(Part B), 611–622 (2015). https://www.sciencedirect.com/sdfe/reader/pii/S0040162514000456/pdf. Accessed 16 Aug 2019 (2015)

Marshall, A.: The Top 6 Reasons to Be Wary of City Rankings, Ranked, CityLab 20 May 2015 (2015). https://www.citylab.com/life/2015/05/the-top-6-reasons-to-be-wary-of-city-rankings/393686/. Accessed 14 Aug 2019

Martin, C.J., Evans, J., Karvonen, A.: Smart and sustainable? Five tensions in the visions and practices of the smart-sustainable city in Europe and North America. Technol. Forecast. Soc. Chang. **133**, 269–278 (2018)

McArthur, J., Robin, E.: Victims of their own (definition of) success: urban discourse and expert knowledge production in the Liveable City. Urban Stud. **56**(9), 1711–1728 (2019)

Meijering, J.V., Kern, K., Tobi, H.: Identifying the methodological characteristics of European green city rankings. Ecol. Indic **43**, 132–142 (2014)

Melo, A.D.: A Marca dos Cidadãos: Intervenção, Ocupação e Subversão na Paisagem Publicitária Urbana. In: Pires , H., Mesquita, F. (eds.) Publi-Cidade e Comunicação visual urbana, pp. 61–89. CECS, Braga (2018)

Melo, A.D.: "Somos todos smart?": co-inteligência, comunicação e sustentabilidade territorial. In: Abreu, J. (ed.) Inteligência Territorial - Governança, Sustentabilidade e Transparência, Idioteque (2019)

Merkelsen, H., Rasmussen, R.K.: Evaluation of nation brand indexes. In: Ingenhoff, D., White, C., Buhmann, A., Kiousis, S. (eds.) Bridging Disciplinary Perspectives of Country Image, Reputation, Brand, and Identity, pp. 69-84. Routledge, New York (2019)

Newburry, W., Song, M.: Nation branding, product-country images, and country rankings. In: Ingenhoff, D., White, C., Buhmann, A., Kiousis, S. (eds.) Bridging Disciplinary Perspectives of Country Image, Reputation, Brand, and Identity, pp. 49–68. Routledge, New York (2019)

O' Sullivan, F.: Death to Livability! CityLab, 26 June 2019 (2019). https://www.citylab.com/life/2019/06/best-cities-to-live-list-monocle-ranking-zurich-vienna/592492/. Accessed 14 Aug 2019

Okulicz-Kozaryn, A.: City life: rankings (livability) versus perceptions (satisfaction). Soc. Indic. Res. **110**(2), 433–451 (2013)

Papp-Váry, Á.: The Anholt-GMI city brand hexagon and the saffron European city brand barometer: a comparative study. Reg. Bus. Stud. **3**(Suppl 1), 555–562 (2011)

Peterson, E.R., Hales, M., Peña, A.M., Dessibourg-Freer, N.: 2018 Global Cities Report - Learning from the East: Insights from China's Urban Success. A. T. Kearney (2018)

Rizzon, F., Bertelli, J., Matte, J., Graebin, R.E., Macke, J.: Smart City: um conceito em construção. Revista Metropolitana de Sustentabilidade **7**(3), 123–142 (2017). ISSN 2318-3233

Rozek, J., Giles-Corti, B., Gunn, L.: The world's 'most liveable city' title isn't a measure of the things most of us actually care about, The Conversation Trust (UK) Limited, August 15, 2018 7.18am BST (2018). http://theconversation.com/the-worlds-most-liveable-city-title-isnt-a-measure-of-the-things-most-of-us-actually-care-about-101525. Acceded 20 Aug 2019

Stremtan, F.: Some consideration regarding collective intelligence. In: 6th Annual International Conference of Territorial Intelligence, "Tools and Methods of Territorial Intelligence", p. 10, October 2008

Vanolo, A.: Smartmentality: the smart city as disciplinary strategy. Urban Stud. **51**(5), 883–898 (2014)

Yigitcanlar, Tan, Inkinen, Tommi: Benchmarking City Performance. Geographies of Disruption, pp. 159–197. Springer, Cham (2019). https://doi.org/10.1007/978-3-030-03207-4_12

Zhang, F., et al.: Privacy-aware smart city: a case study in collaborative filtering recommender systems. J. Parallel Distrib. Comput. **127**, 145–159 (2019)

Mobility Time Style: For an Integrated View of Time and Mobility in Societies with a Future

Catarina Sales Oliveira[1,2] (ID) and Emília Araújo[3](✉) (ID)

[1] University of Beira Interior, Covilhã, Portugal
catarinasalesoliveira@gmail.com
[2] Centre for Research and Studies in Sociology, University of Lisbon, Lisbon, Portugal
[3] Communication and Society Research Centre, University of Minho, Braga, Portugal
emiliarrajo@gmail.com

Abstract. This paper aims (i) to demonstrate the relevance of deepening the study of time usage from the individual and family perspectives and (ii) to put in dialog perceptions and uses of time with daily mobility patterns. It is increasingly imperative to consider mobility and the uses of time as central axes of lifestyles, highlighting the weight of several variables in the definition of lifestyle choices, namely transportation options. This reflection is based on an empirical study carried out in Portugal through interviews in the metropolitan areas of Lisbon and Porto. The analysis leads to the conclusion that, in addition to physical distances people have to cover, the choice of specific means of transportation is strongly dependent on the perceptions and uses of time. It is also evident that time is simultaneously dependent on the way technologies are absorbed into daily life and that time remains a matter of constraint and social opportunity.

Keywords: Mobility · Time · Styles · Lifestyle

1 Introduction

An increasing number of studies have given attention to the notion of quality of life [1] – especially wellbeing – when discussing mobility and travel within the context of modern cities [2, 3]. Most of these state that mobility practices and expectations have a strong impact on individuals and families' decisions and choices throughout their lives [2] conditioning the ways they use time and thereby being a component of people's lifestyles [4]. Authors [4] have claimed that the location of work activities is central in mobility as this strongly influences time use possibilities both in individual and collective terms and determines transportation means (type and forms of use). In this sense, several approaches to the city' spaces and times have fundamentally showed the effects of rationalization of both these dimensions. Later, in the context of globalization, migration and digitization of work further transformations in the form of organization and the spatial functioning of work emerge (each day increasingly more mobile and flexible) creating rather unpredictable configurations of uses of time and transportation.

P. Pereira et al. (Eds.): SC4Life 2019, LNICST 318, pp. 170–183, 2020.
https://doi.org/10.1007/978-3-030-45293-3_13

In Portugal, 42% of the national population lives in Lisbon and Porto metropolitan areas [5]. The development of these areas is intrinsically related to the process of urbanization: fuelled by the historic exodus from the inner country in the sixties of the last century, these cities are currently also experiencing a great wave of touristic influx. Presently, Lisbon hosts two million and eighty thousand active employees - about 27% of the national population [5]. Demographic changes happened in various locations around Lisbon over recent years. These are the cases of cities like Mafra, and Sesimbra which have grown exponentially. The growth in these places is an effect, among others, of the increasing use of private transport and the implementation of public infrastructures such as the river Tejo bridges [6]. This massive growth has gradually triggered the development of an urban continuum between Lisbon, Cascais, Sintra, Loures and Vila Franca de Xira on the north bank, and Sesimbra and Setúbal, on the south. Porto also shows a growth towards more distant places such as Póvoa de Varzim (north) and São João da Madeira (south) [7, 8].

This population growth into further places away from the cities is leading to increasing needs for transport, as the population needs to cover longer distances to access work, services, and other goods. Moreover, the lack of or the weakness of collective and public means of transportation, some of them reaching a rupture point (as happens with the boasts crossing the River Tejo) is leading to increasing use of private cars, which causes problems of traffic and congestion which negatively impact quality of life.

The questions of mobility are therefore complex insofar as poor political intervention concerning transportation solutions and living costs, together with increasing capitalist pressures over certain cities have consequences over people's individual lifestyles, impacting on quality of life. An integrated politics of space and time in the cities, perhaps by improving the technological facilities, would be a way of making cities available to all. An increasing number of studies have been giving attention to quality of life [5, 6] - especially wellbeing – when discussing mobility and travel relationship within the context of modern cities. Most of them state that mobility practices and expectations have a strong impact on individuals and families' decisions and choices throughout their lives [5, 6], the conditioning of the ways they use time thereby being a component of people's lifestyles.

This text explores the concepts of mobility and time within lifestyles, proposing the notion that increasingly, the analysis and the interventions on space – be they physical or digital – must include citizens' perceptions, values and uses of time. In fact, societies are increasingly digitally oriented, as more and more daily activities are accomplished digitally and have become, overall, ever more accelerated. However, citizens must individually deal with a multitude of different time constraints that are sociologically relevant, as they reveal unequal patterns of mobilities, as well as dissimilar accesses to means of mobility and technological trends. This, in course, leads to different uses of kinds of time or time styles (according to gender, age, social classes, and type of job), as well as different lifestyles, and mobility profiles.

2   The Importance of Mobility

There are manifold issues related to mobility and sustainability, particularly in the face of the problem of climate change and the development of adaptation and mitigation strategies that imply deepening the social processes of enormous relevance.

Mobility is a core issue for modern societies. Life choices are related to mobility behaviours and decisions, as each life choice seems to be linked to a specific set of mobility demands. As an example, decisions about work and home taken in a person's early twenties might not be desirable or feasible ten or twenty years later, when responding to family growth [9] or to the process of ageing. In a way, these decisions should all converge into a good life choice. In other words, if mobility has long been known as a feature of human groups, its expression in contemporary society takes on unexpected features that strongly impact society in different realms [10, 11]. International research on mobility has greatly increased in recent years.

Sheller and Urry came to the conclusion that mobility involves such different aspects of the individual and the social world that it actually can be understood as an analytical paradigm; the authors have clearly demonstrated its multidimensionality, thus taking into account the role of technology, cultural expressions and social expectations among other dimensions [12]. Eurostat reports indicate that in Portugal (alongside Norway) car usage is higher than that of the European average, representing 89.8% of the passenger transport [13–15]. The data and Eurostat [15] indicate that transport is one of the main sources of energy consumption in Europe and, as a result, private consumption reaches values close to consumption in industry. The transition roadmap for a competitive low-carbon economy in 2050 [15] stipulates a set of objectives to be achieved over the next 30 years regarding decarbonization, innovation and the adoption of green energy. But the data [16] also indicates that transport costs continue to increase, while the consumption of renewable energies in transport remains low [9]. These results match with the demonstrations of the IEA-International Energy Agency – according to which the consumption of biofuel in road transport will only increase by 1% in these 7 years (2015–2020)

Briefly, all this information helps to support the idea that, alongside any technical and/or scientific changes that involve mobility, displacement and the use of time, are variables and processes of cultural and social character that should be considered, either from the point of view of the positive effects they may cause, or looking to the consequences societies will have to deal with, in the near future, in order to build democratic access to mobility and transportation.

3   Mobilities, Lifestyles and Time Uses

The relation between lifestyles and mobility has been recently explored by Cohen et al. who propose that "lifestyles and forms of mobility increasingly co-mingle in ways that can be crucial to the lives of those who are privileged enough to access them" [4]. At its core, lifestyle is an intricate result of choices that encompasses space and time uses [17]. The connection between lifestyles and mobility supposes free choice and in that sense the concepts of mobilities, lifestyles, and hypermobility [4] are close to the concept of migration lifestyle. Lifestyle conceptualization implies considering the following elements/dimensions: job, housing, and family. It is true that jobs are no longer lifelong and moving (whether actually or virtually) is a main driving force in people's lives. However, the weight of these transformations introduces ever more variations on the patterns of the course of life [18] Therefore, these three usual milestones - work, housing and family - remain as structuring variables, even if only in a mid-term perspective.

Flamm and Kaufmann [19] have proposed that within a world which is becoming increasingly mobile, whilst some people have largely increased their potential for mobility or motility, other are strongly deprived of this ability that negatively affects their quality of life [20] with respect to this, the recent contribution of the concept of mobility justice is of interest. In sum, mobility and travel options cannot be disconnected from the complex web of choices and constraints that a life path is made of [18], being an integrant component of lifestyles. Additionally, behaviours concerning mobilities are initially linked to choices and constraints concerning patterns of using and experiencing time. Mobility requires discussions on time as it is a core element of a lifestyle [17, 21]. Time has been analysed in different scientific areas both as social object, as a resource and a source of meaning. Specifically, in sociology, besides the studies that addressed the connections between time and space [22, 23] researchers from different historical and sociological contexts state the relevance of time usage on people's lives. The assumption that working time is the dominant time that determines the feeling of fulfilment in other times of life, is a core topic of research, alongside increasing social acceleration and the ways it affects people's options and chances, impacting on all life spheres, including on mental and subjective wellbeing. More recently the sphere of work trends - increasing digitisation and automation, flexible working times, globalization and dislocation - have been responsible for the emergence of several new time orders and uses which affect, and in some cases collide with, family time, personal time, or leisure time. These changes have led to alterations in mobility patterns, including the means of transportations used. In fact, one of the reasons families often use the car and other private means of transportation is due to the accumulation of activities they must accomplish during the day, part of them with children and the need to accomplish these as fast as possible [24]. These changes have led to alterations in mobility patterns, including the means of transportations which are being used, and which are increasingly required to be more personalized and flexible. Extensive literature has analysed the expansion of the mobile society. Therefore, one of the pivotal reasons why families keep using the car is the accumulation of activities they must accomplish almost simultaneously along the day. This come to be especially acute in the cases when families must live far from workplaces, schools and health services, in response to the increase in housing prices.

For a general comprehension of the existing studies on mobility, we present the following Table 1:

Table 1. Some themes in the mobility studies and time uses [25]

Traditional themes	Emerging themes	Associated dilemmas and emerging issues
Transport network, timetables, routes and prices	Flexible collective transport Technological adaptation and transport use	Safety of children in parks, public spaces and dwellings
Network accessibility, timetables and circuits, population covered and excluded	Access and use of transport, and new social discriminations and exclusions	Noise pollution in housing areas, mental illnesses and school performance
Quality of services, stops and parking spaces	Speed, increased consumption and reduced rest time	Deadly and incapacitating road accidents
Security and accountability	Forced mobility, speed and fragmentation of family and personal times	Transportation of children, traffic intensity and security
Adequacy of infrastructures and signage adjusted to Mobilities, Lifestyles and choice of transports	Tourism, transport and circulation	Speed, transport and new social, gender and age exclusions
	Energy transition, transport and social values	Transportation, lifestyles and aspirations (school choices and children's extracurricular activities)
The value and consumption of cars	Safety and road coexistence Space-time representations and cognitions	Mental illness in children and young people, panic and time pressure
Circulation, infrastructure and convenience	Virtual time space and driving styles	Accessibility to transport and social exclusion
	Security and social inequality	"Green" energy and social inequality in Access
	Sustainability, gender, climate change and energy	Energy transition, low carbon economy and new inequalities
		Flexibility in the transport network, notably as regards stops and socio-demographic profile of the public.

3.1 Bringing Together Mobility and Time to Understand Mobility Time Styles

In accordance with the above explanation, we can say that the concept of mobility time lifestyles involves three types of elements: present settlements and places of activity (house, work, leisure, family activities); time and duration of (in)activity (day/week/years; morning/afternoon/evening; working day/weekend/vacations, etc.);

and the motivations underlying these activities (inscribed in social and economic constraints and/or emerging from an individual decision). The concept allows overcoming the usual binary readings dealing with how these times and spaces interweave with each other in a certain configuration, while keeping flexibility and diversity in mind. To operationalize the concept, it is necessary to study two main dimensions: (i) the elements concerning what people do and how they do it with regards to time, space and mobility as well as what value - material and symbolic - they attribute to it (linked to subjective and objective class indicators); and (ii) the elements related to people's disposition to face decisions concerning time, space and mobility and its management (mostly linked to subjective class indicators, also inscribed in professional cultures) incorporating the dynamism or mobility of these decisions. Therefore, it is possible to consider that mobility and time lifestyles are result of the intercrossing between three main dimensions: (i) the degree of time-space standardization, (ii) the degree of time-space stability, and (iii) the degree of time-space (self-) coordination.

Each of those dimensions reflect a joint imbricated result between values and practices which imply time, space, and mobility issues.

This paper provides an analysis of two main kinds of mobility time, or "time styles" according to data collected from the study done in the cities of Lisbon and Porto, in Portugal.

4 Method

This research involved 31 in-depth interviews with people who live and work inside of the two Portuguese metropolitan areas of Lisbon and Porto. A purposive sample was employed, choosing people with different family profiles, and distinct working time regimes. The interviews were made throughout one year using an interview grid, which integrated questions intersecting time, space, mobility and lifestyles topics. The interviews were used to collect information about many dimensions concerning mobility and time uses. In this paper the objective is to use the information to stress the strength of argument calling for better understanding of the sociological and comprehensive aspects of time and space appropriations.

Therefore, information was analysed according to the aforesaid themes currently studied: (i) the degree of time-space standardization, (ii) the degree of time-space stability, and (iii) the degree of time-space (self-) coordination. Data about the interviewees socioeconomic profile, gender, age and other information is displayed in the annex.

5 Findings and Reflections

5.1 Profile 1: Liminal and Adjusted Mobility Time Lifestyle

The most relevant and shared feature of this profile emerging across interviews, is the way people mobilize strategies to cope with demands without having to break social rules or give up specific roles/desires. This profile therefore combines high levels of standardization with high levels of desire for stability, and in turn, lower levels of self-coordination of time and space. This style prevails among those interviewees with small children and other dependents, those who undertake more rigid routines. Here, routines play a fundamental role, as it becomes mandatory to have rigidly observed daily plans, linked to the schedules and mobility needs of other family members (children, spouse, etc.). For this section of the population, diaries and calendars are central, so that daily routines can be defined in advance. Therefore, the people exhibiting this profile type seek to control time and travel, and to manage these in a stable way. Whether using public or private transportation, this section of the population needs to have control over space and time (and distance) to ascertain their lives. The following quote is an account by an interviewee relating how predictability allows her to conciliate work and family spheres:

"Compared with the past, when I was always arriving home after 10pm, my current life is better, less stressed. I was [working] in the commercial business back then. [Now] I feel [I have] a shortage of time but that's no big deal, it's normal, everyone would like to have more things done. Now, with this [current] job, I have a stable routine, and I find this is very good and necessary when one has children. I was lucky to have always had a good support network." (Dianna, 38, mother of one, economist)

The following excerpt highlights how daily time is deeply dependent on children's mobility and time needs, in a rigid manner:

"I synchronize my time with that of my two children, 18 and 21 years old [boys], who study Law and History in Lisbon. We always come to and from the station together; sometimes we need to pick the eldest one up at 9pm from the station since there is no decent public transportation to take him home. Our household spends three [daily] hours in transit. I sleep very little." (Kate, 42, mother of two, lawyer)

This prevalent idea about the need to interconnect different mobility needs in a stable way within the same negotiations with time inside the family sphere appears to have a correspondence with individual and family needs at certain moments of their lives as well as with the way people look to their future needs.

For this group, having a car is central as it ensures the possibility of being mobile and arriving at required destinations rapidly. In almost all cases, anxiety and feelings of time pressure come associated with mobility needs. At first sight, this mobility time style can be associated with a low level of individual time-space coordination and a high level of stability, in the sense that people tend to search for steadiness, trying hard to have and maintain a life with a certain degree of stability. They tend to apply space-time discipline also to biographical paths, as they decide whether to undertake, anticipate, or postpone events, considering, in their decisions, the very nature of family members' mobility needs and prospects. In so doing, they also prioritize needs and desires on the scale of their lifetime. The next excerpt provides evidence of the high degree of importance that a time-space-mobility routine may have, thereby reinforce how crucial it can be to structure mobility time styles:

"For sixteen years now that we spend vacations in the same place, at the same time, in August. This year will be the same. I like it very much." (Kevin, 58, father of one, rail infrastructure manager).

5.2   Profile 2: Liminal and Extempore Mobility Time Lifestyle

This profile differs from the previous one as it combines high levels of self-coordination of time and space with elevated levels of stability, even when the individual is faced with high levels of unpredictability. This profile refers to individuals and families that reveal a great need to introduce levels of unexpected activities during the day, without being strict about the need to respect a certain time guideline. There are moments of time/space that can be interchanged in all spheres of life including domestic chores. What distinguishes those who match this style is the wiliness to develop actions without a focus in their planning. In some cases, there is some level of disorganization, while in others it is mainly a matter of flexibility and adaptability. This profile reflects the predominance of flexible working hours with a need to be mobile and often to adapt time demands. Nevertheless, there were also people with flexible working hours within the previous profile, however what differs is their attitude towards this flexibility. Below is a quote of one of the interviewees who shares this mobility time style:

"There is no consistency in my time, although there is a seasonal pattern at work, but there is [consistency] in [some of] my daily activities. I have breakfast relatively early at home, I make calls while I'm in route, I have lunch at the same place [every day], etc. I do not have a regular weekly schedule; I work more frequently during weekends. The concept of free time is something that I do not use because my professional and private lives are very mixed; I am always trying to enjoy holidays [while] combining business and social relationships [which] are in the same group." (David, 58, businessman)

Interestingly, people within this profile share one same distinctive feature: they work in arears that demand flexible time-space arrangements. Much more than those who belong to the previous group, these people also relate difficulties in planning their lives, and their work is consequently thought to be potentially less stable. Thus, they also show less availability to plan or anticipate future choices concerning their mobility prospect. One should note, however, that although some of these interviewees advocate time-space mobility, which is secured by the intense use of cars, they express the willingness to have the possibility to better anticipate their life choices and to be able to plan such choices in a medium time range. In other words, much of the interviewees in this profile would strongly appreciate having more ability to think and plan the future, even though they have different degrees of autonomy to coordinate and master time and space movements. Here, it is relevant to point out that most interviewees are conscientious of the degree of precariousness as well as uncertainty that permeate their lives' choices (mostly those working in the private sector, without working contracts, divorced, and/or with dependent small children).

6   Discussion

The two profiles differ with regards to sociodemographic characteristics.

The first group is composed mainly of married people with small children, employed in dependent work and using both public transportation and private cars.

The second is mainly composed of married people without dependents, working in areas that demand greater flexibility of time. Compared to the former group, these individuals use private cars more intensively.

There are two important ideas to retain: First, mobility as expectancy is mainly ascribed to the second group, as these persons combine mobility needs with professional demands and leisure activities, perceiving cars as the taken for granted means of private transportation. In the case of the first profile, this includes individuals who understand mobility mostly as a determined and defined time-space. For them, most of the actions involving mobility must be prepared according to other schedules, especially if using public transportation.

Additionally, this paper can conclude that the greater distinction between the two groups is not connected to professional activity and its degree of flexibility, but rather with the stage in which individuals are in terms of the position within their life cycle as well as with the existence of small children in the family (who need to be cared for).

We can therefore state that a mobility time style is a complex web of time-space arrangements, which are sculpted according to a set of subjective and objective variables. Such variables also encompass a complex combination of objectivized behaviours (such as car usage, the amount of time allocated to each activity or the distance travelled) and implicit and subjective behaviours that may vary along a life trajectory (plans, projects, dreams, among others). The way people think time and relate to it – in a more or less flexible manner – is crucial to understand to what extent they are also able to alter their mobility habits.

7 Concluding Remarks

This paper has presented some of the motives for which mobility diagnosis is increasingly important to understand the inner difficulties that characterize people's lives concerning decisions of where to live, and how to move to have access to all desired/required the services and goods. In societies such as the Portuguese one, where the consumption of cars is increasingly higher, studies about mobility and time use patterns are ever more needed, to rethink transportation, as well as several other spheres of life, such as work, schools, hospital and health services, culture and consumption in shops [10].

In order to conclude this brief contribution, it is important to remind ourselves of the need for local authorities to involve themselves systematically and directly in the collection and processing of information about people's mobilities, associated with time uses and constraints. The construction of contemporary information databases on mobility flows, motivations and difficulties of the population, implying contact with diverse sources, in addition to individuals or families, thus constitutes a point of great importance, serving as an instrument to support future decision-making.

Acknowledgment. This work was supported by FCT, through the Strategic Financing of the R&D Unit UID/SOC/03126/2019.

Annex

See Tables 2 and 3

Table 2. Socio-demographic profile of people inserted in a liminal adjusted mobility time style

Age	Place of residence	Gender	Means of transportation	Occupation	Family	Work place
32	Montijo	W	Bus	Telecommunications technician	Couple with a baby	Lisbon
34	Setúbal	W	Train	Human Resources assistant	Isolated	Lisbon
29	Setúbal	W	Train	Roaming technician	Couple with a young child	Lisbon
42	Azeitão	W	Car and train	Solicitor (private company)	Divorced couple with two grown-up children	Lisbon
38	Palmela	W	Car and train	Economist	Couple with a teenage daughter	Lisbon
33	Sesimbra	W	Car	Administrative assistant and PhD student	Couple with a daughter of school age	Lisbon
36	Moita	M	underground, ferry and train	Secretary	Couple with a son of school age	Lisbon
56	Oeiras	M	Underground and train	Rail infrastructure manager	Couple with an adult son	Lisbon
30	Cascais	W	Car	Product Manager	Couple, expecting a child (six months of pregnancy)	Lisbon
32	Alverca	W	Train	Secretary	Couple with a baby and a young child	Lisbon

(*continued*)

Table 2. (*continued*)

Age	Place of residence	Gender	Means of transportation	Occupation	Family	Work place
24	Almada	W	Train	Call Center Operator	Isolated and pregnant (2 months of pregnancy)	Lisbon
34	Amadora	M	Car	Human Resources Assistant	Couple with two sons of school age	Lisbon
31	Sintra	W	Train	Commercial Assistant	Couple with no kids	Lisbon
48	Sintra	W	Car	Teacher	Couple with two adult sons	Loures
40	Loures	W	Car and train	Health and Safety technician	Couple	Lisbon
31	Mafra	M	Car	Computer technician	Couple with a small baby and a daughter of school age	Lisbon
36	Barreiro	W	Train or ferry	University lecturer	Couple with a son of school age	Lisbon
29	Alcochete	W	Car	Product Manager	Couple with two young children	Lisbon
35	Lisbon	F	Car	Product Manager	Couple with two children of school age	Lisbon
36	VF Xira	F	Train	Secretary	Couple with a son of school age and a baby daughter	Lisbon

(*continued*)

Table 2. (*continued*)

Age	Place of residence	Gender	Means of transportation	Occupation	Family	Work place
36	Entroncamento	M	Train	Portuguese Railway Company employee	Couple with a daughter of school age	Lisbon
38	Póvoa Varzim	W	Car	Accountant	Couple with a daughter of school age	Porto

Table 3. Socio-demographic profile of people inserted in a liminal extempore oriented mobility time style

Age	Place of residence	Gender	Means of transportation	Occupation	Family	Work place
31	Odivelas	M	Car	Salesperson	Divorced	AML
32	Póvoa Varzim	M	Car	Medical doctor	Isolated (his girlfriend lives in Lisbon)	Porto
32	Lisbon	W	Car	Human resources director	Isolated	Loures
42	VN Gaia	W	Car	Teacher	Couple	VN Gaia
26	Póvoa Varzim	W	Car	Call center operator	Unmarried couple	Porto
58	Azeitão	M	Car	Businessman	Couple	Setúbal
43	Maia	M	Car	Salesperson	Couple	Porto
39	Seixal	W	Car	Driver and Managing Partner of a transportation company	Divorced with a daughter of school age	Seixal
38	Lisbon	M	Car	Marketing Director	Couple with son of school age and a baby	Lisbon

References

1. Schwanen, T., Wang, D.: Well-being, context and everyday activities in space and time. Ann. Assoc. Am. Geogr. **104**(4), 833–851 (2014)
2. De Vos, J., Schwanen, T., Van Acker, V., Witlox, F.: Travel and subjective well-being: a focus on findings, methods and future research needs. Transp. Rev. **33**(4), 421–442 (2013)
3. Wang, D., He, S. (eds.): Mobility, Sociability and Well-being of Urban Living. Springer, Heidelberg (2016). https://doi.org/10.1007/978-3-662-48184-4
4. Cohen, S.A., Duncan, T., Thulemark, M.: Lifestyle mobilities: the crossroads of travel, leisure and migration. Mobilities **10**(1), 155–172 (2015)
5. Pordata: Base de Dados Portugal Contemporâneo. https://www.pordata.pt/. Accessed 01 July 2019
6. Melo, C., Vala, F.: Movimentos pendulares e organização do território metropolitano: distâncias e proximidades nos sistemas metropolitanos de Lisboa e Porto. Revista Portuguesa de Estudos Regionais **5**, 5–34 (2004)
7. Portas, N., et al.: Políticas Urbanas II: transformações, regulação e projectos. FCG, Lisboa (2013)
8. Instituto Nacional de Estatística Proporção de utilização do automóvel nas deslocações (%) por local de residência (2011). https://www.ine.pt/xportal/xmain?xpid=INE&xpgid=ine_indicadores&indOcorrCod=0007135&contexto=bd&selTab=tab2. Access 01 July 2019
9. Cresswell, T.: Towards a politics of mobility. Environ. Plann. Soc. Space **28**(1), 17–31 (2010)
10. Zhang, J.: Revisiting residential self-selection issues: a life-oriented approach. J. Transp. Land Use **7**(3), 29–45 (2014)
11. Montulet, B., Hubert, M., Huynen, P.: Etre Mobile. Vécus du temps et usages des modes de transport à Bruxelles. FUSL, Bruxelles (2007)
12. Sheller, M., Urry, J.: The new mobilities paradigm. Environ. Plann. A **38**(2), 207–226 (2006)
13. Eurostat: Estatísticas sobre o Transporte de Passageiros. http://ec.europa.eu/eurostat/statistics-explained/index.php/Passenger_transport_statistics/pt. Accessed 01 July 2019
14. Comissão Europeia: Roteiro de Transição para uma Economia Hipocarbónica Competitiva em 2050.:http://eur-lex.europa.eu/legal-content/PT/TXT/HTML/?uri=CELEX:52011DC0112&from=EN. Accessed 01 July 2019
15. Eurostat: Consumption of Energy. http://eur-lex.europa.eu/legal-content/PT/TXT/HTML/?uri=CELEX:52011DC0112&from=EN. Accessed July 2019
16. Eurostat: Renewable Energy Statistics. http://ec.europa.eu/eurostat/statistics-explained/index.php/Renewable_energy_statistics. Accessed 01 July 2019
17. Jensen, M.: Defining Lifestyle. Environ. Sci. **4**(2), 63–73 (2007)
18. Zhang, J.: The life-oriented approach and travel behavior research. In: 14th International Conference on Travel Behaviour Research, Windsor, UK, 19–23 July (2015)
19. Flamm, M., Kaufmann, V.: Operationalising the concept of motility: a qualitative study. Mobilities **1**(2), 167–189 (2006)
20. Lucas, K., Jones, P.: Social impacts and equity issues in transport: an introduction. J. Transp. Geogr. **21**, 1–3 (2012)
21. Cockerham, W., Rutten, A., Abel, T.: Conceptualizing contemporary health lifestyles: moving Beyond Weber. Sociol. Q. **38**(2), 321–342 (1997)
22. Hagerstrand, T.: Dynamic Allocation of Urban Space. Saxon House, Farnborough (1975)
23. Harvey, D.: The Condition of Postmodernity: An Enquiry into the Origins of Cultural Change. Blackwell, Oxford (1989)
24. Oliveira, C.S.: Mobilidades em português: paradigma, cultura e potencialidades. In: Araújo, E., Ribeiro, R., Andrade, P., Costa, R. (eds.) Viver emla mobilidade: rumo a novas culturas de tempo, espaço e distância, pp. 10–21. CECS, Braga (2018)

25. Araújo, E.: Questões de mobilidade, tempo e sustentabilidade. In: Araújo, E., Ribeiro, R., Andrade, R. Costa, R. (eds.) Viver em la mobilidade: rumo a novas culturas de tempo, espaço e distância, pp. 146–160. Centro de Estudos de Comunicação e Sociedade, Braga (2018)

Author Index

Andrade, Joana   45
Araújo, Catarina   45
Araújo, Emília   143, 170

Bragança, Luís   45

Conticelli, Elisa   125
Corais, Filipa   143

de Fátima Castro, Maria   45
Duarte Melo, Ana   154

Fedele, Rosario   3
Fonseca, Fernando   125
Fu, Linhao   97
Fuentes Jr., Vivencio C.   31

Houngue, Pelagie   71

Jabbari, Mona   125

Kedowide, Colombiano   71
Kulkarni, Divya D.   83

Marques, Gonçalo   109

Nair, Shivashankar B.   83
Nakajima, Tatuso   97

Oliveira, Benjamim   59
Oliveira, Catarina Sales   170

Paiva, Filipa   15
Paiva, Sara   59
Papageorgiou, George   125
Pedrasa, Jhoanna Rhodette I.   31
Pellicano, Gianfranco   3
Pereira, Paulo   15
Petrova, Elena   125
Pitarma, Rui   109
Praticò, Filippo Giammaria   3

Ramos, Rui   125
Ribeiro, Paulo   125
Ribeiro, Rita   143
Rodrigues, Pedro   59

Sagbo, Romaric   71
Silva, Lígia   15
Silva, Márcia   143
Souza, Pétilin   15

Tondelli, Simona   125

Yang, Zebo   97

Zhang, Mingshu   97
Zhang, Taili   97

Printed in the United States
By Bookmasters